Autism Spectrum Disorders and Visual Impairment

MEETING STUDENTS' LEARNING NEEDS

Marilyn H. Gense and D. Jay Gense

AFB PRESS

American Foundation for the Blind

Printed in the United States of America

Library of Congress Cataloging-in-Publication Data

Gense, Marilyn H., 1952–
    Autism spectrum disorders and visual impairments : meeting students' learning needs / Marilyn H. Gense and D. Jay Gense.
        p.   cm.
    Includes bibliographical references and index.
    ISBN 0-89128-880-5 (pbk. : alk. paper) — ISBN 0-89128-802-3 (ascii disk)
    1. Autism in children.   2. Vision disorders in children.   3. Autistic children—Education.   4. Children with visual disabilities—Education.
    I. Gense, D. Jay, 1957–   II. Title.

    RJ506.A9G46   2005
    649'.154—dc22   2005012386

The American Foundation for the Blind—the organization to which Helen Keller devoted more than 40 years of her life—is a national nonprofit whose mission is to eliminate the inequities faced by the ten million Americans who are blind or visually impaired.

It is the policy of the American Foundation for the Blind to use in the first printing of its books acid-free paper that meets the ANSI Z39.48 Standard. The infinity symbol that appears above indicates that the paper in this printing meets that standard.

PREFACE

W e imagine that most people would find that it takes longer for *two* people to write a book together than it would for someone working alone. Our experience has proven otherwise. We realize how fortunate we are to have the opportunity to share our passion for our chosen field with each other on a daily basis. Our professional lives brought us together, and allowed us to find our respective soul mate; consequently, our journey through life improves each day. Together, we have been able to enhance and improve our writing by sharing together, thinking together, venting together, challenging each other's perspectives, and offering the constructive criticism that ultimately enhanced the quality of the publication. For this opportunity, we will be forever grateful.

We want to thank several people who have helped us along the way. First and foremost, we want to thank the many students who have provided us the opportunity of learning together through our teaching over the years. Each child is indeed unique, and each has afforded us new insights into teaching and learning. We also thank these students' parents and families. Of particular note is Max, the boy whose photo appears on the book's cover, and his mother Julie.

Several colleagues supported us by proofreading early drafts, by contributing photographs, and by offering their insights. In particular, our thanks are extended to Kristine Davis, Jana McFerron, Diane Mitchell, Jane Mulholland, and Anne Olson Murphy. Also, our thanks to our good friend Dr. Kathleen Huebner, who always was available with encouraging words to "keep going, because the book is important—truly."

We are indebted to the staff of AFB Press and the peer reviewers of our manuscript who were able to offer important perspectives and advice. In particular, our warm thanks are offered to Natalie Hilzen for her ongoing support, remarkable editing skills, and consistent words of encouragement.

Our families, and in particular, our parents, have provided us with the support and love that encouraged us to pursue our passions. To them we extend our heartfelt thanks and love.

Certainly, we are excited about completing this publication. While we treasure any influence it may have in improving a child's life, we do not see it as an endpoint. Indeed, we must constantly strive for an enhanced understanding of children with very complex learning needs. Together, we can accomplish so much. Together, we can.

PART 1

Understanding Autism Spectrum Disorders and Visual Impairment

Learning, Teaching, Learning

Over the past 25 years, we have been blessed with opportunities both to teach and to learn from a wide range of students with visual impairments. Each student has been unique in his or her ability to learn, each having individual strengths and challenges in the learning process. Certainly, no two students are alike, and students' experiencing individual success in learning is driven, in part, by teachers' ability to capitalize on individual students' strengths.

LEARNERS WHO ARE NOT "TYPICAL"

During our years working with students with visual impairments, it has been increasingly clear that there is a subset of students whose behaviors differ markedly from those of other students who are visually impaired. Of course, it is difficult to generalize what is "typical," since the impact of visual impairments is as diverse as the students who are affected by them. However, this unique subset of students consistently presents a different challenge, exhibiting reactions, learning needs, and patterns of behaviors that are atypical of most children, whether sighted or visually impaired. These children often have difficulty understanding and learning to use language and communication. As infants, they may begin to babble and then stop. They may develop echolalic (echoing) speech beyond typical development, but may have limited comprehension of the meaning of the words. If they are verbal, their speech may be characterized as monotonous and flat. Furthermore, these students may have difficulty talking about anything outside the immediate context and may be extremely interested in limited topics or objects. Many struggle in the way they relate to peers and adults. Many infants and young children experience a seeming failure to bond and are often socially unresponsiveness. Many engage in compulsive behaviors that involve rigid and obsessive routines. Changes in familiar environments and routines are often upsetting to them. As they grow older, these children are often not interested in being with or playing with other children, appearing to prefer to spend time alone. Both hypersensitivities and hyposensitivities to sensory stimuli are common. Learning characteristics such as these often lead these students to be frustrated, confused, and anxious. Their frustration and confusion, in turn, are often expressed in withdrawal and unusual or unique behaviors and occasionally in aggression or self-injurious behaviors. Most important, these children do not seem to learn and process information in ways that are typical of most children, whether sighted or not.

Consider the following descriptions of three such students.

Miguel

Miguel, age 6, is totally blind. From an early age, he was difficult to comfort, crying constantly unless he was being rocked. He did not babble much and did not attain typical language milestones. His mother said that he was a "late walker." Miguel was not responsive to interactions with his parents and was not interested in typical toys. His favorite free-time activity was to sit on the floor, roll himself into a ball, and spin. This behavior was powerful and nearly impossible to interrupt. If Miguel was walking and was left alone, he would immediately drop down and start to spin. When he learned to say a few words, he would use them for all interactions. He would echo questions in a whiny voice, always using the same inflection.

Miguel was totally disoriented even in familiar environments, appearing unable to use any auditory or tactile information for orientation. He did not like his hands to be touched, pulling away when a teacher attempted to provide instruction tactilely. Furthermore, he was not interested in other children and appeared to ignore their existence, but he enjoyed swimming (being in the water and floating), rocking, spinning, and swinging.

Miguel had difficulty following simple verbal directions. He would stand and wait, drop and spin, or wander without purpose. It was extremely difficult to keep Miguel focused on any task for more than one to two minutes. Miguel's teachers found that each task had to be broken down into minute steps, taught in sequence repeatedly, and paired with frequent reinforcement. Miguel did not benefit from any group instruction, so all instruction was done one on one with a teacher.

Ann

We first met Ann, who is now age 12, when she was in kindergarten, after her mother called to express her concern about Ann's development. Ann had light perception in one eye and could see shadows in the other. At the time, she was attending a regular kindergarten. Her instruction was provided by a teacher of students with visual impairments and a one-to-one instructional assistant. Although Ann was in a regular classroom setting, her interaction with her peers was limited. She would sit next to them in class and could orally list each classmate's name, but she could not seem to connect the name to the particular child.

During group instruction, Ann needed prompting from the instructional assistant to realize that when instructions were given to the group or the class, they were also meant for her. Her verbal skills exceeded her comprehension skills. However, she typically used questions to communicate. For example, she had a toy duck that beeped. Instead of asking for help in turning it on, she would say, "Did the toy go beep, beep, beep?" She initiated and responded to simple greetings if she was paying attention, but preferred to spend time repeatedly singing patterned phrases to herself. Furthermore, Ann had difficulty learning tactilely and was challenged by fine motor tasks. Her toy play was awkward. She used toys not for their intended purpose, but to self-stimulate (for example, flicking toys in front of light) and did not use imaginative play. She loved music, singing, and toys that made noise.

Ann was much more interactive with adults than with children. In addition, she enjoyed Disney movies and would play the same section of a favorite tape repeatedly, starting, stopping, rewinding, and playing the tape over and over. She repeated this behavior hundreds of times. She also would listen to favorite audiotapes, rocking for hours if allowed to do so.

Ann's mother said that Ann "cried most of the time during the first year of her life" and preferred to be in her crib. If her parents took her out of the crib and crossed the threshold of the doorway to her bedroom, Ann would scream.

Ann and her family lived in a rural community. If the neighbors started their lawnmower, Ann would cry, and she covered her ears when the vacuum was turned on. She would only wear certain clothing and could barely tolerate wearing shoes and socks. She gagged when some foods were presented and would eat only mashed, bland food. In addition, Ann was not toilet trained, but it did not appear to bother her to be wet.

Ann's brother John, who is a year older than she, has been blind since birth. In contrast to Ann, he developed language at a typical age and in a typical sequence. John has always had a variety of interests, enjoys playing with toys and other children, and participates in his regular class without additional assistance. John quickly learned braille and has always read and comprehended at his grade level. He learned to use a cane and could easily move throughout the school once he was oriented.

D.R.

When we met D.R., age 15, he had just moved from another state. D.R. is totally blind and his records indicated a diagnosis of mental retardation (an erroneous diagnosis). D.R. was intelligent and able to master academic tasks in his fourth-grade classroom. However, the curriculum was difficult because auditory information seemed to make little sense to him. For example, his braille "read-aloud" skills were exemplary, but his ability to comprehend what he read was negligible. He could read a long passage of text and then repeat the entire passage verbatim. He had a strong interest in audiotapes and would listen to a favorite section of a tape for hours, endlessly rewinding the tape to a prescribed section and listening to it repeatedly.

D.R. preferred to spend time alone during recess. He occasionally tried to engage a peer in conversation, but would always initiate the interaction with the same set of random, unrelated questions. He was troubled that his "friends" did not have the same strong interests as he did.

D.R. lived in fear of the fire bells in the school. He would quickly scurry through the hallways to ensure that he spent as little time as possible in them, on the off-chance that the alarms would be engaged. He quickly figured out the day of the month that the school used for fire drills, and he refused to come to school that day.

D.R. used a long white cane and had received orientation and mobility (O&M) instruction since he was 3 years old. He was easily disoriented and often got lost even in familiar environments in the school, including the library and his classroom. D.R. lived about one block from his school. On some days he could easily travel independently from the school to his home, but on other days, it appeared that he had never traveled this route before; every turn and obstacle seemed to be insurmountable.

D.R.'s behaviors were a classic study in contrast. In school, D.R. was always well behaved, complying with all the rules of the school and his teacher. He was always striving to please adults, and found great pleasure in their complimentary remarks. At home, however, D.R.'s parents often found him to be "hell on wheels." If something did not go his way (for example, if he was offered something other than hotdogs for dinner), his behavior would escalate to the point that it was uncontrollable. When he was sent to his room, D.R. would repeatedly throw his bed against the wall, tear the curtains from the window, throw books and toys on the floor

*and stamp on them, and scream incessantly. Because of his screaming,
D.R.'s parents worried that the neighbors would assume that they were
physically abusing D.R.*

The three students just described represent different needs, abilities, and challenges, yet certain similarities and common themes can be seen in regard to their ability to learn and to process new information. Our quest to gain a better understanding of the unique behaviors and learning characteristics presented by some of our students, and ultimately, to enhance our ability to develop and implement instructional strategies that supported each student's unique style of learning, led us to what has now been more than a 15-year journey in learning about and understanding autism spectrum disorders (ASD). In many cases, the patterns of behaviors and unique learning characteristics presented by some children who are blind or visually impaired have led to an educational diagnosis of an ASD. The implications of an ASD coexisting with a visual impairment are significant and profound for a student's ability to develop, learn, and interact socially, yet information on this dual diagnosis is extremely limited in the professional literature. Even more limited is information that practitioners can use to address the challenges to learning that these children experience.

THE COMPLEXITIES OF AUTISM SPECTRUM DISORDERS

The impact of an autism spectrum disorder on learning can vary from mild to severe, as is discussed more fully in Chapter 1. Children with such a disorder represent a wide spectrum of intellectual capabilities, and ASD can occur concomitantly with other disabilities, including visual impairments, hearing impairments, orthopedic impairments, and mental retardation. Relative to many other disabilities, the study of ASD is comparatively new. As more is learned about ASD, the complexities and learning challenges will become more obvious. The complexities often lead to differences of opinion on diagnosis, causes, and interventions. Currently, no objective biological test can confirm the presence of ASD (Lord, 1997; Lord & McGee, 2001; National Institute of Child Health and Human Development, 2001). Obtaining an appropriate identification requires an assessment conducted by a well-trained team of professionals who are experienced in assessing students with an autism spectrum disorder.

Our journey in learning to understand and provide effective quality educational programs for students with ASD and visual impairment has provided us with a core belief that has guided the information we provide in this book and continues to guide our work with students. We believe emphatically that the educational programs that are designed and implemented for these children *must* address the unique and multifaceted impacts of their dual diagnosis. In addition, teachers and parents need to understand that the educational interventions will vary from those that are typical for a student with only a visual impairment or a visual impairment and other disabilities, such as mental retardation. The diagnosis of autism spectrum disorders is complex, and it needs to be stated clearly that most children with a visual impairment do not have an autism spectrum disorder.

In this book, we address the critical need to evaluate this subset of students and to determine the appropriate identification, plan appropriate programs, and develop appropriate intervention strategies to meet these students' needs. Significant gradations of characteristics and behaviors are associated with ASD, which can range from severe to mild and differ from individual to individual. For this and related reasons, the definition and identification of an autism spectrum disorder continues to be complex. In addition, confusion often arises because behaviors that accompany ASD can mistakenly be attributed to blindness. It is important to recognize that some of the behaviors that are typically associated with ASD resemble those that have historically been associated with so-called blindisms, that are exhibited by some children who are visually impaired. The term *blindisms* is often used to describe unusual or stereotypic (also known as stereotyped) behaviors that are exhibited by some visually impaired individuals, such as rocking, spinning, head swaying, and rhythmic bouncing. Some would argue that these behaviors can be considered "normal" for any child who experiences a visual impairment, and one of the reasons we wrote this book is to alert readers to the need to avoid such generalizations and assumptions. When the combination or patterns of behaviors that are exhibited by a visually impaired child are extreme, or when the intensity and persistence of the behaviors expand beyond developmental norms, we believe that the presence of an autism spectrum disorder, and the implications of it, should be considered. We believe that acceptance of "autistic-like" behaviors without the pursuit of a better understanding of the meaning of those behaviors and the exploration of the possible coexistence of visual impairment and an autism spectrum disorder is doing the child a disservice.

RESPONSIVE EDUCATIONAL APPROACHES

Students with what we have termed ASDVI in this book—the combination of a visual impairment and an autism spectrum disorder—can be gifted, stubborn, endearing, behaviorally challenging, stimulating, and fun; indeed, the descriptions seem endless. Many are undoubtedly the most challenging in-

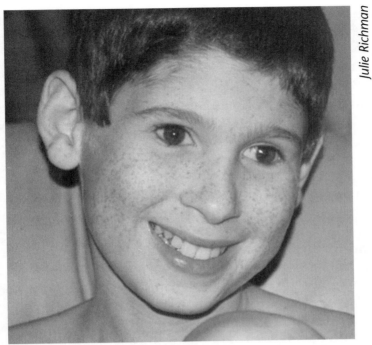

Julie Richman

Students with the combination of a visual impairment and an autism spectrum disorder can be gifted, stubborn, endearing, behaviorally challenging, stimulating, and fun, and assisting them on their path to learning is inordinately rewarding.

dividuals we have taught. At the same time, helping them to "make the connection," gaining their attention, and assisting them on their path to learning has, and continues to be, inordinately rewarding. We believe that each teacher has a responsibility to promote lifelong learning for each student. We also believe that the definition of *teacher* is best applied broadly to include all teachers, parents, service providers, paraprofessionals, and others who work with a student, in that each has a tremendous opportunity to influence and provide guidance to the child. For children with ASDVI, the world can be a confusing mix of sensory inputs that make little sense. For many, the sensory inputs can be overwhelming and may impede learning. Each teacher has the unique opportunity and responsibility to help each child make sense of that input—to learn not to fear it, but, rather, to learn to process it, to manage it, and ultimately to be motivated by and learn from it. A teacher can provide the conditions that support each student's potential for active learning. This potential certainly will vary from student to student, and the conditions and the instruction need to reflect the unique impact of the student's disability. Each teacher must strive to determine those conditions under which each student's learning can be optimized and enhanced. The gift for the teacher, of course, is the student's success.

When working with any student with complex learning challenges, including those with ASDVI, it is sometimes beneficial to consider a "paradigm shift" in thinking about traditional instructional approaches. In *Learning by Heart*, Barth (2001), discussed the concept of educational reform, using the term "thinking otherwise" to mean "to think differently." We propose that effective educational interventions for students with ASDVI are sometimes best designed and implemented by thinking otherwise. Barth presented an analogy that provides a good illustration of this concept by discussing the challenge one may face if one detests the taste of the glue when licking a stamp but knows that the envelope must have a stamp before it can be mailed. Options for dealing with this challenge include (1) licking the stamp quickly and lightly to help ward off the aftertaste; (2) sipping water after each lick of the stamp; or perhaps even (3) attempting to work with the source, corresponding directly with the U.S. Postal Service to encourage it to use a different flavor of glue on the stamps. Alternatively, one could think differently and decide to wet the stamp without licking it or to lick the envelope, rather than the stamp. We challenge each reader to be open to the possibility that for some students, the best programs are discovered by wetting the envelope, rather than by licking the stamp. Indeed, this paradigm shift may lead to the discovery of particularly effective programs.

As you read this book, we encourage you to adopt a broad perspective and be amenable to some new ways of thinking. Be open to the possibility that some visually impaired students who demonstrate unique learning characteristics may have an autism spectrum disorder or other condition. Accept the responsibility to learn *how* each child learns and design teaching strategies accordingly. Also, when a young child who is visually impaired demonstrates behaviors that have been called blindisms, do not ignore these behaviors on the assumption that they correlate directly with a visual impairment, believing that the child will simply outgrow them. Instead, learn why the child is demonstrating these behaviors and strive to learn what they may mean in relation to the child's learning style.

As we share our experiences and thoughts in the following chapters, providing information, resources, and instructional strategies, it is not our intent, nor is it possible, to provide every instructional strategy or tool for working with students with ASDVI. Our intent is provide information and resources that address the areas that we believe are the most critical for students with both a visual impairment and an autism spectrum disorder. What we offer is a framework for understanding this unique set of students, and an approach for developing and implementing interventions that can help open the door to learning. We consider that in this book, we are sharing "craft knowledge," those hard-won lessons and discoveries that we have garnered through years of working with these unique students. The information and resources that we present have been obtained through our direct instruction with students and in working closely and collaboratively with hundreds of teachers, parents, and administrators. They are meant to stimulate thinking, to help each reader perhaps to discover or invent a "better way."

In providing this information, we assume that the reader is familiar with the general requirements of providing special education and related services under the Individuals with Disabilities Education Act (IDEA) and with the concepts of an Individualized Education Program (IEP) or Individualized Family Service Plan (IFSP), as well as the responsibilities of the IEP or IFSP team for developing and implementing programs. Throughout this book, we refer to the responsibilities of the "team," referring to members of either the IEP or the IFSP team who work with the student. Of course, different states have different terms for these teams, but the principles of the team approach still apply. The team includes the parents and, as appropriate, the student. Detailed information on the principles set forth in IDEA is available on the Web sites of many national organizations (see Resources and Additional Readings for some specific sources).

GUIDING PRINCIPLES

As you begin, allow us to set the stage by sharing what has become somewhat of a "mantra" for us in working with students with ASDVI. We consider the following to be a core set of principles that guide our work with these students. We ask that you keep these principles in mind as you read and consider the information contained in this book. Use them as a guiding structure to help make a difference in each student's life.

- **Strive for small doable increments.** Remember that you can not do everything at once. When you design and implement an educational program and break down tasks for the student, move forward with the small doable increments that will enhance the overall "big picture."

- **Expect communication.** A simple but inordinately important concept must be woven throughout the student's curriculum: the student must communicate. If a student is able to meet his or her needs without communicating in a traditional sense, then he or she will not feel the need to communicate. Without the need to communicate, the student will have little need or desire for social interaction. Without social interaction, the student will become increasingly comfortable with himself or herself, which may lead to increased withdrawal, isolation, and self-stimulation.

- **Use positive reinforcements.** Optimally, each student's capacity for learning will be enhanced only when the learning leads to a positive personal gain. Thus, each teacher must be keenly aware of positive reinforcements, remembering that such reinforcers cannot be based on what *you* like or what you *think* the student likes, but what the student clearly demonstrates that she or he likes. It is essential to recognize that for many children with autism spectrum disorder, reinforcements may not be typical. Therefore, it is essential to use each student's personal reinforcers to stimulate learning.

- **Nothing is free.** Design the environment so that the student needs to interact and communicate in order to obtain what he or she wants. Opportunities for success will be enhanced when the student understands that "you have to give something to get something" (such as language, gestures, vocalizations, and movements). Each student's curriculum must be developed to ensure that the expectations are clear and that a response is required.

- **Take responsibility for each student's learning.** If a student is not making progress, in all likelihood the problems lie not with the student, but with the instruction that is being provided. Each teacher needs to examine what is and is not effective in helping a student learn and to recognize that he or she is responsible for the student's learning. The teacher must be constantly aware of the learning opportunities that are being presented through instruction and have a clear understanding of the expected outcomes.

- **Learning, teaching, learning.** Teaching and learning are intrinsically enmeshed and ongoing. If the teacher is not experiencing the joy of learning, chances are good that the student will not either. Try to find the joy that inherently exists in the challenges that you will experience.

The content of this book is presented in two sections. Part 1, "Understanding Autism Spectrum Disorders and Visual Impairment," provides an overview of the conditions encompassed in the term *autism spectrum disorder*. It presents general information on the developmental characteristics of children with ASD and children with visual impairments and discusses the identification of ASD in students who are visually impaired. Part 2, "Program Planning and Instructional Strategies," begins by addressing program planning and core instructional principles, followed by assessment, providing strategies and resources for evaluating students. The remaining chapters are divided into seven content areas that are important to address for any student with ASD and a visual impairment, with the final chapter providing strategies for classroom supports to assist students in the general classroom environment. We recommend that you read the chapters in Part 1 and the introductory and assessment chapters in Part 2 before you apply any of the content presented in any of the remaining chapters in Part 2.

It is important to understand that a disability defines neither the child nor the subsequent special needs that the child may have. Each child presents unique and individualized learning characteristics and learning challenges. The impact of the disability will be influenced by the natural accommodations that the child has learned, by the child's innate strengths and challenges, and by any compensatory skills that the child has been taught. We believe that it takes a community of teachers, including parents, to teach a child with ASDVI successfully. We hope that the information that is provided in this book will enhance the understanding of these unique children and will allow each teacher to capitalize on the gift that each student brings to the challenges of high-quality teaching. Each of us has the opportunity to learn; to teach; and, in turn, to learn again. The goal is not to complete the cycle but, rather, to embrace the fact that this cycle should never be completed. Effective teaching correlates directly with learning. Each child, each situation, and each challenge allow us to enhance our abilities to understand and refine our craft.

Autism Spectrum Disorders: An Introduction

It is estimated that between 1 in 500 and 1 in 2,500 Americans have a condition that is sometimes referred to as "autism," a disorder that typically begins in early childhood (National Institute of Mental Health, 2003). Recent research indicates that the incidence of autism spectrum disorders may occur at an even higher rate. The incidence of the identification of this condition has exploded in the past decade. Currently, the causes and cures remain unknown.

DEFINING AUTISM SPECTRUM DISORDERS

Autism is a neurological brain disorder that profoundly affects a person's ability to communicate, form relationships with others, and respond appropriately to the environment. Its effects on learning and functioning can range from mild to severe and depend on the individual's level of intellectual ability, other co-occurring conditions, and experiences. The learning and thinking styles exhibited are unique but predictable and are different from the behaviors and challenges that are caused by other developmental disabilities (Janzen, 2003). Wing (1997) described the changes in our understanding of this condition over the years. Although there continues to be considerable debate in defining the term *autism,* there is a general acceptance that a continuum or spectrum of conditions and behaviors are encompassed within that term. For this reason, the term *autism spectrum disorders* (ASD) is now used to describe a group of disorders that affect an individual's ability to interact socially, to understand and relate to others, to communicate, and to understand and respond to sensory stimuli and whose symptoms and characteristics present themselves in a wide variety of combinations. These disorders are "unique in their pattern of deficits and areas of relative strengths. They generally have lifelong effects on how children learn to be social beings, to take care of themselves, and to participate in the community" (National Research Council, 2001, p. 1). Although a number of terms, such as *autism* and *autistic disorder,* are sometimes used throughout this book, the term *autism spectrum disorders* will be employed. Autism spectrum disorders are defined by a particular set of behaviors, but children and adults can exhibit any combination of these behaviors in any degree of severity. Two children who are identified as having an autism spectrum disorder can act very differently from each other and display varying and distinct skills. Furthermore, the intensity and severity of the characteristics of autism will affect their learning differently.

A variety of disorders are associated with the term autism spectrum disorders, including autistic disorder, pervasive developmental disorders—not otherwise specified, and Asperger's syndrome, as well as childhood disintegrative disorder and Rhett syndrome (see American Psychiatric Association, APA, 2000; National Center on Birth Defects and Developmental Disabilities, Autism Information Center, 2004). Fragile X disorder is sometimes also included in this term, and readers will encounter variations in terminology such as "high-functioning" autism, and "low-functioning" autism. Although individuals with an autism spectrum disorder are unique in their pattern of deficits and relative strengths, the disorder will fundamentally affect the individual's ability to organize, process, and integrate information.

Autism spectrum disorders are diagnosed by identifying a cluster of behavioral characteristics, with the following caveats:

1. No single behavior identifies an autism spectrum disorder.

2. Behavioral characteristics range from mild to severe.

3. Cognitive abilities range from intellectually gifted to severe impairments.

Common behavioral characteristics that are associated with ASD are identified in four primary areas:

1. **Impairments in communication.** There is a significant delay in or the absence of speech. Language is used in a repetitive manner; that is, words or phrases are repeated with no apparent meaning. Many individuals have difficulty sustaining or initiating a conversation or talk about the same topic repeatedly.

2. **Impairments in social interaction.** Individuals may appear aloof or indifferent, seemingly "locked in their own world." They often lack emotional reciprocity and often have poor relationships with peers.

3. **Restricted, repetitive, and stereotypic patterns of behavior, interests, and activities.** Individuals are often intensely preoccupied with one subject or activity (for example, a child's interest may be limited to one toy or one activity). They may also engage in nonfunctional rituals or routines.

4. **Sensory difficulties.** Individuals demonstrate extreme sensitivity or apparent underreaction to sensory input and unusual, even dramatic, responses to sensory information. They may not be able to regulate sensory information, as is common in typical development.

Specific behaviors that are often observed in each of these four areas are listed in "Impairments in Four Primary Areas of Behavior." Janzen (2003, p. 16) stated that when considering an autism spectrum disorder, it can be "easy to get caught up or sidetracked by the bizarre, unexpected, and colorful details. . . . The details should only serve as clues to understanding the whole picture of autism. If we understand the nature of autism, we will be able to provide the supports that will help those with ASD have a brighter future."

More detailed information on autism spectrum disorders can be found in the *Diagnostic and Statistical Manual of Mental Disorders* (APA, 2000). In addition, a list of Resources and Additional Readings is provided at the end of the book.

DEFINING VISUAL IMPAIRMENT

A great deal of information on visual impairments, their causes, and the implications thereof, is available in the professional literature (see, for example, Corn & Koenig, 1996; Holbrook & Koenig, 2000; Jose, 1993; Pogrund & Fazzi, 2002; Sacks & Silberman, 1998). For the purpose of this book, only a brief discussion is included, to serve as a foundation to identify and understand the range and variety of students with visual impairments and to define the terminology used throughout this book.

In the professional literature and in educational settings throughout this country, there is some variation in the terminology used and in the definition of *visual impairment*. Terms that are typically used and that are encompassed in the term *visual impairment* include *total blindness, low vision, partial sight,* and *functional vision.* A brief description of each is as follows:

Total blindness. Individuals who are total blind have no usable vision and perform tasks through a learning mode other than vision. The term typically refers to a condition in which the individual has only light perception or less vision. The primary learning mode may be tactile, auditory, or a combination of the two.

IMPAIRMENTS IN FOUR PRIMARY AREAS OF BEHAVIOR

Specific behaviors that are frequently observed in the four primary areas of impairment associated with ASD, and the ages at which typical children exhibit these behaviors, are as follows:

Impairments in Communication

- the failure to jabber or to engage in imitative vocalizations (typically seen at 9–18 months)

- the use of gesturing or pointing is lacking or limited (typically seen at 11–19 months)

- the delayed or no use of single words (typically seen at 16–20 months)

- the failure to engage in spontaneous utterances of two-word phrases (not just echolalic) by 24 months

- the development and then cessation of babbling

- the use of echolalic language (the "echoing" of words and phrases) or the use of idiosyncratic phrases more often than is appropriate or past the point of being appropriate for the child's age (these behaviors are typically seen at 24–32 months)

- the lack of joint attention—that is, the ability to coordinate attention to both people and objects

- a delay in the development of spoken language or the lack of development of spoken language

- a marked impairment in the ability to initiate or sustain a conversation with others

- the stereotypic and repetitive use of language or idiosyncratic language

- the lack of varied, spontaneous make-believe play or social imitative play that is appropriate to the child's developmental level

Impairments in Social Interaction

- impairments in nonverbal behaviors, including gestures, eye contact, and body postures

- difficulty with or the inability to develop relationships with peers

- difficulty with or the inability to demonstrate social or emotional reciprocity

- difficulty with age-appropriate social interactions

- difficulty with age-expected play

Restricted, Repetitive, and Stereotyped Patterns of Behavior, Interests, and Activities

- the repetitive, unusual manipulation or use of toys, and other objects

- spinning of objects or self

- compulsive adherence to nonfunctional routines and rituals

- the preference for concrete, repetitive play to the exclusion of varied, spontaneous play

- stereotypic motor mannerisms (such as hand flapping and spinning)

- the persistent preoccupation with "parts" of objects (for example, attending only to the wheels on a toy car)

- the preoccupation with one or more stereotypic and restricted patterns of interests that is abnormal either in intensity or focus (such as an interest only in Disney movies or the Beatles)

- delays or abnormal functioning in symbolic or imaginative play

Sensory Difficulties

- avoidance of gentle physical contact

- extreme or intense preferences for specific foods

- inappropriate responses or no responses to sound

- an apparent insensitivity to pain

- under- or oversensitivity to certain textures, sounds, tastes, or smells

- negative or defensive reactions to ordinary stimuli

Low vision. An individual with low vision has a severe impairment that cannot be corrected to normal through the use of conventional lenses or eyeglasses and "has difficulty accomplishing visual tasks, even with pre-scribed corrective lenses, but . . . can enhance his or her ability to accomplish these tasks with the use of compensatory visual strategies, low vision and other devices, and environmental modifications" (Corn & Koenig, 1996, p. 4).

Partial sight. Individuals with partial sight have vision that is impaired but can continue to use vision as their primary learning mode.

Functional vision. Functional vision refers not to the individual's vision as determined through clinical measurement, but to the extent to which the individual can *use* his or her residual vision to perform behaviors and activities.

Children with visual impairments represent a broad range of abilities, and the impact of their impairments varies widely. Many children have residual vision, with visual functioning varying greatly among them. Many children have concomitant disabilities in addition to their visual impairment. Children with identified visual impairments are typically educated by a teacher of visually impaired students and an orientation and mobility (O&M) specialist. Teachers of visually impaired students receive unique university training and experiences to provide instruction in the expanded core curricular areas (see Chapter 3) for students with visual impairments. These core areas include compensatory or functional academic skills, such as braille and other communication modes, social interaction skills, independent living skills, recreational and leisure skills, career education, use of assistive technology, and visual efficiency skills. The teacher of visually impaired students works with the student and with other members of the IEP team to ensure that the student's curriculum is designed to address the possible needs for magnification, print size, use of braille, use of large-print materials, contrast and lighting, color, tactile or auditory adaptations, and compensatory skills that are necessary to help the student address the implications of the visual impairment. The teacher also supports the core area of O&M, which is taught primarily by an O&M specialist.

The O&M specialist receives unique university training and experience in O&M skills for students with visual impairments. These skills are taught to individual visually impaired students to help them to move through and understand their environment. The O&M specialist provides the primary instruction in the curricular area of O&M and supports the other areas of the curriculum taught by the teacher of visually impaired students. The teacher of visually impaired students and the O&M specialist work closely with other members of the IEP team, including the child's parents, to provide a comprehensive program of instruction.

Individuals with low vision need to be assessed to determine the functional use of their remaining vision. It is essential for anyone who works with students with low vision to understand clearly how an individual student uses his or her vision in order to develop materials and provide instruction that is matched to the student's learning mode. For some students, the use

Each child with an autism spectrum disorder and visual impairment is unique in his or her ability to learn and to process sensory information. Successful interventions depend on understanding each child's strengths and challenges.

of devices that magnify materials may be beneficial. These devices include closed-circuit televisions (CCTVs), magnifiers, and monoculars. Other students may read and prefer large print or braille. Some may respond best to color, while others prefer black-and-white materials. Many students will benefit from enhanced lighting, positioned to enhance their remaining vision.

For students with no usable vision, it is important for the IEP team to determine if they can use information that is presented tactilely (such as braille) or whether they will benefit more from using auditory information. The teacher of visually impaired students assists the team in determining the primary and secondary learning modes for each student to ensure that adaptations and modifications are optimized to meet the particular student's learning style and preferred learning modality.

AUTISM SPECTRUM DISORDERS AND VISUAL IMPAIRMENTS

Although the nature of autism spectrum disorders in children who are visually impaired, particularly in children who are congenitally blind, has long been a topic of interest, there has to date been limited empirical research specifically on the potential dual diagnosis of ASD and visual impairment and the differences among groups of participants. With regard to children with rubella, Chess, Korn, and Fenandez (1971, pp. 116–117) noted that

> *the difference between the autistic and nonautistic rubella children with sensory defects is the use they [the autistic children] make of alternative . . . modes of experiencing. Nonautistic youngsters . . . are very alert to their surroundings through their other senses, especially exhibiting visual alertness and appropriate responsiveness . . . also through seeking of affectionate bodily contact. Some are shy, some slow to warm up, some perhaps wary; but one is impressed by their readiness to respond to appropriately selected and carefully timed overtures. . . . The autistic children neither explore alternative sensory modalities nor manifest appropriated responsiveness. They form a distinct group whose distance from people cannot be adequately explained by the degree or combination of visual and auditory loss, nor by the degree of retardation where this also exists. . . . Whether retarded or not, their affective behaviors do not resemble those of children of their obtained mental age—in fact, there is no mental age for which the behaviors are appropriate.*

Confusion concerning visual impairment and autism spectrum disorders has been sometimes fueled by the appearance of similar behaviors in children who are congenitally blind and children who have an autism spectrum disorder. Children who are blind may have limited concrete experiences and resulting difficulties in cognitive and language development, and their lack of vision can have a profound impact on their social interactions (Jamieson, 2004). Hobson and Bishop (2003) specifically focused on children who were congenitally blind, "among whom features of autism are strikingly common" (p. 336). After they systematically observed the social interactions of two matched groups of children with congenital blindness who did not have autism, they rated social engagement, emotional tone, play, and language. They found that "qualities of social impairment in the more disabled children were similar to those in sighted children with autism . . . the socially impaired children had 'autistic-like' abnormalities in both social and non-social domains" (p. 341). In an earlier study, Hobson, Lee, and Brown (1999) compared a group of nine children with congenital blindness with "autism-like syndrome" with a closely matched group of nine children with autism who were sighted. They found that there "was substantial similarity between the groups, but also suggestive evidence of possible group differences. . . . Research on the psychological development of congenitally blind children promises to yield insights into the nature of autism itself" (p. 54).

Although several others have attempted to explore the relationship, if any, between ASD and visual impairment (Cass, 1996; Gense & Gense, 1994; Jordan, 1996; Morse, Pawletko & Rocissano, 2000; O'Hare, 1996; Pawletko & Rocissano, 2000), correlations have not been established. The fact that ASD is neurological in nature has been highlighted. Are individuals whose visual impairment stems from neurological causes or implications at an increased risk for ASD? Nothing that is presently known about ASD precludes it from occurring with any eye condition, but the potential connection with neurologically based etiologies remains to be explored. Some of the more common etiologies of visual impairment with neurological implications include retinopathy of prematurity (ROP), cortical (or cerebral) visual impairment (CVI), anophthalmia, and optic-nerve hypoplasia:

- **ROP.** ROP is a retinal disorder that causes changes in the retinal blood vessels and may also lead to detached retinas and vision loss. This condition is associated with premature birth. The degree of prematurity correlates with the degree of vision loss.

- **CVI.** In this condition the individual appears to have normally formed eyes and has a normal eye exam. Vision loss is caused by damage to the visual cortex and other visual processing areas of the brain. Visual abilities may appear to fluctuate and may improve with training.

- **Anophthalmia.** Anophthalmia is the absence of the globe (eyeball), usually in both eyes; the condition results when one or both eyes do not form during the early stages of pregnancy during critical periods of the fetus's brain development. The eyelids may appear sunken because of the absence of the globe.

- **Optic-nerve hypoplasia.** In this condition, one or both of the optic nerves are underdeveloped. Vision loss varies from moderate to severe.

When neurologically based visual impairments are experienced by a child who displays a persistent and extreme cluster of behaviors that are typical of an autism spectrum disorder, it is important for the coexistence of these complex conditions to be explored and addressed.

Although research on a dual diagnosis of ASD and visual impairment is limited thus far, it is clear that the implications for development and learning can be profound. Other areas of investigation have included the profound impact of congenital visual impairment on cognitive and linguistic development and social interaction, and the possible relationship between this impact and autistic-like syndromes and developmental breakdowns in children (Cass, 1996; Pring, 2005). A picture of great complexity continues to emerge as our understanding of these relationships evolves.

Each child with ASDVI is, then, unique in his or her ability to learn and to process sensory information. The success of interventions will depend on the educational team's ability to understand each child's strengths and challenges and to design and implement an educational program that is reflective of these strengths and challenges.

2

Identifying Autism Spectrum Disorders in Students with Visual Impairments

How does one accurately determine the presence of both an autism spectrum disorder and a visual impairment? As important, how does one address the development of appropriate educational programs for children who are suspected of having ASDVI? First, it is essential to recognize that there are currently no formal diagnostic tools to establish the co-existence of autism spectrum disorder with a visual impairment. Certainly, a visual impairment can be identified with some precision. Identifying an autism spectrum disorder, on the other hand, can be a highly complex, sometimes more subjective process, and is based on diverse behavioral criteria that are descriptive of clusters of behaviors. For practitioners, it is vital to recognize both disabilities and to understand the effect of their coexistence on individual children.

Historically, since Kanner's description of childhood autism in 1943, there have been descriptions of children with visual impairments presenting a clinical picture similar to autism in sighted youngsters, with some studies citing "stereotypes, autism or echolalia, and self-absorption as frequently occurring features" with blindness (Cass, 1996, p. 1). In addition to the research discussed in the preceding chapter, Fraiberg and Freedman (1964) presented their observations of "ego deviation" in 25 percent to 30 percent of children who are blind. There also is an indication that a significant number of children with visual impairments demonstrate behaviors whose appearance would lead to the diagnosis of ASD in sighted children. These behaviors in visually impaired children, now often referred to as "stereotypical behaviors," are often described as "blindisms," "autistic-like behaviors," or "autistic tendencies"

(Cass, 1996; Hobson & Bishop, 2003; Hobson, Lee & Brown, 1999). However, no research has specifically addressed the statistical prevalence overall of autism spectrum disorders in children who are visually impaired.

As we indicated in Chapter 1, the limited research highlights the need for more study of the identification and prevalence of autism spectrum disorders in children who are visually impaired. However, it is clear that the learning styles of students who are blind or visually impaired *and* have an autism spectrum disorder, are *not* the result of their visual impairment alone. If this were the case, interventions that are typically successful with the majority of students who are blind or visually impaired would also be successful with these students, but they are not. It is critical, therefore, that team members who work with such a student, including parents, strive to understand the unique learning characteristics of the student and the impact of the dual diagnosis and develop individually designed instructional programs that will target the child's specific learning needs.

"TYPICAL" DEVELOPMENT OF CHILDREN WITHOUT DISABILITIES

Before we consider the impact of a disability on learning, it is helpful to have a clear picture of the "typical" development of children who are not disabled. Such knowledge allows professionals to judge the probable impacts of a disability and to develop appropriate educational programs in response to these impacts. Numerous lists and charts that detail the developmental milestones of typically developing children are available. (Online resources include the Web sites of the University of Michigan Health System [www.med.umich.edu/1libr/yourchild/devmile] and the National Network for Child Care [www.nncc.org/Child.Dev/mile1.html].) With this information, one can identify the developmental sequence through which most children grow physically and cognitively. Most children tend to follow the same approximate timetable, generally acquiring the same skills in the same sequence at about the same age range.

In an attempt to gain a better understanding of the learning styles, strengths, and challenges of children who are blind or visually impaired who also have an autism spectrum disorder, it is important to consider what is presently known about the development of children who have such disorders, and the "typical" development of children with a visual impairment, if a descriptor such as "typical" can be used to refer to what is most commonly observed. The similarities and the differences that are manifested in these two disabilities must be carefully considered. It is also essential to recognize that there are no specific behaviors in ASD that may not be found in nondisabled children at one time or another, including children with visual impairments, and such behaviors can be viewed as typical in the context of vision loss. The manifestation of an autism spectrum disorder is the cluster or combination of behavioral deficits and behavioral excesses in the areas of communication routines, social interactions, and sensory processing, as was outlined in the Prologue and preceding chapter of this book.

DEVELOPMENT OF CHILDREN WITH AUTISM SPECTRUM DISORDERS

Children with an autism spectrum disorder do not follow standard patterns of development (Janzen, 2003; Quill, 2000; National Research Council, 2001). In some children, problems may be apparent from birth. For others, behaviors become more noticeable as the child begins to lag developmentally behind children of the same age. Yet another group displays typical development and then suddenly loses the skills they had already acquired (the loss usually occurs between 16 and 36 months of age). These skills by and large are in the areas of communication and social interactions, as we noted in Chapter 1. In addition, children with an autism spectrum disorder display atypical behavior in the two other areas identified in Chapter 1: repetitive behavior and difficulty using sensory information.

In the communication-language area, many children with an autism spectrum disorder remain mute throughout their lives. Others begin to babble and coo, but soon stop. Still others may be delayed in language development, with verbal language skills developing as late as 5–8 years of age. Children with ASD often confuse pronouns. Some children are only able to repeat what they hear (echolalia), whereas others verbalize a "patterned" phrase (e.g., "when's your birthday?") in a variety of different situations, even when this phrase does not pertain to the situation. For children with ASD, facial expressions, movements, and gestures rarely match what they are saying. For those with spoken language, their tone of voice and pitch is often "sing-song" or flat.

In the social realm, most children with an autism spectrum disorder seem to have great difficulty learning to engage in the give-and-take of everyday individual, person-to-person interactions. They take longer to learn to interpret what others are thinking and feeling, and subtle social cues have little meaning for them. Children with ASD have problems seeing things from another person's perspective and hence are unable to predict or understand other people's actions.

Children with an autism spectrum disorder usually display repetitive behaviors and obsessions. These behaviors and obsessions set them apart from other children and are often referred to as stereotypic or self-stimulatory behaviors. Some children tend to perform certain actions (such as rocking, hand-flapping, and spinning) repeatedly. Many develop fixations with specific objects and hence constantly line up cars or arrange Legos in complex patterns, for example. Others demand consistency in the environment and have great difficulty dealing with any kind of change. Furthermore, they rarely, if ever, engage in imaginative play.

In the area of sensory development, students with ASD have difficulty using sensory information to help them develop a "coherent picture" of their environment or of activities that are occurring within their environment. They seem unable to balance sensory input appropriately. Many are hyper- or hyposensitive to certain sounds, textures, tastes, and smells; some even find some sensory inputs to be "painful." Their ability to process sensory information appropriately is "scrambled," which leads them to have extreme reactions to things that would not bother typically developing children. For example, a child may appear not to hear, but then have a strong reaction to the school's fire alarm.

In summary, an autism spectrum disorder affects the individual's ability to communicate, form relationships with others, and respond appropriately to the environment. Some individuals with ASD are high functioning, with intact speech and intelligence. Others are mentally retarded or nonverbal or have severe language delays. They may seem closed off, appearing to be locked into repetitive behaviors and rigid patterns of thinking, making it extremely difficult for others to "enter their world." There is great variability in how the characteristics of autism spectrum disorders manifest themselves and in the subsequent impact on functioning.

DEVELOPMENT OF CHILDREN WHO ARE BLIND OR VISUALLY IMPAIRED

The impacts of a visual impairment on development can be multifaceted and complex, and the implications vary from child to child (Ferrell, 1985; Ferrell, Shaw, & Dietz, 1998; Pogrund & Fazzi, 2002; Warren, 1994). Several critical issues must be considered when one addresses the development of a child with a visual impairment. First, children who are blind have their own individual capabilities and characteristics and approach all learning from a highly individualized perspective. Second, there is great variability in developmental growth. Just as sighted children learn, grow, and develop at different rates within a certain sequence of framework of skills, so do children who are visually impaired. Finally, the impact of a visual impairment can be vast and varying and can alter a child's ability to learn and develop in the same way that a sighted child learns and develops. Thus, a focus solely on comparisons with sighted children may be misleading.

As Lowenfeld (1973) noted, blindness poses three primary limitations: the range and variety of experiences, the ability to move about the environment, and the ability to control the environment and the self in relation to it. The lack of vision or the presence of significant visual limitations can restrict a child's range and variety of experiences and thus will have an impact on the child's overall development. We know that a child who is blind learns about the environment through other sensory channels, particularly the auditory and tactile senses. Neither of these senses, however, provides the depth and detail of information that the visual sense provides. The auditory sense is the primary sense used for developing language and communication, but it does not provide the same information about the size, location, shape, and other characteristics of objects as does the visual sense. The tactile sense can provide information about size and shape, but is limited to objects that can be explored by hand. Information about large objects (including mountains, oceans, and large buildings), minute or dangerous objects (like insects or fire), and "abstract" images (such as a sunset or a rainbow) is not easily understood without the ability to make and understand representations cognitively. For these reasons, the impact of vision loss on a child's cognitive and linguistic development can be profound.

For years, experts in the field of blindness and visual impairment supported the idea that visually impaired children follow the same developmental sequences as do sighted children, although perhaps at a different rate. More recently, however, evidence has been mounting that there may be neither a "typical" rate nor a typical sequence of development for children who are visually impaired. Sighted children use their vision to learn and learn to integrate visual information with information they have gathered through other modalities. When this sense is absent or limited, the processes of learning and growing will be altered. This is certainly not to say that a child who is blind will not develop "normally," but that the process through which the child learns and grows may well be different from that of sighted children. Clearly, the visual sense is the primary learning modality for the majority of children, and if this sense is impaired or nonexistent, learning will be affected.

Project PRISM: A National Longitudinal Study of the Early Development of Children Who Are Visually Impaired (Ferrell et al., 1998) considered the sequence and rate of development of children with visual impairments from birth through age 5. The study, conducted over a period of five years, was a seven-agency collaborative effort and included 202 children with visual impairments, nearly 60 percent of whom had additional disabilities. The investigators used the Battelle Developmental Inventory (BDI; Newberg et al., 1984) as the primary measure of development. The BDI is a standardized instrument that measures behaviors in the personal-social, adaptive, motor, communication, and cognitive domains. It is normed on children with disabilities and includes adaptations for children with visual impairments. Results from this research suggest that the presence of disabilities in addition to visual impairment had a more significant impact on the children's development than did the degree of visual function. In addition, the development of children with visual acuities of 20/800 or worse was significantly different from that of children with visual acuities of 20/500 or better. The development of the latter group approximated that of sighted children if no additional disabilities were present. This finding supports the notion that children use their vision to enhance their understanding of their environment and hence that vision supports their ability to learn from the environment, from interactions with the environment, and from interactions with objects and people in the environment.

Project PRISM has provided important information on the development of children with visual impairment. This research noted the following conclusions:

- When compared to typically developing children, the age of acquisition of 12 developmental milestones (such as reaching for objects, transferring objects from hand to hand, sitting, and crawling) is delayed in children with visual impairments.

- For 5 milestones related to expressive and receptive communication, the median age of acquisition is similar for children who are visually impaired and sighted children.

- Some developmental milestones are acquired in a different sequence by children with visual impairments than by children without disabilities.

Ferrell (2000, pp. 126–127) noted that despite the methodological rigor of the study, two limitations need to be kept in mind: First, all the children received services from specialist agencies for children with visual impairments, and second, the services they received "varied in 'intensity, duration, and frequency'" (Ferrell, 1998, p. 65). Thus, one must be careful not to generalize "about the delicate interactions between children's development and other variables" (p. 65).

IDENTIFYING ASD IN STUDENTS WHO ARE BLIND OR VISUALLY IMPAIRED

How then does one identify a student who is affected by both a visual impairment and an autism spectrum disorder? By working with a team of experienced professionals who are knowledgeable about both areas of disability. By observing the student carefully, and gathering information from family members, past medical and other records, and previous service providers. And by consistently striving to understand the meaning attached to behaviors that are observed. (For a detailed discussion of assessment, see Chapter 4). To help clarify the potential behavioral characteristics of students with ASDVI, Appendix 2A, at the end of this chapter, outlines developmental milestones, behaviors, and learning characteristics that are commonly seen in nondisabled students, students who are blind or visually impaired, and children with ASDVI in the four areas of behavior that define autism spectrum disorder. The charts provided do *not* address every developmental milestone, nor do they address all the behavioral characteristics associated with either autism spectrum disorder or blindness or visual impairment. Furthermore, the behaviors that are identified for children who are blind or visually impaired focus more on behaviors for children who are blind or whose vision is impaired to the degree that they do not rely on visual information for learning. This information is not meant to be used as a tool for identifying autism spectrum disorder in children who are blind. Rather, it is intended to highlight the key areas that often cause uncertainty in the diagnostic process for identifying students with the dual disability and can be used by members of educational teams to gain a better understanding of the potential implications of ASDVI for individual children.

It is important to remember that even children who are developing "typically" and children who are blind or visually impaired may demonstrate behavioral characteristics in one or more of the four areas listed in the charts. It is the combined cluster effect and the pervasiveness of the characteristics that lead to a dual diagnosis of an autism spectrum disorder and a visual impairment. This point is illustrated by the wide variety of behaviors that were observed in six students, each of whom was identified as having both an autism spectrum disorder and a visual impairment. These students' specific behaviors in each of the four areas previously identified are summarized in Appendix 2B to this chapter.

SUMMARY

Children with an autism spectrum disorder have learning challenges that are different from those of most children. So do children with a visual impairment. When a child has both an autism spectrum disorder and a visual impairment, the implications are not simply additive of the two separate disabilities. Indeed, the learning challenges are multiplicative. The *combination* of these disabilities has implications for all aspects of development, including communication skills, social integration skills, cognitive development, and movement. The impact on development and learning is significant and profound.

APPENDIX 2A	Comparison of Development Among Children Who Are Sighted and Typically Developing, Blind or Visually Impaired, and Blind or Visually Impaired with an Autism Spectrum Disorder	
Typical Development	**Blind or Visually Impaired**	**ASDVI**
Communication Behaviors		
Makes cooing and gurgling sounds (3–6 months). Copies speech sounds (6–12 months).	The process of acquiring speech and language appears to be the same for visually impaired children as it is for typical children, but slower physical development, a more restricted range of experiences, and the lack of visual stimulation may cause a child's language development to be slower (Scholl, 1986).	Language develops slowly or not at all. Development is frequently "splintered"; language development may or may not be consistent with typical developmental norms or sequences. May show no interest in communicating.
Uses much jargon (unintelligible speech) with emotional content. Is able to follow simple commands (18 months). Has a vocabulary of 150–300 words (24 months).	Speech is echolalic but for a short duration. Language may be delayed if experiences are limited, but is not distorted. Responds appropriately to language requests; enjoy communication "give and take."	Exhibits concrete understanding and use of language; has difficulty with generalizations. Echolalic; often has difficulty breaking this pattern. The echolalia often leads to patterns of verbal perseveration with idiosyncratic meanings. Has difficulty initiating and engaging in meaningful conversations. The range of "topics of interest" is narrow. Has difficulty maintaining a topic chosen by others; exhibits limited or no conversational reciprocity.

Source: Adapted with permission from M. Gense and D. J. Gense, "Identifying Autism in Children with Blindness and Visual Impairments," *RE:view, 26* (Summer 1994) pp. 55–62. Copyright © 1994, Heldref Publications, Washington, DC.

Typical Development	Blind or Visually Impaired	ASDVI
Understands most simple questions dealing with his or her own environment and activities (36 months). Relates experiences so that they can be followed with reason. May briefly exhibit pronoun reversals. Takes part in simple conversations (2–3 years).	Vocabulary is built through concrete experiences. Can experience difficulty with abstract language because of limited concrete experiences. May reverse pronouns, but such reversals are brief in duration. Difficulties with concepts are common because of the lack of a visual model; once understood, concepts can be generalized. Language development usually follows developmental norms.	Uses words without attaching the usual meanings to them. Uses nonconventional or non-traditional behaviors (such as gestures, pulling) as a form of communication. Has long-term difficulty using pronouns appropriately.
Follows a logical pattern of concept development from the concrete to the abstract.	Language development is based on concrete "hands-on" experiences.	Has apparent lack of common sense; may be overly active or passive. Has difficulty with abstract concepts and often focuses on "irrelevant" information; has a literal translation of language; a literal or concrete understanding of concepts makes generalizations difficult.
Develops language from experience and interaction with the environment; can adjust the topic of interest from an early age.	Learns language from an early age; adjusts the topic of conversation. Had difficulty with abstract concepts for which there is limited "hands-on" experience. Develops a broader understanding based on experiences; is able to generalize information with instruction.	If verbal, may converse but focus on a topic of perseverative interest. Has difficulty generalizing information, even with instruction.

(continued on next page)

Typical Development	Blind or Visually Impaired	ASDVI
Social Interactions		
Responds to his or her name (6–9 months).	Responds to his or name; responses are more defined when paired with tactile contact. Needs to learn that a world exists beyond reach; may exhibit social interest through changing or shifting posture (leaning or turning).	Appears not to hear; does not orient toward sound.
Takes turns while playing with an adult (for example, using actions, sounds, or facial expressions) (6–12 months).	Engages in social give-and-take; seeks to share information or experiences with others.	Has limited, if any, social interests Has a limited understanding of social give-and-take.
Makes simple choices among toys. Mimics another child's play (18–24 months).	Play is sometimes observed to be less "imaginative" and more concrete because of the lack of a visual model. Redirection of an activity is possible.	Plays repetitively; often does not use toys for their intended purpose.
Often indulges in make-believe (48 months).	Because of limited visual references, may have difficulty in observing, organizing, and synthesizing the environment; imitative and make-believe play may be delayed, but can be specifically "taught." Requires a variety of opportunities to learn and to generalize; needs feedback to understand and comprehend some social situations.	Does not engage in sponta-neous or imaginative play or initiate pretend play. Perseverative behavior is a problem, and a redirection of activities may be difficult.

Typical Development	Blind or Visually Impaired	ASDVI
Enjoys playing with other children (3–4 years).	Enjoys playing with other children. Shows social curiosity; is curious about the environment (for example, may ask who may be in the room or where a peer may be).	Prefers to spend time alone, rather than with others; peer relationships are often distorted. Exhibits little social curiosity; may find interactions with others to be unpleasant.
Is able occasionally to use feelings to explain reasons (48 months).	Demonstrates empathy; is able to comprehend another's feelings.	May treat other people as objects; has a limited ability to understand another's feelings.
Enjoys playing organized games with other children (5–6 years).	Enjoys playing organized games with other children. Has difficulty observing, organizing, and synthesizing the environment; requires a variety of opportunities.	Is often anxious and uncomfortable in social situations; prefers to follow routines and rituals. Has difficulty adapting to change.
Demonstrates empathy toward others.	Will acknowledge emotions of self and others. Seeks out others if hurt, sick, sad, or angry.	Appears to ignore when someone is hurt. Shows little bonding with family members

Restricted, Repetitive, and Stereotyped Patterns of Behavior

Reaches for a toy (3–6 months). Puts in and dumps objects from containers (12–18 months). Looks at storybook pictures with an adult (18–24 months).	Stereotypic behaviors (rocking, eye-poke) may occur in novel and unfamiliar situations; management of these behaviors can be accomplished with redirection into meaningful activities that provide sensory feedback; the child learns to control these behaviors when older.	Plays repetitively; toys are not used as intended. May perseverate on a specific feature of a toy (such as spinning the wheel of a car) or may engage in a repetitive action with a toy or objects.

(continued on next page)

Typical Development	Blind or Visually Impaired	ASDVI
	Interests may be limited because of limited exposure; demonstrates an interest in a variety of toys or objects once they are experienced. Historically, stereotypic behaviors have been attributed to the lack of stimulation of the vestibular system. These behaviors occur more in young children and lessen as the children learn to interact with the environment.	The interruption of a favorite activity or of a stimulatory motor behavior (such as hand flapping or rocking from one foot to another) is often met with extreme resistance.
Helps with simple tasks (2–3 years). Follows two-step directions. Uses materials and toys to make things (3–4 years).	Interest may be limited to toys, tasks, or objects that were previously experienced; is able to engage in a variety of activities with adults and peers. Redirection of an activity is possible; response to changes are easier with greater experiences.	Has highly restricted interests; has difficulty being redirected from high-interest toys or objects. Exhibits an extreme interest in one part of an object or one type of object.
Shifts attention from one person, item, or activity to another.	Exhibits typical flexibility in managing changes in routine.	Challenging behaviors escalate when changes in routine or structure are experienced; demonstrates, inflexibility when transitioning between activities. Stereotypic behaviors occur throughout life and are difficult to break. Behaviors increase with anxiety and with stressful situations and can be difficult to redirect.

Typical Development	Blind or Visually Impaired	ASDVI
		May perseverate on a single item, idea, or person; may rigidly perform a seemingly nonfunctional routine. May engage in aggressive or violent behavior or injure himself or herself; may throw frequent tantrums for no apparent reason.

Responses to Sensory Information

Typical Development	Blind or Visually Impaired	ASDVI
Turns head toward sounds (3–6 months). Feeds self with spoon; drinks from a cup (12–18 months). Moves body in time to music (18–24 months). Puts on clothing with a little help (4–5 years). Jumps, runs, throws, and climbs using good balance (3–4 years). Tolerates a normal range of touch, movement, sounds, and smells. Attends to relevant stimuli.	Often has poor posture because of the lack of a visual model; learns to orient to sounds with instruction. Interests may be restricted because of the lack of vision; interests expand with experiences. Exhibits little delay in motor development until the onset of locomotion. Can be easily engaged. Because of the lack of visual stimulation, often creates his or her own stimulation; can usually "redirect" the stimulatory behavior. Uses residual senses to gain information. Attends to relevant stimuli.	Has unusual reactions to physical sensations, such as being overly sensitive to touch or underresponsive to pain; sight, hearing, touch, pain, smell, and taste may be affected to a lesser or greater degree. Unusual postures and hand movements are common and can be difficult to redirect. Commonly perseverates various sensory stimuli. Tactile defensiveness is common and is usually not overcome with time. Often appears not to hear or focus.

A Summary of Specific Behaviors Observed in Six Students with Autism Spectrum Disorder and Visual Impairment

Student	Specific Behavioral Characteristics Observed			
	Impairments in Communication	Impairments in Social Interactions	Restricted, Repetitive, and Stereotyped Patterns of Behavior	Responses to Sensory Information
Tonya (totally blind) An 18-year-old senior in high school; is expected to graduate with a regular high school diploma	Verbal, pedantic speech Converses with adults but not children her own age Impatient if others do not follow her rules	Engages in little inter-action with individuals her own age Stays in own room rather than be a part of family group Has difficulty working with anyone whose ideas are different from hers Speaks fluently about topics of interest, in-cluding politics and music history	Eats the same foods day after day Obsesses on classical music, to the exclusion of all other types of music Performs a task per-fectly one day, but is unable to repeat it if she is distracted by other thoughts Can locate obscure braille classroom notes taken years ago Uses seven straws at one time	Shrinks and moves away from a light touch on the shoulder or hugs Avoids wearing certain clothing because it is uncomfortable on her skin

Student	Impairments in Communication	Impairments in Social Interactions	Restricted, Repetitive, and Stereotyped Patterns of Behavior	Responses to Sensory Information
Robin (low vision) A 14-year-old student in middle school whose curriculum focuses on "functional" life skills; uses large print to read "community" words	Uses a stream of words linked together because she likes how they sound, rather than be- cause of their meaning Vocally repeats rules or situations to herself as she travels from one place to another Is able to recite com- plete conversations "verbatim", but is unable to understand their content	Has difficulty with social judgments; will sit and stand too close to others Does not know her classmates' names Does not initiate interactions	Perseverates on the number 6 Perseverates on win- dows and open doors	

(continued on next page)

Student	Impairments in Communication	Impairments in Social Interactions	Restricted, Repetitive, and Stereotyped Patterns of Behavior	Responses to Sensory Information
Suzy (low vision) An 8-year-old girl presently enrolled in a second-grade classroom; requires significant support from adults to help facilitate inclusion into the curriculum	Vocal language was late to emerge and is limited to familiar phrases and inflections Initiates interactions with adults by asking the same question repeatedly Uses simple, repeated phrases to interact with peers Engages in repeated vocal play; expresses sounds and words through rhythmic patterns	Cried constantly between birth and first birthday Has delayed responses to vocal interactions from other children Plays with toys differently from their intended purpose Has difficulty following directions that are intended for a group Is not interested in what peers are doing	Listens to the same Disney movie hundreds of times Turns on a video to a particular segment and repeatedly plays this segment Has a limited interests in most toys	During infancy, cried when moved between the bedroom and the living room Has tantrums when a neighbor, three houses away, mows the lawn Is frightened of the vacuum; cries when it is in use Flicks her finger and eyes when in sunlight

APPENDIX 2B continued

Student	Impairments in Communication	Impairments in Social Interactions	Restricted, Repetitive, and Stereotyped Patterns of Behavior	Responses to Sensory Information
Bruce (totally blind)	Has a limited understanding of language	Has difficulty following rules	Perseverates about cars	Can identify the makes and models of cars by their sound of the engines
A 25-year-old man who lives with his mother and father; has a full-time job in a supported work site (gardening and lawn maintenance); travels to and from his workplace on the city bus	Becomes stuck on certain questions; asks the same question repeatedly in all environments	Does not engage with peers; has preferred adults his entire life	Walks on tiptoes	Is tactilely defensive; has difficulty reading braille for long periods
	Sings songs backward	As a child did not play with toys	Has tantrums when his daily routine changes or when he is asked to participate in a new activity	Has perfect musical pitch
	Imitates an adult's voice, particulary when repeating "rules" given by the adult	Does not understand teasing or humor	Watches his "favorite" video hundreds of times	
	Engages in perseverative conversations; his topics of interest are limited	Has difficulty understanding other people's perspectives		

(continued on next page)

Student	Impairments in Communication	Impairments in Social Interactions	Restricted, Repetitive, and Stereotyped Patterns of Behavior	Responses to Sensory Information
Amanda (totally blind)	Is nonverbal; has several "odd" vocalizations	Ignores adults and peers	Constantly spins and turns in circles	Prefers to lie on her back, flapping her legs, feet, and hands
A 12-year-old girl whose educational placement is a self-contained classroom; her curriculum focuses on functional living skills	May try to pull a person to get something that she wants	Treats adults as objects Has no observable play skills Does not engage in joint attention (see Chapter 4, Assessment)	Climbs on tables and other furniture	Dislikes clothing on her arms, legs, and feet Has poor motor coordination—is "floppy"; has difficulty grasping Engages in aggressive behaviors

Student	Impairments in Communication	Impairments in Social Interactions	Restricted, Repetitive, and Stereotyped Patterns of Behavior	Responses to Sensory Information
Jimmy (totally blind) A 14-year-old who attends a residential school for students who are visually impaired; his curricula is functional, with a primary focus on foundational communication, daily living skills, and O&M	Vocalizations are often "immediate" echolalia (for example, when the teacher asks, "Do you want a cookie" he repeats, "Want a cookie?") Uses high-pitched inflections Engages in aggressive behaviors (slapping, hitting, or biting) to indicate an undesired activity or food	Has no understanding of or interactions with peers Engages in very limited initiations that are usually based on the desire for food or a favorite activity; his initiation of an interaction is in the form of vocalization of question (for example, "Do you want swimming?") Has no play skills	Perseverates on rocking in a chair or swinging Has extreme difficulty changing routines	Engages in extremely aggressive behavior whose triggers include high-pitched voices, most shoes and socks, and the smells of certain foods

Program Planning and Instructional Strategies

Program Planning and Core Instructional Principles

For students with autism spectrum disorders *and* visual impairment (ASDVI), both the content of and methodology for instruction need to be different from those for students who have only one of these disabilities. Each child and the manner in which he or she learns and develops are highly individualized and unique, so service providers and parents must strive to understand each child's present level of development. According to Ferrell (2000, p. 122)

> *children with blindness and visual impairment learn differently, for no other reason than the fact that in most cases they cannot rely on their vision to provide information. The information they obtain through their other senses is* inconsistent *(things do not always make noise or produce an odor),* fragmented *(comes in bits and pieces), and* passive *(not under the child's control) It takes practice, training, and time to sort all this out.*

For children with ASD, another set of learning difficulties exist. As Arick, Loos, Falco, and Krug (2004, p. 7) noted:

> *A particularly challenging learning characteristic of children with autism is the failure to make critical discriminations when exposed to new learning. For instance, problems with auditory discrimination can make it difficult for the child to connect words to objects and people. This difficulty is sometimes present when the child performs very simple auditory or visual discriminations. Because of this learning characteristic, most behavior—*

analytic curricula developed since the 1960's have included techniques for teaching learners with autism to discriminate among various type of stimuli. These techniques include such discrimination teaching as match-to-sample trials, use of a distractor stimulus, extra stimulus prompting, and within stimulus prompting. . . .

A second and fundamental core learning deficit that is exhibited by children with autism and specifically impedes language development is joint attention deficit. Joint attention is the ability to coordinate attention to people and objects. It involves advanced gesturing such as showing, waving, pointing. Children with autism who have deficits in joint attention have difficulty coordinating attention between people and objects, orienting and attending, and following the gaze and pointing gesture of another person. Acquiring joint attention appears to be a critical developmental milestone in early normal development.

Designing an educational program for students with ASDVI is therefore not as simple as addressing either the visual impairment or the autism spectrum disorder. IEP or IFSP teams must consider how development and learning are or may be influenced by the visual impairment; by the autism spectrum disorder; and, most important, by the combination of the two.

Fundamentally, the IEP or IFSP team will want to be able to answer the question, "How does this child learn?" On the basis of understanding that each student must be approached from the perspective of his or her unique needs, the individually designed curriculum must focus on how the particular student learns. Ultimately, we teach to enhance a child's development. To design a program that leads to this enhancement, the team needs to know where the child functions developmentally, to establish what the child needs to learn next, and to know and understand how he or she processes information (see "Vital Questions: A Conceptual Framework for Instruction and Programming").

To begin to gather the information needed to answer, "How does this child learn?" the team must consider several important related questions:

- What information must be gathered to gain a better understanding of the child's immediate and long-term needs?

- How do we identify and understand the impacts of the disabilities on development and learning?

- How do we develop appropriate educational strategies that best address the child's needs?

Part 2 of this book includes individual chapters that provide information that can be used to answer these questions and to enhance the team members'

VITAL QUESTIONS: A CONCEPTUAL FRAMEWORK FOR INSTRUCTION AND PROGRAMMING

Understanding how a child with an autism spectrum disorder perceives and experiences stimuli and processes information is critical to working effectively with that child. When the members of an educational team begin exploring a student's capabilities and needs and planning educational services to meet these needs, the answers to several questions can provide vital guidance. The following questions provide essential information about a student that can help the team members plan necessary educational services but also indicate the ways in which instruction needs to be delivered to the student. They are therefore keys to both effective teacher-student interactions and successful program planning.

1. How does the student process and manage sensory information? What are the primary distracters that may affect the student?

2. What are the student's primary motivators, preferences, and interests? How can they be incorporated into instruction?

3. Typically, what is the student's attention span? Does the student have particular issues or situations that consistently challenge his or her ability to maintain attention? What strategies can be used to help increase his or her attention span?

4. How does the student manage and deal with change?

5. What are the student's primary strengths and primary challenges? What is the student's primary learning style?

6. What are the present needs of the student in each area of the core and expanded core curriculum? What may the future needs of the student be in each of these areas?

(For an illustration of the way in which these questions can be answered and applied to planning and instruction, see Chapter 8 on orientation and mobility.)

understanding of the child and ultimately supports the development of an effective educational program. This chapter focuses on general considerations for planning programs for students with ASDVI and on core instructional principles that can generally be applied across the curriculum. Also included at the end of this chapter is a brief glossary of terms (see "The Language of Instruction") that are used throughout Part 2. Information that is presented in Chapter 4 guides the team in designing appropriate assessment, while Chapters 5–11 present strategies and resources to address the unique implications of specific curricular content areas. The information provided in the final chapter focuses on general considerations for supporting students in the general classroom environment.

PROGRAM PLANNING

As we discussed in previous chapters, students with an autism spectrum disorder and visual impairment represent a broad range of abilities. Many students will be served best with a curriculum that focuses on functional skills, while others will be fully included in typical grade-level academic course work. Regardless of his or her abilities, however, each student with ASDVI needs intensive interventions and strategies to address the unique manifestations of the dual disability. Effective program planning allows the team to address these needs. The process of program planning is not, however, a one-time activity for students with ASDVI. As is true for all children with disabilities, program planning must be viewed as dynamic, rather than static. Information that is presented in this chapter is intended to help the team

- develop and implement an educational program plan that is based on information that is obtained from assessments

- identify appropriate focus areas of the core curriculum

- design and implement appropriate instructional strategies and tools that can be used to help a student organize and manage his or her environment and understand classroom expectations, which will help to facilitate a positive learning environment

THE FOUNDATION: A CORE CURRICULUM FOR STUDENTS WITH ASDVI

An initial assessment identifies the strengths and needs of the child–information that the educational team uses to design an individualized program that addresses the identified needs. Instructional strategies are used to implement the program, data are collected and analyzed to determine the student's progress, and adjustments are made on the basis of that analysis. The team must recognize that program planning is part of a continuous process, as illustrated in Figure 3.1.

In the educational curriculum that is available to students in schools today, each student's program of instruction reflects a "core curriculum." In a broad sense, this curriculum reflects the educational program that is re-

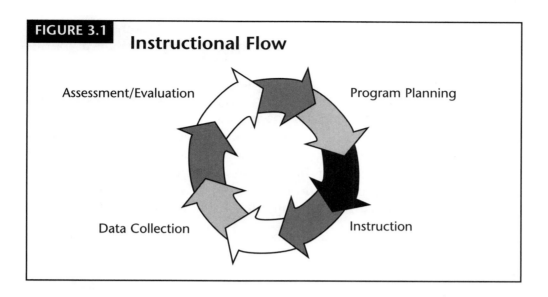

FIGURE 3.1

Instructional Flow

Assessment/Evaluation

Program Planning

Data Collection

Instruction

quired to provide the knowledge and skills that are necessary by the time a student graduates from high school. For many years, the curricular emphasis for all students was solely "academic." However, school reform efforts that have been implemented across the country have expanded this concept, in recognition that many skills other than academic ones are required for successful participation in society.

For students with disabilities, participation in a regular classroom, with access to and instruction in all the same curricular areas as their peers, as appropriate, is essential. For most, however, an expanded core curriculum must be incorporated into program planning. This expanded core curriculum must address the appropriate areas of the general curriculum that are available to all students, as well as the unique curricular focus areas that address the specific impact of a student's disability or disabilities. For the purposes of this book, the term *core curriculum* for students with ASDVI includes both a curriculum that will provide the educational program that covers the core that all students require and an expanded curriculum that addresses the potential impact of both visual impairment and autism spectrum disorder.

The *National Agenda for the Education of Children and Youths with Visual Impairments, Including Those with Multiple Disabilities, Revised* (2004) helped establish the concept of an expanded core curriculum for students with visual impairments in this country. Goal 8 of the National Agenda supports the premise that there are experiences and concepts casually and incidentally learned by sighted students that must be systematically and sequentially taught to the visually impaired student. The core curriculum for visually impaired students is not the same as for sighted students. Indeed, it is much larger and more complex. It is proposed that the term "core curriculum" for students who are vision impaired be used to define the basic educational needs for this population.

Areas of study that are common to visually impaired and sighted students include English, language arts and other languages, mathematics, science, health, physical education, fine arts, social studies, economics, business, vocational education, and history. The expanded core curriculum, unique areas of study for students who are visually impaired, which are typically required for the successful completion of their education and are not common to their sighted peers, include instruction that is needed to address the impact of visual impairment. These disability-specific areas include the following:

- compensatory or functional academic skills (such as the teaching of braille and communication modes)

- O&M

- social, independent living, recreational, and leisure skills

- career education

- listening and visual efficiency skills

- use of assistive technology

For students with ASDVI, the educational program must reflect consideration of this essential core curriculum for both visual impairment *and* ASD, on the basis of needs that have been identified through initial and ongoing assessments.

A core curriculum for students with ASD has not been as specifically identified as that for students with visual impairment. Research has indicated, however, that the following curricular areas may serve as this expanded core (Lord & McGee, 2001, p. 218):

- functional, spontaneous communication skills

- engagement in tasks and play

- social skills

- self-help skills

- fine and gross motor skills

- cognitive skills

- appropriate behaviors

- independent organizational skills

Effective programs for students with ASDVI take into consideration the core curriculum for both disabilities, and are based on the unique needs and abilities of each student. The program must provide the environment and educational strategies that address those needs for the child and the family. The program will need to be designed to include instruction to address the core curriculum for students with visual impairments and the critical skills identified for students with autism spectrum disorders. For example, if a student is a tactile learner, the mode of communication that is identified through the learning media assessment (see Koenig & Holbrook, 1995) may be tactile. Teaching braille using a typical curriculum may make little sense to a student with ASDVI because the student must first learn the connection between the need to communicate and a communication system such as braille. This is where the curriculum for students with autism will overlay the core curriculum for students who are visually impaired. Using the strategies that are appropriate for students with autism, the team will first need to teach the student to engage and communicate appropriately with an adult. The foundational instructional strategies will come from the field of autism (such as the use of such methods as discrete trials, functional routines, and pivotal response training; see "The Language of Instruction" in Appendix 3A of this chapter for definitions) with modifications made to address the student's lack of vision. The overlay of the two focuses and their related processes need to be carefully planned. The following case examples of Timothy and Roy illustrate the different needs and abilities of students with ASDVI and hence the different instructional strategies that are required to teach them.

> Timothy is a kindergarten-age student who is totally blind and has been identified with autism spectrum disorder. Timothy has difficulty understanding night from day. At home, he is allowed to sleep when he is tired and is often awake for many hours at night. As a result, he sleeps on the school bus and often comes to school tired. Since it has been determined that Timothy is a tactile learner, he is being introduced to a tactile object communication system. However, he prefers to use avoiding, crying, pinching, and hitting to communicate. Timothy does not respond consistently to his own name or follow simple directions. He enjoys motor activities, especially swinging and rolling, and has been introduced to an adapted cane. When he is left alone, Timothy sleeps, rocks, or swings. He does not like loud noises, is not aware of others students in his environment, and does not seek out other people, toys, or objects. He eats a few finger foods and needs assistance to scoop and spear food.

Figure 3.2 shows how a program of instruction would be planned for Timothy that would address each of the curriculum areas.

FIGURE 3.2	Planning an Educational Program for Timothy	
Expanded Core Curriculum for Visually Impaired Students	**Core Curriculum for Students with an Autism Spectrum Disorder**	**Program for ASDVI for Timothy**
Compensatory or functional academic skills (such as the teaching of braille) Social, independent living, recreational, and leisure skills Use of assistive technology	Functional, spontaneous communication skills	■ Teach Timothy the systematic use of tactile objects for requesting, following a schedule, and following simple routines for dressing, arriving, and departing ■ Teach Timothy choice making for reinforcements and play activities ■ Consider pairing an auditory output device with a tactile object if Timothy is responding to auditory stimuli
Social, independent living, recreational, and leisure skills Career education O&M	Social skills	■ Teach Timothy to attend to an adult and to imitate simple actions ■ Teach Timothy to share and explore toys ■ Teach Timothy to follow simple commands, both those given by an adult and using a tactile schedule ■ Teach Timothy to go for a walk and locate destinations ■ Teach Timothy to request items
Social, independent living, recreational, and leisure skills	Self-help skills	Teach Timothy to ■ wash his hands

FIGURE 3.2 continued

Expanded Core Curriculum for Visually Impaired Students	Core Curriculum for Students with an Autism Spectrum Disorder	Program for ASDVI for Timothy
O&M		■ participate with a small group for a snack ■ transition between activities ■ follow tactile or auditory routines
O&M	Fine and gross motor skills	Teach Timothy to ■ imitate movements ■ transition between activities ■ to use an adaptive cane to move to functional locations (from the bus to the class-room, and from his home to a car)
Compensatory or functional academic skills (such as braille) Listening and visual efficiency skills	Cognitive skills	Teach Timothy to ■ match objects ■ sort objects ■ label objects ■ follow simple schedule using tactile objects ■ follow directions from an adult
Social, independent living, recreational, and leisure skills Compensatory or functional academic skills (such as braille)	Appropriate behaviors	■ Provide access to and the use of a communication system ■ Provide opportunities for making choices ■ Provide reinforcement with preferred activities

(continued on next page)

Expanded Core Curriculum for Visually Impaired Students	Core Curriculum for Students with an Autism Spectrum Disorder	Program for ASDVI for Timothy
		■ Help Timothy participate in getting out and putting away toys and materials
		■ Provide frequent break times
Compensatory or functional academic skills (such as braille) O&M Social, independent living, recreational, and leisure skills Career education	Engagement in tasks and play	■ Determine toys and activities that are reinforcing for Timothy ■ Offer Timothy choices ■ Stimulate Timothy's interest ■ Teach Timothy to participate in getting materials out and putting them away ■ Teach Timothy how to play with toys ■ Teach Timothy to play in a variety of environments ■ Teach Timothy to take turns
Use of assistive technology Social, independent living, recreational, and leisure skills Compensatory or functional academic skills (such as braille)	Independent organizational skills	■ Teach Timothy to participate in getting out and putting away materials, clothing, toys, and snacks ■ Teach Timothy to follow a tactile or auditory schedule ■ Teach Timothy to follow arrival and departure routines ■ Teach Timothy to participate in dressing, bathing, and toothbrushing routines ■ Teach Timothy to learn whole tasks

FIGURE 3.2 continued

Roy, a fourth-grade student, is a fluent braille reader but does not always understand the concepts involved in what he has read. He has limited social interactions with his classmates, who tease him, and he does not understand the teasing. Roy is highly sensitive to touch and is afraid of loud noises, so much so that he will not engage in activities with his classmates for fear that he will encounter noises or have to touch things he is fearful of. He perseverates on his topics of interest. At home, Roy stays in his room and refuses to complete chores; he screams and hits if forced to do things that he does not want to do.

A program of instruction for Roy will need to include the curricular areas that are identified in Figure 3.3.

CORE PRINCIPLES FOR PROGRAM DEVELOPMENT AND INSTRUCTION

In addition to the need to address the core curriculum, the implementation of certain core principles is a critical aspect of all instructional planning for a student with ASDVI. These principles are typically applied throughout the curriculum and have a profound impact on planning, as well as on interaction between teachers and students (see "Core Principles: A Summary"). First, an educational program should be significantly intense (in hours of instruction, attendance, duration, and amount of progress) to engage the student in systematically planned, appropriate educational activities that address the identified goals. Second, direct, systematic, and sequential instruction must be provided. The program should provide for a teacher—student ratio that provides sufficient opportunity for individualized instruction on a daily basis. Third, students should be given opportunities for instruction and interactions with typically developing peers. Finally, the program should include components for program evaluation, based on an individual student's progress, and the results of the evaluation should be used to inform decisions to enhance or adjust the program. It is critical for persons who are knowledgeable about and experienced in providing interventions that are associated with ASD and persons who are knowledgeable about and experienced in the education of students with visual impairments to work together to make appropriate program decisions.

In addition, several specific key instructional components need to be implemented, including these:

- predictable classroom environments
- use of meaningful reinforcements
- concrete examples, functional hands-on activities, and functional routines

FIGURE 3.3   Planning an Educational Program for Roy

Core Curriculum for Visually Impaired Students	Core Curriculum for Students with Autism Spectrum Disorders	Program for ASDVI for Roy
Compensatory or functional academic skills (such as braille) Social, independent living, recreational, and leisure skills Use of assistive technology	Functional, spontaneous communication skills	■ Develop Roy's conceptual understanding through experience, stories, hands-on activities, and preteaching concepts ■ Use scripts in braille for teaching communication in a variety of situations (both at school and in the community) ■ Teach Roy the use of a portable braille output device to have scripts available in all settings
Social, independent living, recreational, and leisure skills Career education O&M	Social skills	■ Teach Roy social skills using a small social skills group ■ Practice learned social skills in a variety of settings ■ Identify and teach social skills that Roy needs in school, at home, in the community, and at work ■ Teach Roy to travel between activities using peers, as well as a cane ■ Use braille social skills scripts to support learning ■ Teach Roy to follow classroom rules ■ Teach Roy appropriate responses to the conversations of others

FIGURE 3.3 continued

Core Curriculum for Visually Impaired Students	Core Curriculum for Students with Autism Spectrum Disorders	Program for ASDVI for Roy
Social, independent living, recreational, and leisure skills O&M	Self-help skills	■ Pair braille and auditory directions with a step-by-step process ■ Include step-by-step O&M skills for each activity ■ Teach skills in natural settings
O&M	Fine and gross motor skills	■ Teach travel skills for all transitions ■ Teach in environments that Roy will be using ■ Use a portable typing device for writing
Compensatory or functional academic skills (such as braille) Listening and visual efficiency skills	Cognitive skills	■ Preteach new skills ■ Use mapping skills to relate concepts ■ Teach functional, lifelong skills (such as handling money and shopping)
Social, independent living, recreational, and leisure skills Compensatory or functional academic skills (such as braille)	Appropriate behaviors	■ Teach Roy to recognize stress and use skills to monitor himself ■ Teach Roy to accept and participate in new experiences ■ Teach Roy to transition between activities appropriately ■ Teach Roy to use written procedures and checklists to follow rules and perform expected behaviors

(continued on next page)

FIGURE 3.3 continued

Core Curriculum for Visually Impaired Students	Core Curriculum for Students with Autism Spectrum Disorders	Program for ASDVI for Roy
Compensatory or functional academic skills (such as braille) O&M Social, independent living, recreational, and leisure skills Career education	Engagement in tasks and play	■ Teach Roy lifelong leisure activities (biking, walking, table games, and reading) ■ Provide instruction to address Roy's sensory fears ■ Offer systematic instruction to teach daily living skills supported by auditory or braille ■ Identify and practice with Roy lifelong skills that are also used in the work and community environment
Use of assistive technology Social, independent living, recreational, and leisure skills Compensatory or functional academic skills (such as braille)	Independent organizational skills	■ Teach Roy to use braille or an auditory output device for maintaining the organization of assignments, schedules, and activities ■ Teach the whole task, including getting out and putting away materials ■ Break down tasks into concrete steps for teaching

- opportunities to generalize learned behavior

- development of skills with functional outcomes

- positive behavioral supports

Predictable Classroom Environments

Predictable environments refers to the physical arrangement of the classroom in a way that reflects the planning and teaching of the use of space, equip-

CORE PRINCIPLES: A SUMMARY

A number of core principles form the basis of program development and instruction for students who are visually impaired and have autism spectrum disorders. Focusing on these principles is essential in planning an educational program for a student and in delivering instruction:

1. The student's educational program needs to provide significant intensity of instruction in which the learner is engaged in systematically planned, appropriate educational activities addressing identified goals. What is "significant intensity" is determined by a careful assessment of the individual student.

2. Direct, systematic, and sequential instruction needs to be provided. A teacher/student ratio is used that supports individualized instruction on a daily basis.

3. The student should be given opportunities for instruction and for interactions with typically developing peers.

4. Program evaluation needs to be an integral part of the student's educational program, with the results of regular evaluations used to inform decisions to enhance or adjust the program.

In addition, the following emphases need to be integrated throughout instruction:

- the use of predictable classroom environments
- the application of meaningful reinforcements
- the use of concrete examples, functional hands-on activities, and functional routines
- the establishment of opportunities to generalize learned behavior
- the development of skills with functional outcomes
- the extensive use of positive behavioral supports

ment, materials, and activities. Such environments may also include the use of functional daily routines.

Students should have access to their materials, with these materials organized so they can participate in obtaining them to begin an activity and be able to put the materials away when they are finished. For students with ASDVI, movement among and between equipment, materials, and activities in the classroom must be considered. An O&M specialist can assist the team to address these issues (see Chapter 8, on O&M, for further information).

Predictable environments must also take into account the complex sensory issues for students with ASDVI. It does not mean that the classroom must be devoid of any potential sensory stimulation that may produce exaggerated reactions. Rather, the educational team must consider the level of distraction that the sensory environment will cause the student. Depending on that determination, the distraction may be removed or the student can be systematically taught to learn to cope with it.

Use of Meaningful Reinforcement

Since all people are motivated by reinforcement, providing external reinforcement to foster appropriate behavior will enhance the effectiveness of any program. The reinforcement does not have to be elaborate, but it must be of significant strength to provide an incentive for improved performance. Reinforcers are unique to each individual and must be based on an individual's current preferences (see Chapter 4 for strategies for establishing reinforcers). Initially, reinforcement is provided frequently.

Reinforcers are both primary and secondary. Primary (food or preferred items) and secondary (social) reinforcers can be paired together. The ultimate goal is for reinforcement to occur at a natural frequency. Initially, for many students, the reinforcement must be delivered immediately after a student gives the correct response. Once the student is learning and making progress, the delivery of the reinforcement can be delayed until he or she has completed a prescribed number of responses or activities (using token systems, for example), as in the case of Timothy.

Timothy is learning basic attending skills. Since he prefers vibration and swinging, the staff selects either swinging or a vibrating snake for reinforcement, both of which were identified as reinforcing for Timothy during the assessment. While Timothy is sitting in a chair or play area, the staff cues him to respond by calling his name. As soon as he reacts in any way (lifts his head, smiles, reaches, or moves toward an adult), the staff gives him the vibrating snake for a few seconds (reinforcement). This activity is repeated a number of times each day, increasing Timothy's expectation to turn toward the adult by shaping and prompting a closer and closer action of turning his head toward the speaker. Each time he is reinforced for a correct response by getting the vibrating snake.

Eventually, after Timothy consistently responds to immediate reinforcement and is demonstrating an understanding of responding and learning, a delayed reinforcement can begin to be taught using a token system. With this system, Timothy will be socially reinforced for every correct response and given a token or chip. After he has earned two or three tokens (what-

ever the team decides), the primary reinforcement (chosen by either Timothy or the staff) will be given.

For more information on the use of reinforcements, refer to the Resources section at the back of the book.

Functional Experiences and Routines

Most activities in daily life consist of tasks or actions that are performed sequentially, with the series of actions leading to an end goal—that is, they have a purpose or a function. Cooking; working; and even simple tasks, such as getting dressed, are routines in which most individuals participate every day. Students with ASDVI will benefit from instruction that is provided through the functional application of these tasks within the natural routine. Children with ASDVI will not learn what they have not experienced, and children who are visually impaired are not exposed to incidental learning prompted by their observation of the world around them. Therefore, teachers need to create opportunities for learning by *doing* within functional, natural settings. As with all children who are visually impaired, hands-on instruction, using concrete, functional objects and experiences, is necessary for children with ASDVI, especially when teaching new skills. The functional application of skills can be implemented throughout the curriculum. The educational team can use a form, such as the Functional Curriculum Ideas form shown in this chapter, to brainstorm functional applications that are appropriate for a given curriculum area in the elementary, middle, and high school environments. Figure 3.4 gives examples of applications in several curricular areas.

In considering instruction in functional routines, it is important for the team to plan carefully. Janzen (2003) discussed two parts in organizing functional routines for students. These parts will help the team to analyze the student's routines and consider the skills to be taught.

Part 1 consists of establishing the essential components of the routine for the students. A routine can be broken down into the following steps:

1. **Initiation:** What are the naturally occurring prompts or cues that signal the beginning of the activity? For example, a bus pulling up to the school and the driver announcing the arrival at school both serve as natural prompts to begin the school-arrival routine.

2. **Preparation:** What materials, supplies, or activities are needed to get ready for this activity?

3. **Performing the essential steps:** What are the basic steps involved in the activity that will lead to the desired outcome?

FIGURE 3.4 Functional Curriculum Ideas

Curriculum Area: Reading

Elementary	Middle School	High School
Experience stories	Menus	Bus schedules
Area of interest stories	Schedules	Recipes
Classroom rules	Interest area information	Mail
Rules to simple games		Magazines

Curriculum Area: Writing

Elementary	Middle School	High School
Schedules	Letters	Grocery list
Step-by-step instructions	Address and phone numbers	Job application
Making shopping list	Phone messages	Assignment calendar
	E-mail messages	

Curriculum Area: Math

Elementary	Middle School	High School
Money	Measurements	Budgeting
Fractions—real objects	Grocery shopping	ATM Machine
		Checkbook management

(continued on next page)

FIGURE 3.4 continued		
Curriculum Area: Leisure		
Elementary	**Middle School**	**High School**
Table games	Eating out	Participation in fitness club
Swim team	Matching coupons to food labels	Use of community swimming pool
Greeting classmates		Cooking

4. **Termination:** What does the activity or task look like when finished?

5. **Transitioning to the next steps:** What is the next task?

Part 2 involves the team's consideration of the student's specific instructional needs:

1. **Solve the problems:** What problems are likely to occur as this activity is carried out?

2. **Communicate and socialize:** What communication and social skills are important to the successful completion of this activity?

3. **Make choices and decisions:** What choices or decisions are involved in this activity, and which are essential?

4. **Self-monitor:** How will the student know when the end meets the predetermined standard?

Completing these two phases of the process of establishing functional routines will assist the student to be as independent as possible. Applying the appropriate instruction and support strategies will enhance learning and reduce future problem situations for the student with ASDVI.

Opportunities to Generalize Learned Behaviors

Program planning should include systematic opportunities to generalize skills from the teaching setting to the unprompted use of skills in new settings or with new people. In many cases, the skills can be taught in natural environments, so the generalization occurs by virtue of the setting (for example, teaching the student to request a snack at the snack table or at home, rather that at a table used for one-on-one instruction, or teaching dressing skills when getting ready for school, when going swimming, or when putting on a jacket before the student leaves home or school). For other skills, a carefully organized plan will provide instruction from one-to-one work to group work and to the natural environment. Each time the program of instruction is developed, the team must ask the question: If the student performs the skill in the instructional conditions under which the instruction is delivered, will he or she also be able to use the skill at other times and in situations where it is needed? The case of Suzy illustrates this point.

The educational team has determined through the assessment process that Suzy does not have the appropriate communication skills to ask for help. Instead, she uses the repeated vocalization "beep beep beep" when she wants help, even though she is able to use words. The team has developed a communication program in which Suzy learns to use the words "I need help" when she is given a variety of manipulatives to open while seated at her desk. After repeated instructional trials, Suzy learns consistently to ask for help when she is seated at the table. However, she does not automatically understand or use "I need help" in any other situation. The team and the family will need to identify a variety of situations and materials through which Suzy can practice using "I need help" or similar phrases in other settings. When Suzy uses words to ask for help in school, at home, in the community, and with different people, the skill will be generalized.

Skills with Functional Outcomes

Program planning must include a consideration of skills that lead directly to greater independence in the day-to-day world. These skills may include eating skills, dressing skills, and toilet training. They may also include functional, spontaneous communication. As the student with ASDVI grows, these functional skills may become more and more complex. Therefore, when the team is planning a program for a student with ASDVI, it is necessary to give the student opportunities to play, work, and engage in typical activities in the community and with his or her age-mates. To create these opportunities, the team must establish a number of essential factors in the program and adjust them to meet the student's individual needs. These essential factors include

- giving the student the opportunity or skills to make choices that are consistent with his or her age and ability

- providing the student with opportunities to interact socially with similar-age peers

- giving the student adequate breaks and the opportunity to engage in activities that he or she enjoys

- ensuring that the staff are appropriately trained to engage and work with the student

- ensuring that the demands of tasks and instructional strategies offer opportunities to learn and to be positively reinforced

- constantly evaluating and updating the program to offer activities that are based on the sequenced acquisition of skills

- teaching skills in the modalities through which the student learns best

- structuring the learning environments to teach maximum participation and independence

Concurrently, the environment must be structured to maximize opportunities for and efforts to communicate. Teachers must take advantage of "critical teaching moments," since such moments are generally the most functional. For example, when a child is eating a meal or having a snack, it will be more effective to give the student one or two bites and teach him or her to ask for more, rather than to give the child all the food at once. This strategy results in multiple opportunities to practice requesting and naming items in a natural setting.

It is useful to analyze the environment from the perspective of "communication facilitation"—the extent to which the environment provides opportunities and establishes expectations for communication. The communication environment should be designed to allow students to make choices about activities and to engage in activities that are meaningful and pleasurable. Students with ASDVI who do not communicate verbally often demonstrate alternative efforts to communicate that are overlooked, missed, or ignored by the staff or peers, particularly during periods that many teachers consider to be "noninstructional." Transition times between activities, for example, provide a rich opportunity for communication (for instance, What is next? What materials are needed?) In addition, the instructional time can encourage or discourage communication, so, the length of instructional time must be carefully considered. If the activity is too long, the student may lose interest. The time of day and the individuals who are involved in the activity may also have an impact on communication. An instructor needs to understand clearly how he or she expects a student to communicate and ensure that the student has a means of communicating that facilitates interaction.

It will be helpful for the team to take a careful look at the communication environment for each student to be sure that the environment matches the student's skills and needs.

As the team begins to design an effective program for a student with ASDVI, each team member must be well grounded in the foundations of effective instruction. As is summarized in "Instructional Effectiveness: Key Concepts," six aspects or steps serve as a basis for such instruction:

Step 1. The instructor uses appropriate methods to focus the student's attention on the activity or instruction.

Step 2. The instructor uses a hierarchy of prompts to assist the student to complete the skill or activity successfully; and understands the importance of fading prompts to increase the student's independence (see "The Language of Instruction" at the end of this chapter).

Step 3. The instructor shapes the approximation of correct responses and reinforce efforts in the skill-acquisition process.

Step 4. The instructor provides sufficient opportunities to practice using new skills.

Step 5. The instructor designs and implements programs to offer the maximum opportunity to use natural rewards (for example, to ask for toy or to get a toy to play with).

Step 6. The instructor designs and implements programs that allow the student to generalize skills across settings and people.

Programs of instruction should have clear sequential standards for mastery. In general, service providers who deliver instruction need to employ the principles of intensive behavioral therapy, such as applied behavior analysis (ABA), including recognizing when the student has performed the skill that matches the mastery level identified in the individualized program. Various behavioral treatment programs have been used across the country and have helped many children improve their ability to communicate, learn, and interact with others, but to date, ABA has been the most studied, debated, and used. Based on the work of Dr. O. Ivar Lovaas, this intensive structured teaching program involves reinforcing and conditioning techniques and one-on-one work with a child, often 30–40 hours a week, to build social and language skills in minute steps.

With ABA, lessons are broken down into their simplest elements, that are taught using repeated trials in which the child is presented with a stimulus (like "do this" or "touch object" or "look at me"). Correct or appropriate

INSTRUCTIONAL EFFECTIVENESS: KEY CONCEPTS

Effective instruction of students who are visually impaired and have autism spectrum disorders involves the application of certain critical principles and methods, including the following.

1. The instructor uses appropriate methods to focus the student's attention on activities or instruction. The determination of these methods is based on a careful assessment of the student.

2. The instructor uses a hierarchy of prompts to assist the student to complete activities and develop targeted skills and understands the importance of fading prompts to build the student's independence.

3. The instructor shapes approximations of correct responses and reinforces efforts as the student works to develop skills.

4. The instructor provides sufficient opportunities for the student to practice new skills that are being learned.

5. The instructor designs and implements programs to offer maximum opportunities to use natural rewards.

6. The instructor designs and implements programs that allow the student to generalize skills across settings and people.

In applying these principles, it is helpful for instructors to infuse the guiding precepts that were outlined in the Prologue of this book:

- Strive for small doable increments.

- Expect communication from the student (i.e., ensure that the student must communicate as often as possible).

- Use positive reinforcements.

- Design the environment so that "nothing is free" and the student needs to communicate to obtain what he or she wants.

- Take responsibility for the student's learning.

responses and behaviors are rewarded with positive reinforcement, and incorrect or inappropriate responses and behaviors are ignored. At first, the child may be rewarded for doing something that is close to the desired response. Over time, as the child masters the lesson, expectations are raised, and primary reinforcers (like bits of food) are replaced with social reinforcers (such as hugs or praise). As the child masters the skill and generalizes it, it becomes self-reinforcing. Once simple skills like table readiness, imitation, and attention are learned in this way, they can be combined into more complex skills like language, imitation, play skills, and social interaction. (The basic approaches for ABA are outlined in *Behavioral Intervention for Young Children with Autism;* see Maurice, Green, & Luce, 1996.)

To understand and learn, most children with ASDVI require instruction that is provided consistently across environments. Without such consistency, they become confused and may engage in interfering behaviors. Critical characteristics of students with ASD and ASDVI include the difficulty that many of them have in making changes and generalizing information. Offering the instruction with a variety of teachers and in a variety of settings helps these students acquire skills that they will understand and use more readily. Finally, for students with ASDVI to gain new skills, there must be sufficient staff to provide the instruction. In the initial stages of learning, many students will need instruction provided in one-to-one settings. Once they acquire the basic skills, it is essential to expand their learning environments systematically to include those that are offered as part of the general education program.

Positive Behavior Supports

Another fundamental component of program planning is the need to develop a school climate and a home climate that provide a positive, supportive environment and positive expectations. A program and environments that support positive behavior must be orchestrated to address individual strengths and needs. Students with ASDVI benefit most from a highly structured and predictable setting both at school and at home. As is described in the STAR Program (Arick et al., 2004, p. 173), a positive environment should include

- clear and individualized daily schedules

- the availability of visual communication systems (a student's visual communication system would be adapted to address the appropriate learning media of the student with a visual impairment such as Braille or large print)

- a minimum of nonpurposeful auditory stimulation

- an opportunity for children to engage in appropriate sensory stimulation

- clarity and consistency of communication and instruction

- numerous opportunities for positive reinforcement of appropriate behaviors

It is also important to understand that behavioral expectations need to be taught and reinforced by teachers, support staff, and parents. Clear procedures are needed for providing information to students about what is and is not acceptable behavior. Positive behaviors need to be acknowledged and reinforced once they are taught. According to McCart and Turnbull (2004, p. 1),

> the most effective tool [that] teachers have to handle problem behavior is to prevent it from occurring in the first place. Teachers should respond by understanding why a child might be engaging in problem behavior, and then establishing strategies that prevent that behavior from occurring. Problem behavior often occurs in children who are trying to communicate a need. This is often related to:
>
> - A desire to escape from or avoid something (such as school work)
>
> - A desire to obtain something (such as attention from the teacher or peers)
>
> - Or for some internal reason within the child (such as constant moving in the chair because the child has ADHD)
>
> When teachers understand why a child might be having problem behavior, they are better able to respond effectively to that child.

The team must take care to assess the function of inappropriate behavior carefully and develop a behavioral plan to the address the inappropriate and subsequent appropriate replacement behaviors. Additional information on functional behavioral assessment and the development of the Behavior Implementation Plan for individual students is provided in Chapter 7.

SUMMARY

Students with ASDVI need intensive interventions, and educational teams must design and implement curriculum and strategies to address the unique impacts of the dual disability. Program planning is ongoing throughout a student's education, with the process consistently informed through analysis of assessment and evaluation data. Information regarding a core curriculum for students with visual impairment, as well as a core curriculum for students with an autism spectrum disorder, can assist in the design and implementation of a program for students with ASDVI. The instructional principles discussed in this chapter can serve as a foundation for instruction that is integral in starting a child on a path to effective participation in school, work, and life.

The Language of Instruction

Any educational text that is intended to increase the understanding of a unique set of students must use terms and acronyms that are clearly defined or understood. Throughout this book, efforts have been made to define or clarify new or unique terms that may be unfamiliar to readers. Most terms are commonly used and understood by teachers and other team members who work with students with disabilities. However, several terms and applicable educational concepts that warrant further definition are presented here.

Applied Behavior Analysis

Often regarded as the most effective approach in dealing with behaviors that are associated with autism spectrum disorders, *applied behavior analysis,* ABA (sometimes referred to as applied behavioral analysis) is based on the work of Dr. O. Ivar Lovaas and operant conditioning techniques that were first studied by scientists, such as Pavlov and Skinner. It involves the discrete presentation of stimuli with responses, followed by immediate feedback, an intense schedule of reinforcement, the collection of data, and systematic trials of instruction. ABA's highly structured format and intensive delivery have also raised some controversy (Schoen, 2003). According to Arick et al. (2004, p. 6), "the ABA process includes conducting a baseline assessment, implementing a baseline assessment, implementing a behavioral intervention such as discrete trial training or pivotal response training, collecting ongoing data during intervention, making intervention changes based on data collected, reassessing the effect on the target behavior, generalizing the application of the target behavior, and repeating the process as necessary."

Asperger Syndrome

Asperger syndrome is an autism spectrum disorder characterized by communication difficulties in the area of pragmatics. A person with Asperger syndrome typically is extremely literal in his or her understanding of vocabulary and has difficulty using language in social situations. He or she will often engage in repetitive or restrictive patterns of thought and behavior, engage in repetitive routines or rituals, and often exhibit oversensitivity to sounds, smells, and tastes. Most individuals experience problems with nonverbal communication and are challenged by social and emotional interactions and the ability to interact successfully with peers. Speech is usually peculiar due to abnormalities of inflection and repetitive verbal patterns.

Children with Asperger syndrome do not experience severe intellectual impairments, although below average scores on standardized intelligence tests are common. Often these children learn at or above typical rates in certain areas. Areas of ability will differ across individuals (some may learn mathematic concepts easily but have difficulty performing activities of daily living; others may excel in rote memorization, but not be able to answer essay-type questions). Feelings of isolation among individuals with Asperger syndrome are common because of poor social skills and narrow interests.

Discrete Trial

Discrete trial training (DTT) is one method of providing intervention and using the principles of ABA. "Every skill that is selected for instruction is defined in clear, observable terms and then broken down into its component parts. Each component response is taught by presenting a specifically defined antecedent (cue or prompt). When a target response occurs, it is followed immediately by a consequence that has been found to be reinforcing to the learner. Responses other than the target response are ignored. Each antecedent-response-consequence cycle is a learning trial. These trials are repeated many times until the learner performs the response correctly and fluently" (Arick et al., 2004, p. 13). DTT is used to teach receptive language concepts, preacademic concepts and some expressive language concepts, and involves four distinct parts:

- the teacher's presentation
- the child's response
- the consequence
- a short pause between the consequence and the next instruction

This four-part model is the basic framework used in DTT; the programs generally involve several hours of direct one-on-one instruction per day (including high rates of discrete trials) over many months or years.

Errorless Learning

Errorless learning involves procedures that are used to preclude students from performing an incorrect response. For many children with ASD, the way a skill or task is learned the *first* time it is performed will be the preferred way for the skill to be performed from that point on. If the student has made an error in performing the task, it may be difficult to teach the skill without the error. Therefore, errorless learning will be critical for some students.

Functional Routines

According to Arick et al (2004), "even when skills are learned, whether they be in discrete trial setting or in pivotal response training, it is frequently difficult for children to use them in the appropriate contexts without direct cues. One way to effectively address this difficulty is to teach skills within a *functional routine,* which places behaviors under the control of natural cues in the environment" (p. 14). Functional routines include arrival at school, mealtime, toileting, and recess. "Each routine is broken down into simple steps that can be taught using the most appropriate behavioral method" (Arick et al., p. 15). Teaching functional routines supports instruction that can be used to teach the child systematically to participate independently in most typical school and care routines.

(continued on next page)

Pivotal Response Training

Pivotal response training (PRT) is another behavioral method that is used to teach a child "to learn to respond in a more naturalistic child-centered way than he or she would learn using traditional DTT. In PRT, the specific pivotal responses that are targeted are motivation and responsibility to multiple cues" (Arick et al., 2004, p. 14). Like DTT, PRT is based on the four-step sequence: cue, child's response, consequence, and pause. The "trials" within PRT, however, are incorporated into the functional context of the child's environment. In this case, reinforcement is a natural consequence of the behavior that is being rewarded. According to Arick et al., "This technique can be more effective than discrete trial training in increasing [the] spontaneous use of expressive language and [is] primarily used to teach and generalize play, expressive language, and socialization skills."

Prompting and Fading

Prompting refers to any additional stimulus that is provided to a child to illicit a correct response. If the adult says to the child, "What do you want?" and guides the child's hand to the juice cup while saying "juice," the adult is using a physical prompt to get the correct response. Prompting is used in educational settings to help solicit a correct response from a student and to help the student to succeed and feel positive. Good prompting can help the student provide a correct response and increases the likelihood that he or she will give the correct response the next time. There are a number of different kinds of prompting, which can be ordered in a hierarchy, from most to least intervention, as listed here. Physical and verbal prompting are often considered the most difficult to break.

Physical prompt. With a physical prompt, the adult physically assists the student. For example, after the teacher says to the student, "raise your hand," the teacher prompts the student by physically assisting the student to raise his or her hand. A physical prompt may be "partial," as when the teacher touches the student but not control the student's movements or "full," as when the teacher movies the student through the targeted behavior.

Verbal prompt. With a verbal prompt, the adult makes a verbal statement that helps the student provide the appropriate response. For instance, the teacher asks, "What is this?" while holding a bowl and says "bowl," and then the student says "bowl."

Modeling prompt. With a modeling prompt, the adults models the requested behavior, so the student can imitate it. For example, when the teacher tells the student, "Push your chair back," then pushes his or her chair back to show the student. Modeling prompts require the student to be able to imitate. For students who are blind, modeling prompts may require some physical prompting.

Gestural prompt. With a gestural prompt, the adult uses an arm, a hand, or facial movements to communicate specific information about what the student is to do. For instance, when the teacher asks the student to "stand up," he or she then prompts the student by raising his or her hand, to model the upward movement.

Positional prompt. With a positional prompt, the adult positions an object closer to the student so the student is more likely to choose that object. For example, the teacher says "find the ball" and then ensures that the ball is closer to the student than any other toy or object.

Fading the prompt, which means supporting the student's weaning from the need for a prompt, is accomplished by gradually reducing the strength of the prompt. Independence comes by eventually fading the prompt entirely. It is important to fade a prompt as quickly as possible, so the student does not become unnecessarily dependent on it.

When working with students with ASDVI, all members of the educational team need to be aware of the verbal and nonverbal cues they are providing unconsciously or unintentionally because the student may learn to become dependent on these unintended cues. For example, when the student is asked to identify various objects, and the objects are always placed in a particular place or position, he or she may learn to use that position as a prompt.

Reinforcement

A *reinforcement* is provided to reward correct responses or behaviors or to solicit desired ones. A reinforcer is anything that the student finds motivating and would select in a free-choice situation. Reinforcers can be tangible (such as food) or may be abstract (such as listening to music, going for a walk, or being allowed a "free-choice" activity). Typically, when a student is learning a new skill, reinforcement is provided frequently. It can be provided when the student initiates the desired behavior or response or can be used in the absence of undesired behaviors.

Shaping

Shaping is the process by which successively closer approximations of a behavior, skill, or task are reinforced. It supports the identification of reasonable goals to be established and gives the student many chances for success as he or she learns new skills. Shaping refers to the process of increasing the level of expectation for the correct response. Using the example of juice, when the adult says to the child, "What do you want?" he or she may initially accept any vocalization to mean juice. Through practice and reinforcement, the adult eventually shapes the behavior, so the child has to say "j" for juice, then "ju," and then "juice." Shaping provides the student with positive feedback for small changes in behavior.

Task Analysis

Task analysis involves breaking down the behavior, skill, or task into its identifiable component behaviors, skills, or tasks. For example, the steps involved in hand washing include (1) finding the sink, (2) turning on the faucet, (3) using the soap dispenser, (4) rubbing the hands under the water, (5) turning off the faucet, and, (6) drying the hands on a towel.

Assessment

Assessment is a vital foundational process that guides the members of the educational team to understand the individual student and allows them to formulate an accurate identification of the student's needs in relation to autism spectrum disorder and visual impairment. In the United States, to receive special education services, a child must first be determined to be eligible by having a specific disability. This is what is referred to as an "educational diagnosis." To be determined to be eligible, a child must meet the criteria for eligibility and must be determined to need specially designed instruction.

It is important not to confuse a medical diagnosis with an educational diagnosis. A medical diagnosis indicates the presence of specific characteristics that are caused by or reflect autism spectrum disorder from a medical perspective and are defined in terms of anatomical, metabolic, and neurological processes. An educational diagnosis indicates the presence of characteristics and behaviors that are associated with ASD and the identified need for specially designed instruction, leading a student to be considered to have ASD. In general, medical diagnoses are based on the criteria listed in the *Diagnostic and Statistical Manual* (DSM) (APA, 2000) that are used to determine diagnoses in this country. In contrast, educational diagnoses are based on the criteria that each state uses to determine educational eligibility for services for disabled children, including those with visual impairments and ASD. Each state's criteria address the DSM criteria in some form. Since these criteria vary from state to state, it is important for the team members who are conducting the assessment and determining a student's eligibility for services to be familiar with their state's criteria. It is also important for the team to include individuals who are specialists in relevant areas to avoid the inappropriate labeling of children, as well as labeling of children, as well as the recommendation of inappropriate programs and instruction. However, any team can use the information that is provided in this chapter and apply it to their respective state's criteria.

Assessment will provide information that can be used to identify the presence of ASD and visual impairment and be the basis of an appropriate intervention plan. It is used to "build a picture" of the child. Assessment is "fluid" in that it is ongoing, with relevant information changing as the child acquires new skills. The assessment of the child does not end with the identification; rather, the members of the educational team continue to learn and use new information as they continue to work with the child. The new information allows the team members to update their knowledge of the student's current level of educational performance. Initial assessment and ongoing subsequent assessment should be conceptualized as one component of the overall instructional "flow," as was discussed and illustrated in Chapter 3, with each component providing information that is relevant for the next.

COMPONENTS OF ASSESSMENT

To provide the supports and instructional strategies that a student with ASDVI needs, the team must have a clear picture of the child's development, and understand how the child learns new information, uses information that he or she has been taught, communicates, and interacts with people and with the environment. A comprehensive assessment will provide this information.

The information that is collected during an assessment supports the development of the IFSP or IEP and the instructional strategies that will be used. As instruction is provided and the student learns new skills, the original assessment must be updated, providing opportunities for enhanced instructional strategies and continued learning.

The picture of the child that is developed and maintained will include information in three major areas:

- profile of development

- profile of the student's learning

- profile of sensory interactions

The development of these three areas forms the basis of the assessment and will provide the team members with the information that they need to understand who the child is, how she or he processes information, and how she or he uses that information to make sense of the world and participate in it. Information will be collected both informally and through the use of standardized assessment tools.

Profile of Development

Careful documentation of the child's developmental history will help the team establish the child's developmental milestones, identify the presence or absence of behavioral characteristics that are associated with ASD, determine the extent of the child's functional vision, and identify areas of concern. The profile will include information that is related to the presence, absence, and quality of the development of language, social interactions, interests, behavioral patterns, and sensory responses. More specifically, the team will look for the development of characteristics that may be associated with an autism spectrum disorder that are related to the child's development in the domains just mentioned. A simple table of these learning domains can be used to identify relevant developmental information, as provided in the examples in Figure 4.1.

In addition to this information, the team should review and document any relevant medical information, including a family history of ASD, and should identify the nature and onset of the visual impairment, and the type and onset of behavioral characteristics that are associated with ASD. While some behavioral characteristics of ASD appear early in life, some may not appear until 12–34 months of age. Since many individuals with visual impairments are often not referred for evaluation for ASD until they are at least 5 years old, it is necessary to review relevant developmental information that helps to document the behavioral characteristics of the child. The earliest possible identification is important for appropriate program planning and intervention; many children with ASD are now being identified at 2 to 3 years of age.

Since a student with ASDVI may exhibit different behaviors and reactions in different settings, it is necessary to observe and interact with the student in all the environments to develop a whole picture of him or her. For example, Ozonoff and Dawson (2002) and others have explored information that they gained from reviewing a videotape of a child's first birthday party. Observations of behaviors that were exhibited during the party may demonstrate early social indicators of ASD. Parents and teachers can provide a wealth of information that may not be revealed during other elements of the assessment.

If the child is of school age, the educational team may prepare a school history that focuses on how well the child has done in school academically and socially and that includes information on significant behavior, learning difficulties, or other issues that have been documented over the years.

FIGURE 4.1

Sample Developmental Profiles

4-Year-Old Student Who Is Totally Blind

Age	Source	Language	Social Interactions	Interests	Behavior	Sensory Interactions
11 months	Developmental pediatrician's report	No babbling	Does not alert to parent's voice	Does not respond to the musical mobile	Cries repeatedly	Arches back when parent attempts to hold
24 months	Teacher's report	Does not imitate sounds	Has trouble with joint attention	Becomes upset at attempts to introduce new toys	Is not walking; rocks on hands and knees repeatedly	Mouths toys and other objects repeatedly
36 months	Preschool teacher	Repeats some words if highly motivated (water)	Has trouble with turn taking	Prefers to swing, play in water, or sit	Does not initiate any activities	Resists touching anything new with hands
		Does not initiate requests	Is not interested in the other children in the class	Will listen to the same tape over and over	Needs prompting to complete simple tasks	Resists being touched by others

46 months	O&M specialist's report	Does not use concepts, such as in, on, and under	Does not greet others	Does not move to most sounds	When left alone, will wander without purpose	Covers ears and cries at certain sounds
48 months	Parent interview	Will use a few words repeatedly	Prefers to play by self	Loves anything to do with water	Cries; has tantrums when daily routine is changed	Will eat only mashed potatoes, pudding, and similar soft foods
		Does not follow simple directions	Responds to adults but not children	Listens to Disney videos over and over	Has trouble sleeping, wakes up in the middle of the night	Will not keep shoes and sock on; will not wear long sleeves

(continued on next page)

FIGURE 4.1 continued

12-Year-Old Student with Low Vision

Age	Source	Language	Social Interactions	Interests	Behavior	Sensory Interactions
4 years	Pediatrician's report	Odd voice quality	Flat affect, rather business-like for a young child	Will play only with musical toys, repeats action over and over	Difficult to redirect from a preferred activity	Is worried about what he would have to touch as part of the exam
Birth–12 years	Parent's report	Spoke words at an early age, began decoding words at age 4, reads words far beyond his age but has difficulty applying meaning	Has difficulty making and keeping friends; only wants to talk about music, is not interested in activities that the family enjoys	Played with tape recorder over and over. Would start and stop in the middle of songs to hear certain sections repeatedly	Has never wanted anyone to touch his things; lines up tapes in room and becomes upset if they get moved	Will not touch balloons or things made of soft rubber or soft plastic; worries about fire drills in school and ambulances when riding in the car
11 years	Classroom teacher's report	Has trouble following general group directions	Has difficulty with group projects, has trouble getting started	Tries to get others to listen to him talk about classical music	Has a hard time changing to a new activity if he has not had time to complete the entire first activity	Gets annoyed by other students whispering, making noises
12 years	Teacher's report	Has difficulty with abstract concepts	Has trouble initiating and sustaining interactions	Is very interested in classical music	Has difficulty when other students break the rules	Has perfect pitch

Profile of Student Learning

The co-occurrence of autism spectrum disorder and visual impairment presents itself in "idiosyncratic developmental pathways" (Jordan, 1996). Without a clear recognition and understanding of the unique problems that are caused by ASDVI, the team will have great difficulty developing an effective program of instruction and effectively educating a student with ASDVI. The goal of the profile of student learning is to provide information so that each person who encounters the child knows (1) how the child learns new information (for example, his or her learning media), (2) what strengths the child displays and the conditions in which she or he is most effective, and (3) what motivates the child to attend and to learn (his or her likes, dislikes, reinforcers). Figure 4.2 provides a sample Profile of Student Learning that can assist the team to determine learning modes, interests, reinforcers, strengths, and sensory needs. This information will assist in answering these three questions.

The Profile of Student Learning can be developed using a variety of processes and tools, including standardized assessments, such as behavioral rating tools and communication assessments, and informal tools, such as observations, interviews, and checklists. Each process is discussed briefly in the section of this chapter entitled Gathering the Information. Samples of tools that can be used to collect accurate data pertaining to the child appear in Appendix 4A to this chapter.

Profile of Sensory Interactions

The process that the brain uses to organize sensory experiences into useful information that enables an individual to organize and make sense of his or her world, particularly when the person cannot perceive the world visually, may be significantly affected by the co-occurrence of an autism spectrum disorder and visual impairment. If the individual has problems registering sensory input effectively, then he or she will have difficulty with subsequent steps in the integration process. Extreme responses to sensory input (hypersensitivities and hyposensitivities), including the basic sensations and perceptions of touch, taste, sight, hearing, smell, and motor movement, are common. It is critical for the assessment team to identify how a particular child processes, manages, and regulates sensory information so they can plan and implement appropriate interventions that effectively address the sensory issues.

When the student does not process sensory information appropriately or if the sensory information is painful, experiences can be confusing and difficult. When the sensory systems do not work as expected, the student may over- or underreact to common situations at school, at home, and in the community, his or her entire life may be disrupted.

FIGURE 4.2 — Sample Profile of Student Learning

Primary Learning Modes	Strengths	Interests/ Reinforcements	Sensory Needs	Other
Verbal	Responds to simple directions that are delivered in a calm voice	Swimming	Loose-fitting clothing	Becomes agitated with high-pitched voices
Tangible symbols paired with auditory output device	Makes choices between two activities	Chips	Slip on shoes, cotton socks	Perfumes and other strong scents can cause aggressive behavior
	Likes activities that provide motion and movement	Apples	Multiple vestibular activities every day—swinging, rocking, spinning, rolling, and therapy ball	Bites or hits if he is confused
	Swimming	Rocking chair	Pushes or pulls weighted objects	Easily disoriented
	Walks on a track using a guide rail or uses a treadmill	Country music	Wears a weighted vest when walking between destinations	
	Will initiate a verbal request for favorite reinforcers (chips, french fries, swimming)	Gum	Uses a weighted lap pillow when at the work table in the classroom	
		French fries		
		Beanbag chair		

The student with ASDVI may register or modulate sensory information poorly. Examples of the poor registration of sensory information include

- sensory stimulation that is over- or underregistered
- "overreactions" to some things yet little attention paid to others
- an appearance of "nonresponse" to pain
- frequent spinning or whirling behaviors
- picky eating habits

Poor modulation may cause reactions that are over- or underresponsive to the situation. Examples of poor modulation or integration include

- An over sensitivity to touch, hugs, and other forms of physical contact
- a strong preference for certain types of clothing (for example, the child will only wear shorts or only sandals, not his or her "regular" shoes)
- a strong reaction to specific textures (such as an antipathy to anything made of plastic)
- alarm and resistance to new experiences and situations
- the appearance of withdrawal from sensory stimulation

To establish a profile of sensory interactions, it is important to consider how the student functions in the environments in which she or he regularly interacts, including home, school, and community settings. Information should be collected in response to auditory information, visual information, taste, smell, touch, and movement and body position. The auditory and visual information that is collected to establish the appropriate learning medium for students with visual impairments will provide valuable information about the child's learning style. For the purpose of the sensory profile, information on responses to visual and auditory information will focus on reactions to these sensory stimuli (such as "avoids contact"; "is bothered by lights, but not in connection to visual impairment"; "holds hands over ears"; "does not respond to name"; "seems oblivious to the environment"; and "responds negatively to common noises").

The following are several examples of students with sensory processing difficulties that illustrate the potential impact of sensory difficulties on a child with ASDVI:

Randy is fearful of touching balloons. His fear causes him to refuse to participate in any parties, particularly birthday parties. His lack of participation has made it difficult for him to establish and maintain friendships.

April is so sensitive to the feel of clothing on her skin that she wiggles, fusses, and often strips off many of her clothes and her shoes. Even when the weather is cold, windy, or rainy, she prefers to wear shorts, a tank top, and no shoes.

Ann is extremely uncomfortable with loud noises. From birth until about age 2, she would cry and be unsettled for hours when the neighbors mowed the lawn or if the vacuum was turned on. Now a fifth-grade student, her parents hesitate to take her places for fear that she will begin to cry and have a tantrum.

Tony has an acute sense of smell, so much so that he can locate individuals by smell and has aggressive behavioral outbursts when his teacher wears strong perfume. He also he has strong food preferences. He can smell food cooking at a great distance and reacts with aggressive behavior toward himself and others when he smells food that he does not want or like—behaviors that often appear to be unprovoked.

Jane often "pops up" out of her seat in her classroom, flaps her hands, and hops up and down for several seconds. This effort is her attempt to control her need for adequate vestibular input and to help keep herself in "balance."

Terri has difficulty learning braille because of extreme tactile hypersensitivity. She cries, screams, and pulls away when a teacher attempts to help her guide her fingers lightly across various textures or braille letters or words and when she is involved in other fine motor activities. She has repeatedly been described as "tactilely defensive," yet she craves hugs, and asks to be carried around like a baby.

PREPARING FOR THE ASSESSMENT

In the following sections, greater attention will be given to clarifying and guiding the team in completing an assessment of the child to build the picture of the child and prepare for instruction.

Asking Critical Questions

Before the assessment is conducted, it is helpful for the team to begin by identifying some critical questions that will help guide it. These questions allow the team to plan the assessment and to determine who should participate in it, what data need to be gathered to build an accurate picture of the child, and the environments in which the assessment will be conducted. Critical questions include these:

1. What do we need to know about this child? (This is a simple question, but one that is often overlooked.)

2. Why will the information that is gathered in the assessment be important?

3. What behaviors, if any, is the child exhibiting that are causing concern for the family and the educational or school team?

4. Where are the behaviors occurring?

5. What is the child not able to learn or do as a result of the behaviors?

These questions also help guide the team in making decisions about the training and experience requirements of the professionals who will conduct the assessment. If the team suspects that the student has an autism spectrum disorder, it will be vital to include an evaluator who is skilled in assessing students with ASD. Because the student also has a visual impairment, it would be ideal to use an evaluator who is experienced with both disabilities. Unfortunately, because of the low incidence of ASDVI, few professionals are trained and experienced in evaluating both conditions. Therefore, it is essential to include a professional who is highly experienced in the early development of children with visual impairments who will work in conjunction with the ASD specialist. These team members, along with the parents, will serve as the core of the assessment team. Parental involvement in the assessment process is crucial, since the parents know and understand the child's behaviors, strengths, and challenges better than does anyone else. Additional team members may include a communication specialist, an occupational therapist, an O&M specialist, the classroom teacher, an early childhood specialist, and any other service provider who can help answer the questions regarding who the child is as a student.

Gathering the Information

The following "general principles" of observation (adapted from Lowscence, 1994) can help guide the team in gathering accurate information to build the picture of the child. These principles will apply when the team uses both standard and informal methods of assessment.

1. Assess the student across a variety of settings (such as the home, play group, toddler group, preschool class, recess, music, social studies, math, and lunch). A series of brief observations that represent the student's environments is preferred to one lengthy observation in a single environment.

2. Observe the student in the presence of different individuals (including his or her parents, siblings, teachers, and peers).

3. Examine the student's behaviors when the student is confronted with the demands of various tasks (for instance, during individual play, group play, independent activities, written work, group work, and unstructured activities).

4. Observe the student at different times of the day (such as in the morning and afternoon and before and after lunch).

5. Seek information from multiple respondents (including teachers, parents, paraprofessionals, support staff, and peers).

6. If possible, assess the student in a variety of potentially stress-invoking scenarios (such as an unexpected change in routine, disruption of a favorite play activity, instruction with a high level of verbal content, and academic demands that are higher than the student's instructional level).

7. Talk to the student, if possible; some insights can be gleaned just by asking the right questions.

8. Consider the value of observation during other assessments. Observing the student while he or she is taking an achievement or intelligence test can provide valuable insights and can assist the team in selecting appropriate sensory assessments.

9. Look for patterns of, as well as differences in, performance across multiple variables. These patterns can provide valuable insights for developing interventions.

10. Consider the environmental or assessment setting as a critical component for understanding the student's behavior (for example, the number of children in and the size of the preschool setting, the student's proximity to the teacher, the arrangement of desks and lighting, and noise levels).

Students with ASDVI display a wide variation in levels of skills. Thus, it is the responsibility of the assessment team to select assessment tools that can be used to determine if the child has ASD and to provide the team with precise, current information regarding

- the child's strengths

- the history of the child's development

- the child's present levels of development or educational performance

- the interventions or strategies that have and have not been effective

- the child's communication skills and abilities

- the child's ability to interact with adults and peers

M.H. and D.J. Gense

In assessing students, it is vital to identify reinforcers that are powerfully motivating to the individual child and that can reinforce learning. For this student, swinging is the reinforcement.

- the existence of behavioral deficits or excesses (exhibiting too much or too little of a particular behavior)

- the child's responses to sensory information

- the child's motivators (what motivates the child to attend? what motivates the child to learn new information?)

This information can be gathered by using both standardized and informal assessment tools and methods. Educational teams use informal assessment both to support and to inform formal, or standardized, assessment procedures. The collection of information through observation is often thought of as informal assessment, as is information that is obtained in interviews with parents or previous teachers and by using teacher-constructed tests.

FORMAL AND INFORMAL ASSESSMENT TOOLS

Many standardized and informal methods are available to assist an educational team in assessing a child. In general, they can be categorized as follows. Formal or standardized assessments include

- behavior rating tools

- cognitive assessments

- social skills inventories

- adaptive behavior assessments

- communication assessment

Informal tools and methods include

- functional observations

- interviews

- checklists

The standardized and informal assessment tools described in the following sections have been successfully used to assist teams in gathering information and developing a picture of a child with ASDVI. It is not an exhaustive list, and new tools continue to be developed that can be applied with this type of student.

Formal or Standardized Assessment

BEHAVIOR RATING TOOLS

A number of behavior rating tools are used to indicate the probability of an autism spectrum disorder. These tools are used not to identify an ASD, but to determine the presence of the behavioral characteristics of an ASD. The tools are generally designed to be completed by parents or service providers who are familiar with the child.

The behavior rating tools have been developed and standardized for use with students who are sighted, and many have components that assess the visual use and strength of the student. Although the tools were not designed or standardized specifically for use with visually impaired students, the first three tools may be more useful for students with visual impairments than the last three.

Behavior rating tools, which are discussed in the following sections, include

- Autism Diagnostic Observation Schedule–Generic (ADOS-G)

- Autism Behavior Checklist (ABC)

- Gilliam Autism Rating Scale (GARS)

- Childhood Autism Rating Scale (CARS)

- Gilliam Asperger Disorder Scale (GADS)

- Asperger Syndrome Diagnostic Scale (ASDS)

ADOS-G

The ADOS-G (Lord, Rutter, DiLavore, & Risi, 2000) is a semistructured assessment of communication, social interaction, and play or the imaginative use of materials for individuals, toddlers through adults, who are suspected of having ASD or another pervasive developmental disorder. It is a combination of two earlier instruments, one intended for adults and children with language skills that are at least at the 3-year-old level, and the other intended for children with limited or no language, as well as additional items developed for verbally fluent, high-functioning adolescents and adults. The ADOS-G consists of four modules, each of which is appropriate for children and adults who are at different developmental and language levels, ranging from no expressive or receptive language to verbal fluency. Offering standardized materials and ratings, the ADOS-G gives a measure of autism spectrum disorder that is unaffected by language. It can be used with a wide range of children and adults.

ABC

The ABC, a subtest of the *Autism Screening Instrument for Educational Planning* (ASIEP-2; Krug, Arick, & Almond, 1993), is a screening instrument for non-adaptive behaviors that is used to see how an individual "looks in comparison" to others. The ABC addresses the following skill areas:

- sensory

- relating

- body concepts

- language

- social and self-help behaviors

The ASIEP-2, which is appropriate for individuals from toddlers aged 18 months to adults, provides a development scale for autism or related disorders. It combines multiple measurement and information sources and emphasizes an interactive approach to development, behavior, and contexts.

GARS

Appropriate for students aged 3–22, the GARS (Gilliam, 1995) helps identify and diagnose autism spectrum disorder in individuals and estimate the severity of the problem. Items on the GARS are based on definitions of ASD that were adopted by the Autism Society of America and the DSM-IV (APA, 1994). These items are grouped into four subtests that describe specific measurable behaviors:

- stereotyped behaviors

- communication

- social interaction

- developmental disturbances

CARS

Brief, convenient, and suitable for use with any child aged 2 or older, the CARS (Schopler, Reichler, & Rochen Renner, 1986) makes it much easier for clinicians and educators to recognize and classify children with autism spectrum disorder. The CARS distinguishes mild to moderate from severe ASD. The 15 items of the CARS include Relationships with People, Imitation, Affect, Use of Body, Relation to Non-human Objects, Adaptation to Environmental Change, Visual Responsiveness, Auditory Responsiveness, Near Receptor Responsiveness, Anxiety Reaction, Verbal Communication, Nonverbal Communication, Activity Level, Intellectual Functioning, and the clinician's general impression.

GADS

The GADS (Gilliam, 2000) is used to evaluate individuals, aged 3–22, with unique behavioral problems who may have Asperger Syndrome and differentiate them from those who have autism spectrum disorder or other related pervasive developmental disabilities. The 32 items, divided into four subscales, describe specific, observable, and measurable behaviors. A parent or professional who knows the child provides documentation about the essential behavioral characteristics of Asperger's disorder that are necessary for a diagnosis.

ASPERGER SYNDROME DIAGNOSTIC SCALE (ASDS)

The ASDS (Myles, Bock, & Simpson, 2001) is a quick, easy-to-use rating scale that can help determine whether a child, aged 5–18, has Asperger syndrome. Anyone who knows the child or youth well can complete this scale. Parents, teachers, siblings, paraeducators, speech and language specialists, psychologists, psychiatrists, and other professionals answer 50 yes-or-no items in 10 to 15 minutes. The instrument provides an AS Quotient that indicates the likelihood that an individual has Asperger syndrome. The 50 items that are included in the ASDS were drawn from five specific areas of behavior:

- cognitive

- maladaptive

- language

- social

- sensorimotor

Although these tools can assist in the identification of autism spectrum disorder in children who are visually impaired, it is clear that additional research is needed to develop a deeper understanding of the core deficits of students with ASDVI to develop more refined behavior rating tools to determine the presence of ASD in children who are visual impaired.

COGNITIVE ASSESSMENTS

Children with ASDVI have unique patterns of development. Most have unique strengths that can be used to enhance their learning in areas that they find difficult. Cognitive deficits are interwoven with social and communication difficulties. Since there has been no research on the use of standardized IQ tests for students with ASDVI, and no IQ tests have been normed on these students, standardized IQ tests should be used cautiously with students with ASDVI.

Some assessment tools that can assist the educational team in developing a picture of the child with ASDVI by providing information on cognitive development include the following:

- The Battelle Developmental Inventory (Newborg, Stock, Wnek, Guidubaldi, & Svinicki, 1984), designed for children from birth though age 8, tests across several different developmental domains, including cognition, motor, self-help, language, and social skills.

- The Bayley Scales for Infant Development (Bayley, 1993) is designed for children aged 1 month through 42 months. It assesses areas of mental, motor, and behavioral development.

- The Carolina Curriculum for Infants and Toddlers with Special Needs (2004) is an assessment and intervention program that is designed for children with mild to severe special needs. It is divided into more than 20 logical teaching sequences across five major domains: cognition, communication, social adaptation, fine motor, and gross motor.

- The Hawaii Early Learning Profile (HELP) (1988) for preschoolers aged 3–6, is a curriculum-based tool. It helps focus on a child's strengths as well as needs, provides adaptations for assessing each skill, and promotes high expectations for all children. HELP covers 622 skills in six developmental domains: cognitive, language, gross motor, fine motor, social, and self-help. Each domain is organized into specific skills, starting at age 3 and sequenced through age 6, in month-by-month increments.

■ The Oregon Project for Visually Impaired and Blind Preschool Children (Anderson et al., 1991) consists of 640 behavioral statements that are organized in eight developmental areas: cognitive, language, socialization, vision, compensatory, self-help, fine motor, and gross motor. Each of these eight areas contains skills that have been developmentally sequenced and arranged in age categories: birth–1, 1–2, 2–3, 3–4, 4–5, and 5–6 years. All major skills that a visually impaired child needs to prepare for the first grade, such as prerequisites for O&M and braille, are included.

It is important to remember that measures of cognitive abilities alone are not sufficient to gain the entire picture of an individual child and how the child processes and uses information.

SOCIAL SKILLS INVENTORIES

Children with ASDVI demonstrate impairments in their relationships with their peers, use of nonverbal communicative behaviors, use of imitation, and capacity for symbolic or dramatic play. Their interactions are often characterized by low rates of initiation and low rates of response. Although, research on visual impairment may have indicated similar areas of impairment, one critical difference between visually impaired children and children with ASDVI is the low responses of children with ASDVI. Once they are introduced to and taught early social skills, young children who are visually impaired will initiate, attend, and respond at typical rates, although their nonverbal gestures may not be at a rate of sighted children. In contrast, young children with ASDVI require intensive, directed interactions to improve their social responses. Even with intervention, these children, often appear aloof and passive or exhibit odd interactions (such as the use of odd language, obsessive talk about certain topics and a lack of understanding of others).

Observing the social repertoire of a young child with ASDVI with their familiar, typical peers provides information about the child's current social behavior that cannot be determined any other way. Behaviors to assess include

■ initiations of interactions

■ responses to interactions

■ lengths of utterances

■ interest in others

- level of social play

- turn-taking abilities

The Play Interest Survey (Quill, 2000), a copy of which is included at the end of this chapter, offers a tracking system for identifying play interests. This information can be used to teach students play skills, as is discussed in Chapter 6. The materials that are suggested in the survey may be modified for children with visual impairments by using toys and objects from *Let's Play: A Guide to Toys for Children with Special Needs* (published annually by the American Foundation for the Blind, the Toy Industry Foundation, and the Alliance for Technology Access).

There are assessment tools that provide a range of information on social development. The Vineland Adaptive Behavior Scales (Sparrow, Cicchetti, & Balla, 2005) and the Scales of Independent Behavior–Revised (Bruininks, Woodcock, Weatherman, & Hill, 1996) provide an overview of social functioning, although not a detailed look. Preschool curriculum assessments often contain a social subscale. The HELP, the Carolina Curriculum for Infants and Toddlers with Special Needs, and the Oregon Project for Visually Impaired and Blind Preschool Children have been standardized for visually impaired children.

In *Do-Watch-Listen-Say,* Quill (2000) provides a detailed assessment tool, entitled Assessment of Social and Communication Skills for Children with Autism. The tool has two purposes: It assists the team in identifying both communication and social skills for children aged 3–8 and can be used as a curriculum guide for instructing students.

ADAPTIVE BEHAVIOR ASSESSMENTS

The Vineland Adaptive Behavior Scales (Sparrow et al., 2005), and the Scales of Independent Behavior–Revised (Bruininks et al., 1996) are widely used to assess the everyday living skill that an individual learns in the process of adapting to his or her surroundings. Good adaptive behavior and the absence of behavioral problems promote independence. Information that is collected from these scales will assist the team in planning a student's educational program.

COMMUNICATION ASSESSMENT

Since communication is one of the specific deficit areas in ASD, it is critical that a careful assessment of the student's functional communication be completed in different environments and under various conditions. ASD includes core deficits in verbal and nonverbal communication. The team must identify the child's interest in communicating, determine how and when the child communicates, and identify what the child understands when others communicate. A speech and language specialist who is experienced in assessing students with ASD and students who are visually impaired will be an essential member of the assessment team.

To obtain a complete picture of the communication and symbolic abilities of children with ASDVI, the team needs to use a combination of assessment strategies, including interviewing people who are significant in the child's life and observing the child in everyday situations.

One significant area of communication that needs to be addressed is *joint attention*. Joint attention refers to the ability to in orient and attend to a social partner, shift one's gaze between people and objects, share affect or emotional states with another person, follow the gaze and point of another person, and draw another person's attention to objects or events for the purpose of sharing experiences (Lord & McGee, 2001). This is an area in which the combined skills and experience of the team in both ASD and visual impairment is critical. The evaluators must differentiate between difficulties in joint attention that are due to the lack of vision and deficits in joint attention that are due to an autism spectrum disorder. One of the clarifiers will be the team's ability to understand "how" the student processes and reacts to information that is presented. The team members will need to enhance their observational skills, so they can recognize difficulties in joint attention that are due to the lack of experience (commonly associated with a visual impairment), and the non-conventional forms of communication that can indicate problems, including those with joint attention (associated with ASD). The Communicative Functions form, included at the end of this chapter, can be used to collect data on an individual student. Chapter 5 addresses strategies for teaching communication skills.

Another significant area of communication that needs to be assessed is the discrepancy between expressive and receptive communication. Students with ASDVI often differ in their ability to produce words (expressive communication) and their ability to understand the meaning of words (receptive communication). Some of them, typically those who are higher functioning, may be verbal, but their understanding of language is not at the same level unless it is in their area of intense interest. For others—those who are non-verbal—their understanding of language may be at a significantly higher level than their ability to produce speech. For lower-functioning students, this discrepancy between expressive and receptive communication is one of the areas that separates them from students with mental retardation. Individuals with mental retardation tend to have similar expressive and receptive levels of communication.

For some students, an assessment of their need for or use of an augmentative communication device may be needed. Augmentative communication systems are designed to assist individuals to communicate using symbolic forms, such as objects, pictures, line drawings, or words, that represent the

LEVELS OF SYMBOLIC REPRESENTATIONS

If the student uses the following means of communication:	The student's level of communication is:
Body and limb movements, gestures, vocalizations	Presymbolic
Symbolic gestures and vocalizations, tangible symbols (object, pictures)	Concrete symbolic
Speech, sign language, printed language, braille, abstract shapes, abstract graphics	Abstract symbolic

Source: C. Rowland and P. Schweigert, *Tangible Symbol Systems* (rev. ed.). Portland: Center on Self-Determination, Oregon Health Sciences University, 2000.

actual item, person, or activity. The main function of such an assessment is to determine whether the child requires augmentative communication assistance and, if so, to determine that appropriate augmentative communication devices or systems are selected to meet the child's needs. An augmentative communication assessment will provide information about an individual's level of symbolic representation and needs for communicating with these symbols. The "Augmentative Communication Assessment Protocol for Symbolic Augmentative Systems," developed by Gamel-McCormick and Dymond (1994), which appears in the chapter Appendix, is an easy-to-use protocol that can help point teams toward the characteristics of a system that will work for the student who is being assessed. "Levels of Symbolic Communication" will help the educational team decide which symbolic representation an individual student needs—information that the team can use to determine the best medium through which instructional supports and strategies can be delivered. In addition, the educational team can use *Analyzing the Communication Environment (ACE)* (Rowland & Schweigert, 1996) to recognize natural cues that stimulate the student's communication and to design the social and physical environment to provide more of these cues by embedding opportunities in natural, functional activities.

Informal Assessment Tools and Methods

FUNCTIONAL OBSERVATIONS

Behavioral observations provide information on specific behaviors that a student exhibits and the conditions under which the behaviors are seen, including the frequency, duration, and intensity of the behaviors. The student's behavior is recorded as it occurs, and the compilation of information is recorded systematically to assist in interpretation. The observations can be done in a prescribed situation (such as during testing) or in a natural situation (for example, in the classroom, at recess, at home, or in a store). They also provide information on discrepancies across settings and environmental conditions.

Members of the educational team may need to enhance their observational skills, they can learn to recognize how the nonconventional forms of communication that a child uses can indicate his or her particular needs, social and emotional states, desires, and preferences. Observation is a primary tool for identifying a child's strengths, and the observer must be skillful in collecting objective data to determine the learning strengths that are embedded within the child's unique performances. The purpose of the observation is to understand what the child does well and under what conditions. This information will be used as a springboard for planning the child's program. Additional information on methods of behavioral observation can be found in *Assessment of Children: Behavioral and Clinical Applications* (Sattler, 2002).

Several pieces of information are essential to identify for each student. First, as with all students with visual impairments, the child's primary learning media must be identified. The *Learning Media Assessment* (Koenig & Holbrook, 1995) can be used to gather information for the student with both a visual impairment and an autism spectrum disorder. Of particular relevance are three assessment forms (samples of which are included at the end of this chapter):

- Use of Sensory Channels

- General Learning Media Checklist

- Functional Learning Media Checklist

Although the information that is gathered through these tools is designed mainly to determine whether an individual with a visual impairment learns primarily using print, braille, or another medium, each can also be used to provide information about how a child with an ASD is processing information. The tools allow the team to observe and interact with the child, watching to see if she or he responds best to visual, auditory, or tactile information. Each of the forms prompts the observer to consider the child's responses to various learning materials and teaching methods. The child's preferred media (visual, tactile, or auditory) is identified and can be used to identify overall trends and preferences. Figure 4.3 shows how the Use of Sensory Channels form can be used to chart some of the observed activities of a student who is blind to identify that this student is primarily an auditory learner.

FIGURE 4.3   Sample Use of Sensory Channels Form

Observed Behavior	Sensory Channel		
Locating classroom door	V	T	(A)
Reading a book (prefers tape)	V	T	(A)
Following a list of simple directions	V	T	(A)
Learns words to song	V	T	(A)
Identifies the make and model of a car by sound	V	T	(A)
Cannot track braille dots with fingers	V	T	(A)
	V	T	A
	V	T	A

☑ Probable Primary Channel: _____ Auditory _____

○ Probable Secondary Channel(s): _____

Source: Reprinted with permission from A. Koenig and C. Holbrook, *Learning Media Assessment of Students with Visual Impairments* (2nd ed.). Copyright © 1995, Texas School for the Blind and Visually Impaired, Austin.

Second, the team will need to determine the student's preferences. Such information can be collected during interviews with the child and his or her parents and teachers and from direct observations. The information on the child's likes and dislikes will be helpful in determining how to establish attention, how to motivate learning by using preferred activities, and to how establish motivating activities that the child can engage in, in his or her free time, among other things. A simple Preference Checklist (see the sample included at the end of this chapter) will provide valuable information about the child's preferences.

INTERVIEWS

The profile of development can be completed by interviewing the parents, guardians, or other family members; the child (when appropriate); and other service providers with extended knowledge of the child. When conducting the family interview, be sure to arrange a time when both parents are available and conduct the interview in a setting that is free of distractions. For a portion of the interview, it can be helpful to have the child present, so the parents can demonstrate the child's specific characteristics or the assessor can interact with the child for clarification. Remember to probe and stimulate the parents' thinking by associating questions with specific events or periods (such as birthday parties, family vacations, shopping, haircuts, doctors' appointments, and play dates with other children). Two different sample family interview forms, a Family Questionnaire and a Family Interview form, are provided at the end of this chapter.

CHECKLISTS

SENSORY INTERACTION CHECKLISTS

A number of assessment tools are available to assess sensory information and to develop a sensory profile. It can be helpful to refer to resources on sensory processing, sensory organization, and sensory integration. The terms *sensory integration* and *sensory processing* are often used interchangeably to refer to the process by which the brain registers, organizes, and interprets information from a person's sensory systems (movement, touch, sight, sound, smell, and taste). Dunn, Saiter, and Rinner's (2002) article offers guidance for understanding and planning interventions for individuals with Asperger syndrome. In addition, the ERIC Clearinghouse on Disabilities and Gifted Education (ERIC EC) has a Web site http://ericec.org with a database of information on sensory integration. Occupational therapists also can provide information on sensory processing.

Three commercially available checklists can assist the educational team in determining how well an individual processes sensory information in daily life. These tools are the Infant/Toddler Sensory Profile, the Sensory Profile, and the Adolescent/Adult Sensory Profile. Each tool is designed to evaluate sensory information processing and to identify sensory processing patterns.

The Infant/Toddler Sensory Profile (Dunn, 1999) consists of 36 items for children from birth to age 6 months and 48 items for children aged 7 months to 36 months. The caregiver questionnaire contains items that are divided into sensory systems.

With the Sensory Profile (Dunn, 1999), the team can determine how well a child, aged 3–10 years, processes sensory information in daily situations and the effect of the sensory system's effect on functional performance can also be profiled. The results of Sensory Profile, when considered with other evaluation data, will yield insights about the child that can be used for diagnostic purposes and intervention planning.

With the Adolescent/Adult Sensory Profile (Brown & Dunn, 2002), the team can identify the patterns and effects of sensory processing on the functional performance of students aged 11 years and older. Students can evaluate themselves using the Self-Questionnaire. The possible contributions of sensory processing to a student's patterns of daily performance can also be evaluated and used to support the development of strategies that optimize the desired sensory environment. The Adolescent/Adult Sensory Profile is designed as a trait measure of sensory processing characteristics. That is, an individual answers questions on how he or she generally responds to sensations, rather than on how he or she responds at any given time. Thus, the instrument is able to capture the individual's more-stable and enduring sensory processing characteristics. The Adolescent/Adult Sensory Profile contains 60 items, with 15 items in each quadrant, that cover the sensory processing categories of taste/smell, movement, vision, touch, activity level, and audition; these categories are distributed throughout the quadrants.

The Sensory Profile Observation form (see the sample at the end of this chapter) serves as an example that can be used to collect information for the sensory profile. Careful observation and reports by the child's parents and teachers will assist the team in collecting this information. The team can use the form to record repeated choices, as well as the child's behavioral reactions to stimuli that are presented visually, auditorially, and tactilely and by taste and smell. For example, how does the child react to the smell of various foods? Does the child select only foods with certain textures? How does the child react to various clothing materials? Does the child mouth inedibles? How does the child react to background noise or lighting?

Additional Sensory Profile resources include *Building Bridges Through Sensory Integration: Occupational Therapy for Children with Autism and Other Pervasive Developmental Disorders* (Yack, Sutton, & Aquilla, 2001) and the *Sensory Integration Inventory–Revised for Individuals with Developmental Disabilities* (Reisman & Hanschu, 1992). *Building Bridges* is a practical resource for parents and professionals that presents many strategies and ready-to-use activities for sensory learning for children with autism spectrum disorder or another pervasive developmental disorder who experience abnormal sensory processing and impaired motor planning.

The *Sensory Integration Inventory–Revised* is designed to assist occupational therapist in determining whether clients with severe and profound mental retardation would benefit from sensory integration treatment in the tactile, vestibular, proprioceptive, and general-reactions are as. Its use is also applicable for many students with ASDVI, as it explains how each item is an indicator of sensory integrative dysfunction and presents alternative explanations for behaviors that are often presumed to be primarily psychosocial in origin.

In addition to identifying how an individual student with ASDVI responds to sensory information, it will be helpful for the team to identify the sensory demands of the environments in which the student participates, including lighting, noise, crowding, temperature, and odors. The Checklist for Assessing Environmental Demands, which is included in *Understanding the Nature of Autism* (Janzen, 1996) can help team members to identify these demands. The checklist (see the sample included at the end of this chapter) should be used in combination with information on the student's learning style and sensory profile. The information can be used to determine if the environment presents significant stress for the child and whether or not adaptations are appropriate or necessary or whether specific instruction should be provided to teach the child to better tolerate the environment.

REINFORCER AND INTEREST ASSESSMENTS

It is vital that the team identify reinforcers that are powerfully motivating to the child because when these reinforcers are used appropriately, they provide a direct link to maintaining attention and learning. Reinforcers, in the instructional context, increase the rate of learning, the strength of new learning, and the likelihood that the behavior will reoccur. A reinforcer may occur naturally, as a result of the action or effort, or may be added during instruction to achieve the desired result (Janzen, 2003). It will be helpful to the team and the family to identify current reinforcers and continuously to develop new reinforcers as part of the ongoing assessment of the student with ASDVI.

In the process of identifying reinforcers, it is important to seek a variety of reinforcers that can be used to help expand the individual student's repertoire of potential interactions. A reinforcer is something that is powerful to the individual, but may not necessarily be elaborate or what another person may typically think of as reinforcing. For example, a child may find a particular toy reinforcing, not because of the toy itself, but because she or he is motivated to spin the wheels on the toy. To gain a better understanding of the reinforcing qualities for the child, it will be helpful to try to understand the salient features of the reinforcer, since as these features can be used to develop additional similar reinforcers or reinforcing activities. Because different reinforcers have different values, it is important to have a range of reinforcers for different levels of behavior. Observing the student will help the team identify reinforcers for a variety of environments or levels of behavior. A reinforcer needs to be something that an individual would select in a free-choice situation. Thus, setting up free-choice situations and exposing the child to the situations may help the team identify reinforcers. Some simple forms, such as the ones shown in Figures 4.4 and 4.5, can be used to identify information that will be critical for designing and implementing educational programs. The examples that are shown in these forms illustrate how the forms can assist in identifying, tracking, and developing reinforcements and interests.

It is important to remember that children can become satiated on a reinforcer at any time, and when they do, the reinforcer will lose its power to be motivating. For that reason, it is critical to continue to add to the list of

FIGURE 4.4   Sample Student Interests*

Home Interests	Similar Interests	School Interests	Similar Interests	Community Interests	Similar Interests
Rocking in rocking chair	Rocking horse Treadmill Swinging Wagon Spinning office chair	Swinging	Sit-n-Spin Mini trampoline Radio Flyer Racer Bicycle	Riding in car	City bus Horseback riding Carousel Train Bicycle
Stares at bright lights Filters light through fingers	Flashlights Bubble wands Water blocks Tornado bottle Windup toys Paint	Flipping paper	Notes to school office Shredding Unpacking boxes Recycling chores	Playing in water	Swimming Hot tub Landscape crew Car wash work Laundry work
Plays in sink	Water plants Wash dishes Clean the tub Make juice	Waving plastic bags	Pom-poms Flags Dance with scarves Folding clothes Parachute play	Listening to music videos	Go to movies Concerts Music class Work at video store Download music Work at music store
Disney videos	Musical toys Musical instruments Tape or CD player Musical push toys Play microphones	Reading facts on baseball cards	Rules for games Directions for cooking Schedules	Running aimlessly	Walk on path or track Walk a pet Ride a bike Collect and return shopping carts

*Begin by identifying home, school, and community interests. Then identify similar types of activities that can be used to expand the student's interest areas.

Note: The sample is not representative of one student; rather, it is representative of a variety of students in an effort to stimulate a creative way of thinking about the possibilities.

FIGURE 4.5 | **Sample Reinforcer Development***

Toys/Objects	Auditory Stimuli	Visual Stimuli	Movement Stimuli (swinging, vibrating, and so forth)
Balls Pull toys Push toys Musical toys Tape recorder	Musical toys Tapes or cds Balls in a container Rattles Rainstick Sing-along videos	Lights Flashlights Pictures Photos Flags Metal bowls Bubbles Mirrors Slinky	Swings Scooter board Therapy ball Roller skates
Tactile Stimuli	**Taste/Smell**	**Food**	**Other**
Vibrating snake Vibrating pillow Bumble ball Koosh ball Water table Sandbox	Aromatherapy candles Lifesavers	Crackers Candy Gum Juice Fruit	Games Social interactions

*This form can be used to identify toys, objects, and other stimuli that the student finds reinforcing.

Note: The sample is not representative of one student; rather, it is representative of a variety of students in an effort to stimulate a creative way of thinking about the possibilities.

Source: Adapted from EC Cares (Early Childhood Coordination Agency for Referrals, Evaluations, and Services), Lane County Early Intervention/Early Childhood Special Education Program planning and assessment materials, Eugene, OR.

reinforcers. An effective way to develop reinforcers is to make associations with established reinforcers and potential new reinforcers (Leaf , McEachin, Harsh, & Boehm, 1999) For example, consider Gaby, a student with multiple disabilities, including a visual impairment, a hearing impairment, and ASD. One of Gaby's primary reinforcing activities involves "flipping" pieces of paper in front of her eyes and mouth and shifting the paper through her fingers. In an attempt to expand her reinforcers, the team looked for other material besides paper that Gaby might find stimulating. During recreation, part of her exercise (and reinforcement) was to shake cheerleaders' pom-poms. To dust her room, she used a big, loosely strung feather duster. Eventually, the team was able to "build upon" this reinforcement theme; as described in Chapter 10, her fixation with paper flipping led her to a job as a "paper shredder" for a group of county offices.

OTHER CHECKLISTS

The Social Interaction Checklist and Student Daily Schedule at the end of this chapter offer several ideas for collecting relevant information from school settings. These checklists provide information about the skills the child has or needs to participate successfully in school settings. Once the present skills are identified, the team can address areas of weakness.

SUMMARY

The goal of assessment is to build a picture of the child so that each member of the educational team clearly understands how the child learns. This information is critical for designing and presenting instruction that makes sense to the child. The foundation of learning begins with this understanding. Building a picture of the child takes time and teamwork. This process, done well, will lay the groundwork for successful learning. It will also help the team to make learning fun, since the instruction will be matched to the child's learning style and will be based on practical application. It is also important to remember that assessment is an ongoing process. As the child learns, the picture evolves, and instruction is adjusted.

Play Interest Survey

Child's name: _____   Date: _____

Directions: 1. Rate the child's play interest on a scale of 1–3.
      1 = Does not like   2 = Shows some interest   3 = Likes a lot
      Leave the rating column blank if there has been no opportunity
   2. Check each toy or game if age-appropriate solitary play is observed
   3. Check each toy or game if age-appropriate social play is observed

Exploratory play	Rate	Solitary	Social
Bubbles			
Bumble ball			
Busy bead mazes			
Cause-and-effect toys			
Crawl longer drum roll			
Kaleidoscope (low vision)			
Macaroni bin			
Mirrors (low vision)			
Paint bags			
Tonka light and sound vehicles			
Sandbox			
Tops			
Matchbox rescue nets			
Water table			
Windup toys/sound			

Physical play	Rate	Solitary	Social
Ball			
Basketball and hoop			
Beanbags			
Bicycle			
Bowling			
Exercise equipment			
Hopscotch			
Hula hoop's			
Jump rope			
Playground equipment			
Rollerskates or ice skates			
Seesaw			
Sit 'n spin			
Swing			
Trampoline			

Manipulatives	Rate	Solitary	Social
Beads and laces			
Build-and-stack sets			
Colorforms			
Lite-Brite			
Lock and latch board			
Magnetic mazes			
Marble run			
Mr. Potato Head			
Nesting dolls			
Parquetry blocks			
Pegboards			
Puzzles			
Sewing cards			
Shape sorter			
Viewmaster			

Constructive play	Rate	Solitary	Social
Bristle blocks			
Building blocks			
Duplos			
Erector set			
Gears building set			
Lego models			
Legos			
Lincoln Logs			
Magnablocks			
Pop beads			
Snap blocks			
Tinkertoys			
Tool bench and tools			
Train and connecting tracks			
Vehicles and roads			

Source: Adapted with permission from K. A. Quill, *Do-Watch-Listen-Say: Social and Communication Intervention for Children with Autism.* Copyright © 2000, Paul H. Brookes, Baltimore, MD.

Music	Rate	Solitary	Social
Dancing			
Exercise video			
Fingerplays			
Karaoke machine			
Keyboard			
Marching band			
Microphone			
Musical instruments			
Musical toys			
Rain stick			
Rhythm sticks			
Sing-along video			
Songs			
Tape recorder			
Tapes and CDs			

Social Games	Rate	Solitary	Social
Catch			
Chase or tag			
Dog, dog, my bone is gone			
Duck, duck, goose			
Hide and seek			
London Bridge			
Mother May I?			
Musical chairs			
Parachute play			
Peekaboo			
Red light, green light			
Rough and tumble			
Simon says			
Tickle games			
Twenty questions			

Other preferences	Rate	Solitary	Social
Spins objects			
Throws objects			
Sifts objects through fingers			
Watches objects fall			
Shakes objects for noise			
Smells objects			

Other interests	Rate	Solitary	Social

Favorite solitary activities

Favorite social activities

Communicative Functions

Name _____ Date _____

Observer/Interviewer _____ Informant _____

Communication behaviors	Protest	Refusal	Rejection	Request for Object	Request for Action	Situations*
Generalized movements						
Changes in muscle tone						
Vocalizations						
Facial expressions						
Orientation						
Touching another person						
Manipulating/moving with another person						
Acting/using objects						
Assuming positions						
Going to places						
Conventional gestures						
Depictive actions						
Withdrawal						
Aggressive/self-injurious						
Other: Echolalia						
One word speech						
One word sign						
Combined words						

*Identify situations in which the child exhibits each of the five communication functions. Identify the communication behaviors observed.

Source: Reprinted with permission from D. Chen and J. Kote Kwan, *Starting Points: Instructional Practices for Young Children Whose Multiple Disabilities Include Visual Impairment.* Copyright © 1995, Blind Children's Center, Los Angeles, pp. 59, 61, 62.

Augmentative Communication Assessment
Protocol for Symbolic Augmentative Systems

The questions in this protocol are designed to help you collect information with which you can make decisions about symbolic augmentative communication systems for the students with whom you are working. The questions are in no way comprehensive and can not anticipate all the needs and variables of all students and their communication environments. The protocol will, however, help point you toward the characteristics of a system that will work with the student you are assessing.

Part I: Student Skills

A. Expressive Communication

What methods does the student currently use to expressively communicate?

■ Request objects, items:

_____
_____

■ Continue an action:

_____
_____

■ Stop an action:

_____
_____

■ Request social interaction:

_____
_____

■ Express a feeling:

_____
_____

■ Make a choice:

_____
_____

■ Initiate an interaction:

_____
_____

Source: Reprinted with permission from M. Gamel-McCormick & S. Dymond, "Augmentative Communication Assessment Protocol for Symbolic Augmentative Systems," Training and Technical Assistance Center— Old Dominion University, Norfolk, VA, 1994. Retrieved from Informational Topics at www.ttac.odu.edu.

(continued on next page)

■ Terminate an interaction:

_____

_____

■ Request assistance:

_____

_____

■ Other communication:

_____

_____

_____

_____

_____

_____

B. Cognitive Skills (including receptive communication characteristics)

1. Does the student have object permanence?

_____

_____

2. Does the student have an understanding of cause and effect?

_____

_____

3. Does the student have an understanding of means–end actions?

_____

_____

4. Review the hierarchy of symbolic communication. According to his or her cognitive abilities, what is your best determination of which level the student understands symbolic representation?

_____

_____

_____

_____

_____

_____

C. Motor Skills

1. In what position is the student able to optimally move and respond?

_____

_____

2. What reliable, predictable motor movements does the student have?

_____

_____

3. Does the student have a hand preference? _____ If "yes," what hand?

_____

_____

4. Does the student have the ability to reach?

_____

_____

5. Does the student have the ability to grasp?

_____

_____

6. Does the student have the ability to grasp and release?

_____

_____

7. Is the student able to isolate a finger? _____ If "yes," which finger(s)?

_____

_____

8. Is the student able to point?

_____

_____

9. How much hand and wrist strength does the student have?

_____

_____

10. Can the student manipulate objects? _____ If "yes," what type?

_____

_____

11. Can the student sort through objects or pictures? _____ If "yes," what type?

_____

_____

D. Visual Skills

1. What is the students' visual acuity? (What size objects can the student see best?)

_____

_____

2. What is the optimal lighting/contrast for the student to see an object, picture, or drawing?

_____

_____

(continued on next page)

3. Can the student fixate on an object, photograph, or drawing? _____ Which of these is his or her best medium?

_____

_____

4. What distance is optimal for the student to fixate on an item?

_____

_____

5. In what position should the object be for the student to be able to optimally fixate on it?

_____

_____

6. Can the student scan a visual display of items? _____ If "yes," in what medium (objects, photographs, drawings)?

_____

_____

7. How many items can the student scan before loosing interest?

_____

_____

8. How much time does the student need to scan an array of that size (in seconds or minutes)?

_____

_____

E. Auditory Skills

1. At what decibel level does the student best hear?

_____

_____

2. What frequency levels does the student best hear?

_____

_____

3. Can the student localize to sound? If "yes," how precisely?

_____

_____

Part II: Settings Where Communication Will Take Place

A. What are the settings where the student will use his/her augmentative communication system?

Setting 1: _____

Setting 2: _____

Setting 3: _____

B. What are the benefits and drawbacks of each of these settings in relation to the student's skills and abilities?

Setting 1: _____

Setting 2: _____

Setting 3: _____

Part III: Probable Content of Communication

A. What types of communication will probably take place using the augmentative system?

□ greetings

□ initiations

□ requesting

□ request continuation of an action/activity

□ stop an action

□ request a social interaction

□ express a feeling

□ terminate an interaction

□ request assistance

□ ongoing discourse

B. Will specific vocabulary be needed? _____

If "yes," identify the preliminary vocabulary that probably will be needed from the student's point of view (important events, activities, people, etc.)

_____

_____

_____

(continued on next page)

Part IV: Probable Recipients of Communication

A. *With what groups of people will the student be communicating?*

Group 1: _____

Group 2: _____

Group 3: _____

Group 4: _____

B. *At what symbolic level do each of these individuals process information?*

Group 1: _____

Group 2: _____

Group 3: _____

Group 4: _____

C. *What types of information are important for each group to understand from the student?*

Group 1: _____

Group 2: _____

Group 3: _____

Group 4: _____

Part V: Student Preferences

A. Tactile Preferences

Does the student have tactile preferences? If "yes," what are they?

_____

B. Visual Preferences

Does the student have visual presentation preferences? If "yes," what are they?

_____

C. Positioning Preferences

Does the student have positioning preferences? If "yes," what are they?

_____

D. *Interaction and communication preferences (include people, places, events, activities, etc.)*

_____

_____

_____

E. *Other student preferences that may influence the use of an augmentative system:*

_____

_____

_____

Part VI: Family and Caregiver Preferences for Communication Modes/Methods

A. *What preferences/concerns do the student's family express regarding an augmentative communication system?*

_____

_____

B. *What do the student's family members want the augmentative communication system to do?*

_____

_____

C. *What preferences/concerns do the student's caregivers express regarding an augmentative communication system?*

_____

_____

D. *What do the student's caregivers want the augmentative communication system to do?*

_____

_____

Use of Sensory Channels

Student _____

Setting/Activity _____

Date _____ Observer _____

Observed Behavior	Sensory Channel		
_____	V	T	A
_____	V	T	A
_____	V	T	A
_____	V	T	A
_____	V	T	A
_____	V	T	A
_____	V	T	A
_____	V	T	A
_____	V	T	A
_____	V	T	A
_____	V	T	A
_____	V	T	A
_____	V	T	A
_____	V	T	A
_____	V	T	A
_____	V	T	A
_____	V	T	A
_____	V	T	A

☐ Probable Primary Channel: _____

○ Probable Secondary Channel(s): _____

_____

Source: Reprinted with permission from A. Koenig & C. Holbrook, *Learning Media Assessment of Students with Visual Impairments* (2nd ed.). Copyright © 1995, Texas School for the Blind and Visually Impaired, Austin.

General Learning Media Checklist

Student _____

Date _____ Evaluator _____

DISTANCE

Use of vision	Use of touch	Use of hearing	Learning Materials	Use of vision	Use of touch	Use of hearing	Teaching Methods
V	–	–	Pictures	V	–	–	Pointing
V	–	–	Alphabet strips	V	–	–	Gestures
V	–	–	Wall clocks	V	–	–	Facial expressions
V	–	–	Calendar	V	–	–	Demonstration
V	–	–	Felt board	V	–	–	Modeling
V	–	–	Flip chart	–	–	A	Oral instructions
–	–	A	Environmental sounds	–	–	A	Verbal prompts
V	–	–	Timelines	–	–	A	Verbal guidance
V	–	–	Number line	–	–	A	Verbal descriptions
V	–	–	Posters, wall maps	–	–	A	Questioning
V	–	A	Videos, movies, TV	–	–	A	Class discussions
V	–	–	Transparencies	–	–	A	Lectures
–	–	A	Tapes, records, CDs	V	T	A	_____
V	T	A	_____	V	T	A	_____
V	T	A	_____	V	T	A	_____
V	T	A	_____	V	T	A	_____
V	T	A	_____	V	T	A	_____
V	T	A	_____	V	T	A	_____

Notes:

(continued on next page)

Student _____

NEAR

Use of vision	Use of touch	Use of hearing	Learning Materials	Use of vision	Use of touch	Use of hearing	Teaching Methods
V	T	–	Pictures	V	T	–	Pointing
V	T	A	Toys	V	T	–	Gestures
V	T	–	Clay	V	–	–	Facial expressions
V	T	–	Paint	V	T	A	Demonstrations
V	T	–	Crayons	V	T	A	Modeling
V	T	–	Stencils	V	T	A	Prompts, guidance
V	T	–	Puzzles	V	T	A	_____
V	T	–	Board games	V	T	A	_____
V	T	–	Real objects	V	T	A	_____
V	T	–	Models	V	T	A	_____
V	T	–	Flash cards	V	T	A	_____
V	T	–	Worksheets, workbooks				
V	T	A	Personal watch, clock, timer				
V	T	–	Desk calendar				
V	T	–	Desk number line, timeline				
V	T	–	Math manipulatives				
V	T	–	Money				
V	T	–	Abacus				
V	T	A	Calculators				
V	T	–	Maps, atlases				
V	T	–	Globe				
V	T	–	Charts, diagrams				
V	T	A	Measuring devices				
V	T	A	Science materials (such as lab equipment)				
V	T	A	Language Master				
–	–	A	Tapes, record albums, CDs				
V	T	A	_____				
V	T	A	_____				
V	T	A	_____				
V	T	A	_____				
V	T	A	_____				
V	T	A	_____				

Functional Learning Media Checklist

Student _____

Date _____ Evaluator _____

DISTANCE

Use of vision	Use of touch	Use of hearing	Learning Materials	Use of vision	Use of touch	Use of hearing	Teaching Methods
V	–	–	Pictures	V	–	–	Pointing
V	–	–	Conventional calendars	V	–	–	Gestures
–	–	A	Environmental sounds	V	–	–	Facial expressions
V	–	A	Community environment	V	–	–	Demonstration
V	–	–	Environmental signs	V	–	A	Modeling
–	–	A	Tapes, records, CDs	–	–	A	Oral instructions
V	–	A	Videos, movies, TV	–	–	A	Verbal prompts
V	–	–	Posters	–	–	A	Verbal guidance
V	–	–	Felt board	–	–	A	Verbal descriptions
V	T	A	_____	–	–	A	Questioning
V	T	A	_____	–	–	A	Class discussions
V	T	A	_____	V	T	A	_____

Use of vision	Use of touch	Use of hearing	Adaptive Communication Systems and Materials
			Unaided Communication Systems
V	T	–	Sign Language
V	T	–	Gestures
V	T	A	_____
V	T	A	_____
			Aided Communication Systems
V	T	A	Communication boards
–	–	A	Tape recorders
V	T	–	Picture communication books
V	T	A	Technology-based communication systems (such as speech synthesizers)
V	T	A	Primitive communication devices (such as real objects, miniatures)
V	T	A	Other augmentative communication devices
V	T	A	_____
V	T	A	_____

Source: Reprinted with permission from A. Koenig & C. Holbrook, *Learning Media Assessment of Students with Visual Impairments* (2nd ed.). Copyright © 1995, Texas School for the Blind and Visually Impaired, Austin.

(continued on next page)

Student _____

NEAR

Use of vision	Use of touch	Use of hearing	Learning Materials	Use of vision	Use of touch	Use of hearing	Teaching Methods
V	T	A	Real objects, materials	V	T	–	Pointing
V	T	–	Full size, scale models	V	T	–	Gestures
–	T	–	Positioning equipment	V	–	–	Facial expressions
–	T	–	Adaptive mobility devices	V	T	A	Demonstrations
V	T	–	Adaptive eating devices	V	T	A	Modeling
V	T	A	Washer, dryer	V	T	A	Prompts
V	T	A	Kitchen appliances	V	T	A	Guidance
V	T	–	Money	–	T	–	Physical manipulation
V	T	A	Telephone	–	T	–	Restraint
V	T	A	Calendar boxes	V	T	A	_____
V	T	A	Switches	V	T	A	_____
V	T	A	Timer	V	T	A	_____
V	–	–	Mirror	V	T	A	_____
V	T	A	Language Master	V	T	A	_____
–	–	A	Tapes, records, CDs	V	T	A	_____
V	T	–	Conventional desk calendar				
V	T	A	Adaptive vocational devices				
V	T	A	Behavior management charts				
V	T	A	Adaptive measuring devices				
V	–	–	Pictures				
V	T	–	Clay, paint, crayons				
V	T	A	Toys				
V	T	–	Stencils				
V	T	A	Puzzles				
V	T	A	Board games				
V	–	–	Light Box				
V	T	A	Personal watch, clock				
V	T	A	_____				
V	T	A	_____				

Preference Checklist

Name: _____

Date: _____

Preferred Activities*	Setting/Materials	Nonpreferred Activities*	Setting/Materials

*Consider toys, objects, people, and activities.

Source: Adapted with permission from EC Cares (Early Childhood Coordination Agency for Referrals, Evaluation, and Services), Lane County Early Intervention/Early Childhood Special Education Program planning and assessment materials, Eugene, OR.

Family Questionnaire

Name of Child: _____

Date of Birth: _____

Names of family members being interviewed: _____

_____

_____

Name of interviewer: _____

Date of interview: _____

This questionnaire will assist the educational team in understanding more about the child's family routines and interactions in daily life. Please include all family members and significant caregivers in the interview process.

1. *Describe your child's typical morning routine as listed below. Include your child's typical behaviors, what adults/siblings may do during the routine, and what, if anything, you might want to change about these activities.*

   Waking:

   Morning hygiene:

   Dressing:

   Breakfast:

   Preparing for school:

   _____

2. *Describe your child's typical after-school routines. Add any additional activities that you wish. Include what adults/siblings typically do during this routine, and what, if anything, you might want to change about these activities.*

   Transitioning from school:

   After-school activities:

   Dinner:

   Evening activities:

   Evening hygiene:

   Bedtime:

   Sleeping:

   _____

Source: Reprinted with permission from Pennsylvania's Initiative on Serving Students with Autism Spectrum Disorder, "Autism Select Team Training 2002 Assessment Packet," pp. 9–11. Retrieved from Pennsylvania Training & Technical Assistance Network, ftp://ftp.pattan.k12.pa.us/pattan/Autism/Protocol.pdf.

3. *Which of the above activities occur most easily for your child? Why do you think this is so?*

4. *Which of the above typical activities appear most difficult for your child? Why do you think this is so?*

5. *What are your child's favorite activities, interests, and past times? Describe how your child pursues these interests.*

6. *What are your child's dislikes? How do you know this?*

7. *How does your child communicate with adults at home?*

8. *In what family outings does your child participate?*

9. *How does your child respond to changes in your typical routine?*

10. *How does your child get your attention?*

11. *Who are the most important adults and children in your child's life?*

12. *What would you like to see your child accomplish now and in the future? List your ideas and prioritize.*

Family Interview

Name of Child: _____

Date of Birth: _____

Names of family members being interviewed: _____

_____

_____

Name of interviewer: _____

Date of interview: _____

1. Describe any concerns, problems, or specific issues you have concerning your child.

2. Describe your child has an infant (crying/not crying, stiff, resisted being held, eating patterns, sleeping patterns)

3. As an infant, could you tell what your child needed? How?

4. When did your child's first cooing and babbling occur?

5. If you have more than one child, how is this child different?

6. What does your child do when he/she wants to show you something?

7. How does your child gain your attention or the attention of others?

8. How does your let you know if he/she needs help?

9. Does your child repeat words or phrases? When? What phrases or words?

10. Does your child respond to your interactions? The interactions of peers?

11. Does your child converse with you? Others? Can your child vary the topic? Will your child participate in nonpreferred topics?

12. When did your child begin to talk? What is your child's voice like? Pitch? Inflections?

Source: Reprinted with permission from Oregon Statewide Regional Autism Services, Oregon Department of Education, Salem, OR.

13. How does your child entertain himself or herself?

14. Does/Did your child enjoy infant/toddler social games? (peek-a-boo, pat-a-cake)

15. How does your child interact at parties, social activities?

16. What does your child like to do with an adult? With peers?

17. How does your child react to strangers?

18. How does your child react to pain?

19. How does your child react to someone else being hurt? Sad?

20. Does your child understand social rules? (e.g., waiting in line, asking for help, waiting turns)

21. Does your child have difficulty changing routines? Going to new places? Trying new tasks?

22. What toys does your child like? How does he or she play with them?

23. What are your child's strengths?

24. What things are difficult for your child to learn?

25. Does your child have any repetitive or compulsive habits or movements?

26. How does your child respond to sound? Tastes? Smells? Touch? Textures?

27. Describe your child's sleeping patterns.

28. Describe any behavior or discipline problems your child exhibits.

29. What is your child curious about?

30. How does your child learn new skills?

Sensory Profile Observation Form

Name _____ Date _____

Sensory Area	Oversensitivity / Hypersensitivity Behaviors	Undersensitivity / Hyposensitivity Behaviors	Comments
Vision			
Auditory			
Touch			
Taste			
Smell			
Movement			

Source: Reprinted with permission from Oregon Regional Autism Services, Oregon Department of Education, Salem, OR.

Checklist for Assessing Environmental Demands

Student: _____

Environment: _____ Date: _____

Use this checklist to identify and determine which adaptations may be necessary. Match the learner's sensitivities and deficits to: (1) the level of environmental stimulation and (2) the demands of the activity. Note examples.

1. Nature and level of the activity and environmental stimuli (Consider the intensity, frequency, and duration of stimuli.)

   ☐ Noise—Subtle (echoes, fans, lights, halls, street) people (talking, singing, shuffling feet or paper)

   ☐ Noise—Intense (whistles, bells, trains, loudspeakers, machinery)

   ☐ Visual—Objects (pictures, mobiles, lights and shadows, bulletin boards, materials on open shelves), surfaces (wood grain, reflecting, or patterned), people (glasses, jewelry, movement)

   ☐ Odors—People, materials (perfumes, glues, paint, paper), cafeteria, cleaning supplies, nearby businesses (bakery, factory, service station)

   ☐ Touch—People (crowding, touching, holding hands, physical assistance or touch for reinforcement), materials (textures of fabrics, furniture, sticky or rough materials)

   ☐ Movement (Vestibular)—Demand for getting up and down, reaching, stooping, moving about, moving up or down inclines, sitting or standing in one place)

   ☐ Taste—Meals and snack foods, exploratory tasting activities for young children

2. Demands of the event (work or activity)

   ☐ Complexity of the language used in directions

   ☐ Requirement for written work

   ☐ Time pressures

   ☐ Need to keep several thoughts together in a sequence

   ☐ Need for generating new motor and/or verbal responses

   ☐ Requirement for solving problems, using judgment, making decisions

   ☐ Clarity of the beginning and end of the activity or routine

(continued on next page)

□ Waiting requirements (for bus, before/after transitions, for help, in line)

□ Participation with others (cooperative teams, assembly lines, competitive activities, partners, large or small groups)

3. New or unfamiliar events

Activity:	□ New	□ Familiar
Materials:	□ New	□ Familiar
Location:	□ New	□ Familiar
Staff members:	□ New	□ Familiar
Peers:	□ New	□ Familiar

Other new: _____

_____

Student Interests

Home Interests	Similar Interests	School Interests	Similar Interests	Community Interests	Similar Interests

Reinforcer Development

Toys/Objects	Auditory Stimuli	Visual Stimuli	Movement Stimuli (swinging, vibrating, and so forth)
Tactile Stimuli	Taste/Smell	Food	Other

Source: Adapted from EC Cares (Early Childhood Coordination Agency for Referrals, Evaluations, and Services), Lane County Early Intervention/Early Childhood Special Education Program planning and assessment materials, Eugene, OR.

Social Interaction Checklist

Summary Sheet

Student's Name: _____ School Year: _____

Teacher: _____ Class: _____

Use the space below to summarize teachers' information collected from direct observations of the student. Highlight items scored either 4 or 5 to assist in determining trends. Use a heavy line to separate reporting periods.

Frequency	Consistently	Often	Sometimes	Seldom	Never
Intensity	No Problem		Moderate		
	1	2	3	4	5

Date														
Instructor's Initials														
Behavior														
1. Plays with peers during break.														
2. Responds to questions from peers.														
3. Participates in games with other children in the classroom.														
4. Participates in games with other children at breaks.														
5. Has particular peers with whom the child interacts.														
6. Participates in group activities in the classroom.														
7. Appears to enjoy time spent in group activities.														
8. Responds to teacher questions during large group instructions.														
9. Talks with other children in the classroom at the appropriate times.														
10. Helps other children with tasks.														
11. Shares material goods with other children.														
12. Shows concern (verbal or non-verbal) for the problems of others.														
13. Shares feelings at appropriate times.														
14. Interactions with adults seem to be of a positive nature.														
15. Interactions with children seem to be of a positive nature.														

Reprinted with permission from Willamette ESD Special Programs, Salem, OR.

Student Daily Schedule

Name _____   Date _____

Directions: Fill in the name of each subject and the name of each teacher. Place an X in the appropriate column to show whether you always, frequently, sometimes, seldom, or never have difficulty during this time, period, or place. The intent is to have the student fill in the schedule. It may also be used as a data-recording tool for staff conducting observations of the student.

If you **always** have difficulty during this time, period, or place, put an X in the box opposite number 5.
If you **frequently** have difficulty during this time, period, or place, put an X in the box opposite number 4.
If you **sometimes** have difficulty during this time, period, or place, put an X in the box opposite number 3.
If you **seldom** have difficulty during this time, period, or place, put an X in the box opposite number 2.
If you **almost never** have difficulty during this time, period, or place, put an X in the box opposite number 1.

Time, Period, Place	Before School	1st Period	Hall	2nd Period	Hall	3rd Period	Hall	4th Period	Lunch	5th Period	Hall	6th Period	Hall	7th Period	After School
Subject															
Teacher															
Rating															
5															
4															
3															
2															
1															

Communication

Communication is an interactive exchange between two or more people to convey needs, feelings, or ideas. As a child develops, he or she learns to understand what is being communicated by others (receptive communication) and learns to express his or her needs and make others understand his or her feelings and ideas (expressive communication). Communication includes language systems (speech, sign language, written language, and other graphic symbols), as well as gestures, body language, and facial expressions. Learning objectives to build *language* are aimed primarily at expanding a child's vocabulary and grammatical complexity. In contrast, *communication* is a social exchange. Language is only one vehicle that is used to communicate. Nonverbal messages, such as eye gaze, gestures, facial expressions, and other expressions of affect, are equally important vehicles of communication. Effective communication can exist in the absence of language, as shown by the communication behavior of infants. Furthermore, as Quill (1995, p. 76) noted, "language can exist in the absence of communication, as is often observed in children with autism." These children use words, but the words do not have meaning.

Communication deficits are a critical characteristic of students with autism spectrum disorder, with many children having difficulty acquiring speech and language. Other communication deficits include the lack of verbal imitation, of nonverbal communication, of spontaneous joint attention (described in Chapter 4) and sharing, and of interests in other people; echolalia, both immediate and delayed (discussed later in this chapter); the inability to take turns; and difficulty with social conversations. In contrast, most children with visual impairments typically do not have difficulty developing speech and language. Vocal and verbal imitations are usually not a problem for these children, but without visual feedback, some aspects of communication may be slow to develop and must be specifically taught. These aspects of communication include the nonauditory forms of communication, such as eye contact, understanding facial expressions, and other nonverbal gestures (waving, pointing, and nodding). Visually impaired children can learn to use these skills effectively when naturally occurring events are used to teach the skills. The curriculum for students with visual impairments must reflect instruction in appropriate communication modes that match their individual learning styles and needs, which may include the use of braille, large print, print with the use of optical devices, regular print, tactile (object) symbols, sign language, or audiotape-recorded materials.

The communication characteristics of students with autism spectrum disorder and visual impairment will seem similar to those of individuals with ASD. One area that will be difficult to assess is nonverbal behaviors. Because of the child's visual impairment, the educational team may struggle to differentiate whether the child's lack of nonverbal communication is due to the lack of vision or to the presence of ASD. It is important to remember that impairments in nonverbal communication are one aspect of ASD that needs to be considered. As was just noted, students with visual impairments who demonstrate difficulty with nonverbal communication can be taught to use nonverbal communication through traditional means and will generalize the skills in a variety of settings. Those with ASDVI have trouble understanding and using these skills, and the deficits will need to be addressed with specific instruction and intensive opportunities to practice and generalize.

Students with ASDVI present a wide variety of skills and deficits in the area of communication development. Thus, the team must take time to observe and assess the student carefully to understand how a student communicates. Without this understanding, an effective intervention plan will be difficult to implement. Once the team establishes the student's level of communicative means and functioning as is discussed in Chapter 4 and using the Communicative Functions form in Appendix 4A, the strategies in this chapter will assist the team to begin expanding the student's functional communication.

INSTRUCTIONAL STRATEGIES: GENERAL PRINCIPLES

Entire books that focus on the development of communication skills for students with ASD are available (J. Baker, 2003; Bondy & Frost, 2001; Hodgdon,

1995, 1999; Quill, 1995, 2000). This chapter highlights the areas of communication skill development that are often the most challenging for teams that work with students with ASDVI.

Opportunities for communication occur many times in any activity. Since students with ASDVI have difficulty sorting out the meaning and relevance of the communication, the educational team needs responsibility to provide experiences and activities that help the student learn to understand the meaning of the communication. To be motivated to cooperate with attempts to teach communication, the student must understand that by participating, he or she will gain access to the items or activities that he or she desires (Sundberg & Partington, 1998).

Before any instructional strategy can be introduced, the instructor must establish rapport with the student with ASDVI and help the student to learn that the instructor will deliver reinforcing items and activities. Initially, it is best to approach the child while he or she is not engaged in a highly reinforcing activity by himself or herself. It will be more productive to allow the child to gain access to the highly reinforcing items through the instructor. For example, if a boy whose most reinforcing activity is playing with a train has access to the train any time he wants and does not have to communicate or interact with anyone to get it, he will have no need to communicate. On the other hand, if the boy is motivated to play with the train and the instructor controls access to the train by requiring him to use some form of communication (such as any sound, the sound "tra," the word *train,* a picture of train, an object signifying train, or a voice-output device that says "train"), he will learn the power of communication and will learn that by interacting with others, he will get the things that are pleasurable to him. The interaction may go something like this: The instructor has several toys on a table, including a train. She brings the child to the table and sits across from him. The instructor begins to play with the train and then stops. For a child who has some babbling, she says "train." After any verbal response, the instructor gives the boy the train for a few seconds. For a nonverbal child, the initial interaction may be that the child attends to the instructor and is then given the train. This is just one example of the way in which a reinforcer is used to gain interaction and communication with a child.

The process for identifying appropriate instructional strategies will be based on information that was obtained in the assessment (see Chapter 4). This information will lead the team to establish clear goals and objectives. Once the goals and objectives have been established, the team can develop and implement specific instructional strategies that lead to their acquisition. In the process of selecting and providing instructional strategies it is important for the team members to work on *increasing spontaneity* and *building generalization* across environments and people. In the design of the individual program, the following steps are critical for mastery and help to be implemented across the program:

1. the functional skill is developed;

2. the skill is present without adult prompts;

3. the skill is generalized across adults, peers, and groups; and finally,

4. the skill is generalized across familiar and new contexts (Quill, 2000).

The following example illustrates how the four steps are implemented. In Step 1, the child is taught the names of the items, such as food, toys, or activities, that he or she desires. If the child likes the Bumble ball toy, instruction begins by making a connection between the Bumble Ball and a vocalization (or movement, or word, or picture), depending on the child's level of functioning. The idea is to pair the desired object with a word or with some symbolic representation, so the child understands that when she says "ball," she will get the ball. In the second phase, the child learns to say "ball" without an adult prompting her to say it. She will be able to ask for the ball when she sees it or touches it briefly and is asked "what do you want?" In the third step, the child will be able to use the word *ball* with a variety of different people. In the fourth step, the child will be able to use the word *ball* appropriately with both adults and peers at school, at home, and in different play settings.

In this chapter, four areas of communication deficits that are associated with students with ASD and, in turn, with students with ASDVI are addressed. Although these four are not the only deficits that children may experience, they are often the most challenging for students with ASDVI and include

- spontaneous vocal language

- echolalia

- nonvocal language and the use of augmentative communication supports

- social conversations

SPONTANEOUS VOCAL LANGUAGE

The empirical evidence in the area of ASD supports the use of contemporary behavioral approaches in which naturalistic teaching methods are used to foster the development of language. These approaches use systematic teaching trials, or instructional periods, that have several common ingredients: they focus on the child's interests, they are interspersed into a variety of activities, they are embedded in the natural environment, and they use natural reinforcers (Lord & McGee 2001, p. 53).

Arranging the Environment

To elicit spontaneous vocal communication, the instructor must systematically arrange the environment to provide motivation. The following six strategies can be used to provide this motivation.

STRATEGY 1

Arrange the physical environment to increase the student's need to communicate. Materials and motivators should not magically appear and disappear in front of the student. The student with ASDVI must be taught that objects exist in the environment and understand that he or she plays a role in gaining access to the objects. The student will then have functional communication opportunities to gain access to materials, toys, food, and activities.

STRATEGY 2

Use toys, objects, food, and activities interests as opportunities to initiate communicative activities. The child can not have free, unlimited access to toys, materials, food, or activities, or there will be no reason for him or her to communicate. Thus, the team needs to develop the mindset that "nothing is free" to the child. The team must expect communication from the child for the child to gain access to the toys, materials, and activities. In the earliest stages, the communication may include movement, reaching, touching, or simple vocalizations. The level and sophistication of the communication that is expected must increase over time, and it is critical for every member of the team to understand and follow this philosophy. Through a process of prompting responses and shaping vocalizations (see "The Language of Instruction" in Chapter 3), the child will learn to understand the power of communication.

Many of the early forms of vocal language consist of requesting. Requesting is usually taught first because it results in direct benefit to the learner (they get what they want). Parents and instructors need to provide an environment that requires and reinforces requesting (Sundberg & Partington, 1998). They also need to analyze the student's day at home, at school, and in the community to determine all the opportunities the student has, or they can create, to use a language system to make a request—for objects, food, a turn or help. Figure 5.1 presents some examples of how a simple tool can be used to analyze and plan opportunities for promoting communication and to enhance and expand these opportunities as the child progresses.

FIGURE 5.1   Requesting Opportunities

Reinforcement	What the instructor will do	What the student will say (vocalization, picture, device, sign)
Student 1: *Vocal, with low vision*		
Applesauce	At snack time, place an unopened snack on the table with a spoon; show the item and ask the student "What do you want?"	1. "help" or 2. "open" or 3. "want" Repeat until the applesauce is eaten or student has vocalized several times.
Toy Bumblebee	Show the toy and ask the student "What do you want to play with?"	1. "toy" 2. "bumblebee" 3. something similar
Toy piano	Show the toy and ask the student "What do you want?"	1. "toy" 2. "play" 3. "piano"
Rocking horse	Show the horse and ask the student "What do you want?"	1. "horse" 2. "ride" 3. "play"
Reinforcement	**What the instructor will do**	**What the student will do (picture, device, sign)**
Student 2: *Blind, uses a tactile object*		
Vibrating tube	Show the toy and ask the student "What do you want?"	1. point to the object 2. touch a piece of the object that represents the vibrating tube
Musical toy	Turn on the toy and turn it off. Ask student "What do you hear? What do you want?"	1. touch the toy 2. touch the object that represents the toy
Goldfish Crackers	Show the student a bowl with crackers or a package of crackers. Ask the student, "What do you want to eat?"	1. point to the package or bowl 2. touch the object that represents the cracker
Rocking Chair	Show the student the chair and rock it back and forth. Ask the student, "What do you want?"	1. rock the chair 2. touch the object that represents the rocking chair

An approach for creating opportunities for communicating can be adapted from *Do-Watch-Listen-Say* (Quill, 2000), as illustrated in the following example. The first level of instruction begins with interactions between the child and the instructor. The second moves to small-group instruction, while the third focuses on generalization of the skill. (See Appendix A in *Do-Watch-Listen-Say* [Quill, 2000] for additional communication activities that can be used or adapted for students with ASDVI.)

Communication Skill: Requesting an Object or Toy

Possible Communication Modes to be Taught:

Gesture: reach, move adult's hand, open palm request
Communication mode: speech, sign, photograph, voice output, braille, print

Level 1 Activity: Adult-Child Interaction

Setting: *Open area of room*
Materials: *Bumble Ball*

> *Procedure:* Place the Bumble Ball in the child's hand; turn it on and off. Say "Bumble Ball" (or other appropriate words the student is working on). Reward any communicative attempt. Prompt (e.g., move the child's hand to turn the toy on, say the sound "*b*") and shape (e.g., accept movement toward ball or any vocalization) as needed, and fade the prompts as quickly as possible. Give the child a chance to play with the Bumble Ball for several seconds following the communication. Repeat as many times as possible, or until child loses interest.

Level 2 Activity: Small Group Instruction

Setting: *Play Area*
Materials: *Bubble wand that emits sounds*

> *Procedure:* Blow bubbles paired with sounds toward the small group. Experiment to see what each child alerts or responds to. Pause, wait, and watch for the children to respond. Respond to the child's communication by repeating the action he or she enjoys. If there is no response, prompt (e.g., guide the child's hand toward the bubbles, have child touch bubble wand, say the sound for "*b*," repeat the word *bubbles*) as appropriate. Repeat the activity; work to fade any prompts and increase expectations for communication.

Level 3 Activity: Generalization of Skills

The following are some examples of opportunities that can be used to help the child generalize learned skills:

- requesting music to be turned on in the music area

- requesting a snack from a closed container

- requesting a book from the bookshelf

- requesting a paper towel to dry hands in the bathroom

- requesting a straw to drink milk from the carton

- requesting a toy from a closed container

- requesting a toy from the toy shelf

STRATEGY 3

Use the child's apparent social interests as opportunities to initiate communicative interactions. For example, a child may enjoy swinging on his or her father's knee. Use the social interaction between the father and the child to initiate communication, such as a body movement to indicate more swinging or a vocalization to indicate that the child wants to continue. Many children enjoy rhythmic social games that are found on sing-along tapes. The tapes may be used to initiate communication for the names of songs, turning on the tape, and singing, among a few examples.

STRATEGY 4

Reinforce all attempts to communicate, accepting any and all communicative means. If a child with ASDVI is going to learn to use vocal language, then he or she must learn to understand that vocal behaviors have meaning. The teacher must be alert to all attempts and provide the link to developing more-formal communication. For example, if a child and an adult are in the play area and the child touches a toy, the adult should view it as an attempt to communicate about play and the desire to interact with the toy. The adult can reinforce the communication by saying the name of the toy or "You want to play." If the child pounds a spoon on the table during mealtime, reinforce the attempt to communicate by saying (after interpreting what the child may be trying to indicate) "You are finished" or "You want more."

STRATEGY 5

View every moment as a potential opportunity to build communicative interactions. Assist members of the team to be alert to communicative attempts. Learn which adults and peers are able to interact successfully with the child and identify the strategies they use that are effective (adapted from Quill, 2000, p. 98). Use information that was collected in the assessment of motivators and reinforcers, plus the social and communication assessment (discussed in Chapter 4), to help understand situations that may motivate the child to communicate.

STRATEGY 6

Implement a strategy of "communication temptations and motivations" (adapted from Wetherby & Prizant, 1997). The following is a list of ideas that can motivate communication:

- Saturate the environment with interesting objects with which the child will come in contact (visually, auditorally, tactilely) that will motivate the child to ask for help to obtain an object.

- During snack time, wait for the child to request an item before you get the snack. Do not give the entire snack at once, but repeat the opportunity to request.

- Reinforce attempts to communicate.

- Vary the tasks that are used during a teaching session. Do not allow the child to become bored.

- Intersperse tasks that the child already knows when the child is learning new tasks.

- Activate a windup toy, let it run down and then hand it to the child.

- Initiate a social game that the child enjoys. Play the game until the child expresses pleasure. Stop and wait for the child to imitate some aspect of the social game (such as tickling, bouncing, or rocking).

- Place food or an item in a container that the child can not open. Show the child the object and wait for him or her to attempt to communicate.

- Roll a ball to the child several times. Pause and wait for the child to communicate.

- Put an object that makes noise in a container. Hold the container and wait for the child to communicate.

- Give the child materials for an activity of interest. Keep a necessary piece for completion of the activity and wait for the child to request it. (For example, if the child enjoys painting on large paper, give him or her the paint and brushes, but not the paper; wait for the child to request the missing paper.

■ Analyze the child's environments. See what interests the child and create opportunities to intersperse communication throughout the activities in these environments. Be a "detective" and search for clues for opportunities to communicate.

Intervention Strategies

In addition to these strategies, there are a number of *systematic* intervention strategies that are designed to develop and enhance spontaneous vocal communication, including Pivotal Response Training and the Picture Exchange Communication System.

PIVOTAL RESPONSE TRAINING

Pivotal Response Training (PRT) is an intensive behavioral intervention that was specifically developed to teach language and play skills to children with autism spectrum disorder (Arick, Falco, Krug, & Loos, 2004). This method of instruction for teaching language creates multiple opportunities to communicate using a natural context. The procedure resembles the way in which one interacts with typically developing children and is especially effective for teaching generalization across environments and people, maintenance of skills, and motivation.

PRT focuses on training in which the child directs the activity by making choices. The reinforcer has a specific relationship to the desired behavior (for example, when the child says "ball," he or she gets the ball, not praise). The child is reinforced for communicative approximations or attempts in the early stages of development. As the child gains skills, more sophisticated communication is expected.

The procedure that is followed includes four steps:

1. The teacher places objects, toys, and food in the environment and arranges the environment so it is conducive to activities that are interesting to the student. For students who are visually impaired, it is helpful to use toys and materials that make noise, provide light, or contain pleasing textures, rather than containing visual elements. The area should include items that are age appropriate, with opportunities for the student to explore what is available.

2. The teacher encourages the student to select items by providing a stimulus or cue or otherwise giving the student an opportunity to respond (e.g., making the child aware of an electronic toy by activating the noise or bright lights). The student selects an item by showing an interest in it (such as simply by turning his or her head toward the item when it is presented or smiling or laughing) or by reaching out to get it. By knowing

the child, the teacher will have a sense of what the child is interested in and how the child demonstrates that interest. The teacher is alert to such signals and gives the child the opportunity to interact on the basis of the interest that the child has demonstrated.

- The student vocalizes to gain access to the item (response); vocalization could be paired with a symbolic representation (an objects, picture, or auditory output device).

- The teacher and child play or otherwise interact with the item. In so doing, the child receives reinforcement and learns the consequences of his or her behavior and how to take turns.

- The teacher pauses, so the child gets a few seconds to interact with the item.

- The teacher repeats the process and changes the stimulus if the child has selected a new item of interest.

PICTURE EXCHANGE COMMUNICATION SYSTEM

The Picture Exchange Communication System (PECS) was developed to foster spontaneous communication (see Bondy & Frost, 2001). The focus is on teaching the child that communication is an exchange and facilitating the emergence of speech. Since some children may not develop vocalizations, pictures can be used as symbolic cues that serve as the augmentative communication system for them. Many teachers use Boardmaker—a graphics database containing over 3,000 pictures to produce such pictures, but object cues (an object or part of an object used to refer to or represent a person, place, activity, or object) or photographs can also be used.

The procedure that is followed when using PECS is this:

1. The child hands a picture to a person in exchange for receiving the desired object. To teach the child to do so, the teacher uses motivating toys, foods, or activities to build the child's requesting skills; labeling (naming items and objects) comes later in the process.

2. The teacher systematically expands the distance that the child needs to travel to locate a person to convey a message (by choosing destinations at increasingly distant locations).

3. The teacher systematically increases the time that the child needs to persist to get another person's attention.

4. The teacher systematically teaches the child to discriminate among different PECS symbols.

M. H. and D. J. Gense

Picture Exchange Communication System (PECS) symbols. As students learn to exchange the symbols for a desired object from another person, the system helps them develop spontaneous communication.

For students with ASDVI whose vision does not allow them to use pictures, other communication modes can be used. These modes may include a tactile symbol system, braille, sign language, voice output devices, or a combination of these modes. The recommendations are not exhaustive, but they serve as a framework for developing spontaneous vocal language.

ECHOLALIA

Echolalia, the repetition or echoing of verbal utterances that are made by another person, is common in children with ASDVI. There are two types of echolalia: *immediate* echolalia and *delayed* echolalia. Immediate echolalia is the repetition of words or phrases that were just spoken, whereas delayed echolalia is the repetition of words or phrases after some delay or lapse of time. Both forms of echolalia serve a specific purpose and have communicative functions for the individual. Echolalia is a common means that typically developing children use to learn language. Children with ASDVI who use echolalia longer than is expected in typically developing children appear to be "stuck" at this point in their development of languages.

The first step in identifying appropriate instructional strategies to address echolalia is to determine the function of the echolalic behavior. The behavior may be directed toward a social partner, to request something, or to reciprocate in response to a social partner. It can also be used to initiate communication (to request, call to a person, or protest) or to maintain exchanges (turn taking or providing information). For some students with ASDVI, echolalia may be a form of self-stimulation. A careful analysis of the function or functions of the echolalia will help the team identify the skills that the child is lacking. Such an analysis can be completed by collecting samples of language across multiple settings, including both familiar and unfamiliar environments or activities. Intervention programs can then be designed to address the function that the echolalia serves. For example, when the child repeats the phrase "Do you want apple?" the child *may* mean that he or she wants an apple. It *may* also mean that the child wants adult attention something to eat or perhaps simply likes the sound of the words rolling his or her tongue. The team members will need to determine the message that the child is trying to convey to design appropriate intervention strategies. They can do so by observing the child, the situation, and the environment and making an educated determination about what the child is trying to express. If the purpose is to gain the attention of an adult, the child can then be taught appropriate strategies to get attention. The team members must become detectives of language functions. That is, they must identify the clues that the child provides and then use these clues to solve the communication problem.

There are a number of instructional strategies that can be used to address echolalia. For example, you can try responding literally to the student. If the student echoes "Do you want juice?" after being asked the question, respond by saying "No, thank you," followed by "I think you want to tell me something, though." Then use another communication prompt (for example, a cue, such as giving the picture or an object to the student) to prompt the student to say "juice" (Heffner, 2000).

Another strategy is called the "Cues–Pause–Point Method" (Heffner, 2000). It involves selecting 10 questions from each of the following three content areas making sure that the child does not know the answers to the questions:

1. identification (for example, ask the name of an object)

2. interaction (for example, "How are you?")

3. factual (for example, "What city do you live in?")

During a baseline period, ask the questions and record the child's answers in one of three categories: echolalia, incorrect response (when the response contains an irrelevant word), or correct response (when the answer is appropriate). Training consists of the following four steps:

- Training Step 1: Teach the child to respond verbally to cards with labels that are used to prompt the correct answers to the 30 questions. For example, for the answer to the question, "What is this object," show the student the card that is labeled with the name of the object. The cards can utilize braille, pictures, objects, or an auditory system, depending on the appropriate learning media that have been identified for the student. Continue training until the student can label each card.

- Training Step 2: Use a system to indicate a "pause" prompt to request silence while you are asking a question (see Heffner, 2000). Ask the questions (from the original set of questions) and point or touch the student's hand to the correct response card. Reinforce each correct answer with verbal praise or a reinforcer.

- Training Step 3: Ask the questions without using the prompt cards. Provide reinforcers for the correct responses.

- Training Step 4: Fade the feedback and reinforcers until all are eventually eliminated.

This method can be viewed as teaching scripted responses instead of having the student echo back vocalizations. The teacher is attempting to break the echoing pattern and to replace the pattern with scripted responses. Now, instead of the student repeating back exactly what is said, he or she repeats a scripted response to the question. For more information on this approach, refer to information available on the Web site of the Autism Home Page (http://groups.msn.can/theautismhomepage; see the Resources at the back of this book).

Another strategy employs the use of peer or adult models to prompt a correct response. For example, at mealtime, teach the child with ASDVI to make choices. First tell the child (or show him or her, using an object, braille, or picture prompts) what is available. Then give a verbal prompt, such as "We have juice or milk" "What do you want?" I want ____," and wait for the child to respond. Another adult or peer can prompt the response. When the child responds, he or she is reinforced with the actual item. After the child can successfully and spontaneously answer with one word, systematically fade portions of the prompt. Say, for example, "We have juice or milk, what do you want?" The child responds, "juice."

Another possibility to address echolalia is to consider using augmentative verbal production devices (discussed in the following section) for students with ASDVI who demonstrate little evidence of communicative intent.

Finally, reducing specific repetitive questions can be helpful in addressing echolalia. Repetitive questions are a form of echolalic behavior and may serve a variety of functions for students with ASDVI. The team needs to become increasingly familiar with the student to understand the purpose behind the questions. Depending on the function of the questions, one or more of the strategies just listed may be useful.

NONVOCAL LANGUAGE AND THE USE OF AUGMENTATIVE COMMUNICATION SUPPORTS

Some students with ASDVI have difficulty developing vocal communication skills and may benefit from augmentative communication supports. As was described in Chapter 4, augmentative communication systems use symbols, such as objects, pictures, line drawings, or words, that are used to optimize the child's communication skills. The assessment and development of appropriate augmentative systems is complex. Numerous resources that provide in-depth information are identified in the Resources that are listed at the end of this book. This section addresses the critical components of providing instruction for students with ASDVI who have limited or no effective vocal language.

Any intervention approach should involve teaching students to be both initiators and receivers of information. As with the issues involved in developing spontaneous vocal language, the student with ASDVI must have something to communicate about and a desire to communicate. Daily routines and communicative exchanges should be planned, so the student has multiple opportunities to interact with others. In addition to recognizing natural cues that stimulate communication and designing the social and physical environment to provide more of these cues as discussed in Chapter 4 (see Rowland & Schweigert, 1996), the team needs the child's learning style and preferred media, using the Learning Media Assessment (Koenig & Holbrook, 1993), also discussed in Chapter 4. For example, a student whose primary learning medium is tactile may use an object symbol system, a braille symbol system, or a combination of the two. For a student with ASDVI whose primary medium is visual, the primary medium may be pictures, print, or a combination of the two. For a student whose primary medium is auditory, many different auditory output devices can be used to assist the student to learn and use communication. A number of devices are listed in the Resources for this chapter. Selecting a device will also depend on the sophistication of

Students whose primary learning medium is tactile may use object symbols, such as these, for communicating about their daily routines.

the communication that is needed. In addition, the team will need to consider the ability of the augmentative system to prompt communication, the device's portability and speed, the ability to expand to higher or formal levels of communication, and the ease of understanding for the communication partner.

For many students, the team may have difficulty knowing the student's level of understanding for using a symbolic system (his or her level of representation) to replace or supplement vocal behavior. Thus, it is essential for the team members to establish the level of representation that the child needs before they determine what augmentative system may be appropriate. The "Guide to Help Establish Your Student's Level of Representation" (Davidson & O'Meara, 1997) can assist the team in making this determination (see Figure 5.2). This guide will help the teacher to determine the best match for the student. It will help sort out whether the student can understand and use objects, pictures, line drawings, written words, or a voice output device. In response to questions in the guide, a pattern will be established as to the level of response that the student is able to provide. A picture system will not be appropriate for a student who cannot recognize pictures, either visually or cognitively. On the other hand, if the student is primarily an auditory

FIGURE 5.2

A Guide to Help Establish Your Student's Level of Representation

What is the student's "level of representation?" What materials will the student communicate with receptively and expressively? Cognitively, what symbols can represent real-life things and events for the student?

- Objects
- Parts of objects
- Colored photos
- Black-and-white photos
- Colored line drawings
- Black-and-white line drawings
- Printed words/braille

You may start where you think your student is and move backward if you are unsure or if your student is not succeeding at that level. *Do not make a final determination of the level of representation without probing all levels.*

A. Questions to consider when determining skills at the object level:

	Yes	No
1. Does the student have object permanence?	____	____
2. Does the student have cause and effect?	____	____
3. Does the student have means-ends relationships?	____	____
4. Can the student match like-objects?	____	____
5. Can the student receptively identify objects?	____	____
6. Can the student label objects"	____	____
7. Can the student functionally use objects?	____	____
8. Can the student match objects to activities?	____	____

B. Questions to consider when determining skills at the colored-photo level:

	Yes	No
1. Can the student match colored photos to objects/activities?	____	____
2. Can the student match like colored photos?	____	____
3. Can the student receptively identify colored photos?	____	____
4. Can the student label colored photos?	____	____

Source: Adapted with permission from J. Davidson and P. Omeara, "A Guide to Help Establish Your Student's Level of Representation," Columbia Regional Program, Autism Services, Portland, Oregon, May 1997.

(continued on next page)

FIGURE 5.2 continued

C. Questions to consider when determining skills at the black-and-white photo level:

	Yes	No
1. Can the student match like black-and-white photos?	___	___
2. Can the student match black-and-white photos to objects/activities?	___	___
3. Can the student receptively identify black-and-white photos?	___	___
4. Can the student label black-and-white photos?	___	___

D. Questions to consider when determining skills at the colored line drawing level:

	Yes	No
1. Can the student match like colored line drawings?	___	___
2. Can the student match colored line drawings to objects/activities?	___	___
3. Can the student receptively identify colored line drawings?	___	___
4. Can the student label colored line drawings?	___	___

E. Questions to consider when determining skills at the black-and-white line drawing level:

	Yes	No
1. Can the student match like black-and-white line drawings?	___	___
2. Can the student match black-and-white line drawings to objects/activities?	___	___
3. Can the student receptively identify black-and-white line drawings?	___	___
4. Can the student label black-and-white line drawings?	___	___

F. Questions to consider when determining skills at the printed word/braille level:

	Yes	No
1. Can the student match like printed/braille words?	___	___
2. Can the student match printed word/braille to objects?	___	___
3. Can the student receptively identify printed/braille words?	___	___
4. Can the student read printed/brailled words?	___	___
5. Can the student do above with upper-case letters?	___	___
6. Can the student do the above with lower-case letters?	___	___

FIGURE 5.2 continued

You may be able to obtain the above information through a combination of formal assessment, interview, and observation.

Some important points to consider:

- Many variables related to the stimulus item can make a difference in your student's understanding, (e.g., size, color, interest level, clarity, and background information in photos).

- Use stimulus items that are meaningful and motivating to the student.

- Remember when choosing a representational level for your student's communication system, choice boards, etc., use the level where your student's skills are firm—that is, he really knows what these items represent in his daily life. Remember, if you know a few words in French and half of the German language but are fluent in English, English would be your main mode of communication.

- If your student is not independent, ask yourself: What does she not understand and how can you help her understand it?

- Consider adding information with lower levels of representation; for instance, hand the student his coat to signal it is time to go outside or add a picture cue for a student who typically understands the written word. Consider adding information on a yellow self-stick note.

- Providing information at a simpler level of representation than the student typically needs might be needed at any time, particularly if your student is under stress.

- These are guidelines. We hope they are helpful. We recommend using the school-parent team to determine levels of representation.

responder, a voice output system may make more sense. The guide can be used in combination with information that the team has already collected on the Learning Media Assessment and Learners Interests forms (see Chapter 4: Assessment), and from observations that were implemented to complete this guide.

Teaching the Use of an Augmentative Device

Using symbols for communication requires an exchange between a nonvocal individual and a partner. The process consists of five phases (adapted from Marriner, 2001):

1. **Prompt exchange.** A prompt exchange is an interactive exchange of a symbol between a nonspeaking student and an adult communication partner. In this phase, the student is taught to use a symbolic representation of vocal communication to interact with an adult for a desired item. The exchange is made so the student gets a highly reinforcing item or activity. Initially, the adult prompts (physically guides) the student to make the request using a symbolic representation (an object, picture, written word, or auditory output device). This exchange is done repeatedly for many different requests, with the amount of physical prompting faded until the student completes the exchange independently of the adult.

2. **Increasing spontaneity.** Once the student has learned to make the exchange in a instructional setting, the teacher sets up the environment to assist the student to use the exchange in a functional setting. If the student has learned to exchange an object representing juice for the actual juice, then the object needs to be made available to the student to request juice spontaneously, not just when the student is learning the exchange process.

3. **Discrimination among symbols.** In this phase, the student learns to select from two or more symbolic representations that are presented at the same time. For example, the symbol for juice and the symbol for work are presented at the same time, and the student learns to choose the correct item.

4. **Sentence structure.** In this phase, the student adds components to the exchange, such as "I want," "I need help," or "I'm done." Pictures, objects, words, or voice output are designated to indicate the additional sentence structure and are added to the instruction process just as the words are taught.

5. **Additional communication functions and vocabulary.** In this phase, the student's additional communication needs are met by adding symbols to meet the needs of communicating in different settings and different environments. Such symbols may also be used to give the student directions, such as for making a bed, for cooking, or for completing other functional routines.

Using this process, the teacher must set up the environment so the student with ASDVI is motivated to exchange a symbol (communicate) to obtain a highly motivating objects or activity. A system for organizing symbols will be essential so the student can efficiently locate the needed symbols. For individuals who use a tactile symbol system, the team may find useful the article, "A Standard Tactile Symbol System: Graphic Language For Individuals Who Are Blind and Unable to Learn Braille," (Hagood, n.d.). This article discusses a process for coding symbols by shape and texture to represent different categories of meaning. New symbols should be introduced within the context of an activity prior to using them to "schedule" or follow routines. Symbols should be stored in predictable locations.

Through the use of augmentative communication systems, students with ASDVI can be taught to express their needs and desires. Some children may also learn to speak, and the augmentative system can then be paired with vocal utterances to enhance vocal communication.

For example, Chris uses a Cheap Talk, a communication device from Enabling Devices that allows an individual to push a switchplate to produce a brief recorded message. Chris's Cheap Talk has three switchplates, each representing a different message. For mealtime, pushing the first switchplate causes the device to say "I want a drink," and a cup is attached to the switchplate with Velcro. The second message says "I want to eat," and a spoon is attached. The third says "I am finished" and has no object on the switchplate. Both the objects and the vocal communication can be quickly changed for the classroom setting to express different messages, except that "I am finished" never has an object on it and is always programmed to say "I am finished."

The augmentative system or systems must be carefully determined by the team and must be matched to the student's primary learning style and learning medium. A student may require several types of systems, depending on his or her needs at home, at school, and in the community.

Social Conversations

Teachers and parents must create ways to teach, develop, and sustain social interactions. Students with ASDVI can learn to enhance their conversational skills in an environment that is orchestrated to meet their needs. Many students will need to be taught and practice skills with an adult before they use the skills with peers, initially using their strengths and interests as the motivation to participate in these conversations. It will also be important to increase the student's participation in social contexts. Students should be given opportunities to use conversational skills in naturally occurring situations, using reinforcement to encourage the expansion of conversation. (Social Skills are discussed in more detail in Chapter 6.)

In the initial stages of understanding the development of conversations, the student with ASDVI should be able to describe a topic. A simple approach to teaching this skill begins by selecting a topic, preferably one in which the student is interested. Once the topic is selected, the student can be taught to identify things that he or she knows or wants to say about the topic. For example, a student may be interested in birthdays, but struggles to know what to say or ask when discussing birthdays with his or her friends. By identifying different concepts that are inherent in birthdays—such as "date," "party," "presents," and "cake"—the student learns to expand his or her ability to converse with friends. The student can be taught to ask and answer questions on the topic and to present important ideas. This structure allows him or her to identify appropriate content related to the topic of interest.

Other strategies, including the use of scripts, topical questions, conversation games, video or audio modeling, and comic strip conversations, can be used to expand the verbal skills of students with ASDVI at various ages, as described next.

SCRIPTS

A scripts may be developed to address a specific conversation or social interaction. The script is then used in a role-playing or actual situation with a peer to help the student learn what to say. For example, a student may have difficulty initiating conversations at lunch. The teacher may observe several lunch groups, noting the general topics and flow of conversation that the student's peers use. The teacher then writes a script to help the student with ASDVI manage the conversational and social situation. An example of a script may be as follows:

> *Student with ASDVI: "What do you want for Christmas?"*
>
> *Partner: "I really want a video game. How about you?"*
>
> *Student with ASDVI: "I want the* Men in Black II *DVD. Have you seen the movie yet?"*

Some scripts consist of a set of cues or rules that are developed to help the student to maintain a conversation. The cue cards are prepared in the student's learning media and are kept with the student to refer to during conversations. The following is an example of a script that uses cue cards (Freeman & Drake, 1996, p. 31):

> 1. *When you want to say something to someone, say their name first to get their attention.*
>
> 2. *Always look at the person you are talking to.*
>
> 3. *Face the person you are talking to or turn your body toward them.*
>
> 4. *Always listen to what the other person is saying.*

Topical Questions or Comments

The teacher selects a topic, starting with one in which the student is interested. The student then identifies a variety of questions, writing them down using his or her primary learning mode (for a student who does not use writing, the teacher can record his or her questions and answers at the beginning stages). The student then answers the questions, and the responses are written down. The questions and answers can be formatted so the student can see their relationship to communication. Graphic symbols, objects, or pictures that are added to the words can help establish connections with the vocabulary. Through this process, the student with ASDVI learns the structure of a conversation, acquires knowledge of a topic, and learns new vocabulary. Conversations can be enhanced through this carefully planned process of preview, review, and practice.

Conversation Games

Conversation games (Freeman & Drake, 1996, p. 54) are played with a spinner and a list of topics that are of interest to the child. The spinner will have the following sections on it: what, where, why, how, who, and when. All materials should be prepared in the student's primary medium, such as print, braille, pictures, objects, or a voice output device. The student selects a topic card, spins the spinner, and asks an appropriate question, depending on where the spinner lands. For example, with the topic "Disney movies," if the spinner lands on "why," the student can ask, "Why do you like Disney movies?" Once the student understands the game, many variations can be added; for example, topics can be expanded, answers can be written down, and peers with additional interests can be added. Each variation helps to widen the student's conversational repertoire.

Video or Audio Modeling

Video modeling can be used in a variety of ways to enhance conversation. To use this strategy, videotaped examples of peers who are engaging in a variety of conversations will be needed, initially focusing on a particular skill and later expanding the conversations to others. This strategy may be of the greatest benefit to a student with low vision, although a student who is blind can follow a distinctly focused conversation when the video includes concrete audio descriptions. Students with ASDVI can view and model communications that are displayed in the videotapes. This approach may be particularly useful with students who are already interested in videotapes. One advantage of using videotapes is that the video can be paused, allowing the teacher to provide the prompt for the student at the appropriate time. It also allows the teacher to reduce other stimuli and hence to focus on the interaction. It is important to use peers—especially those the student knows well—as the models in the videos in trying to enhance interactions and conversations. Begin by using videos with short segments, focusing on a close-up of the action that you want to model.

In the beginning, the student may simply use the videotape to identify appropriate interactions. As his or her skills improve, the student can practice these skills in conjunction with the video. The practice involves the student reviewing the appropriate interactions with an adult alone or as part of a student group, stopping the video to explain key points, practicing the skills, and assessing performance. Eventually, the student can be videotaped or audiotaped in a variety of interactions, and the video can be used to monitor and reinforce appropriate conversations.

Comic Strip Conversation

This method, developed by Gray (1994), provides students with a visual record of the spoken interaction. In comic strip interactions, communication exchanges are shown in a cartoonlike drawing, with multiple exchanges presented on a single page. The drawings illustrate ongoing communication, emphasizing what people say and do and what people may be thinking. Comic strip conversations can be adapted for students who are braille readers by using tools, such as Inspiration software (see the Web site www .inspiration.com/contact_us/index.cfm) and a tactile graphics enhancer. This software provides diagrams and outline views to help students comprehend concepts and information. Braille can be added with a slate and stylus or with braille labels.

The conversation that is depicted in the comic strip can be about any topic and can be simple or complex. The concrete representations help the student understand what different participants in the conversation are saying and thinking and to identify and understand each person's role in the conversation.

SUMMARY

Communication and language deficits represent one of the characteristic critical areas of children with autism spectrum disorders. As with all learning characteristics associated with ASD, the communication challenges for children vary from mild to severe. For some children, oral language abilities may appear typical, and communication deficits may be manifested primarily in difficulties with social communication and interactions. For others, development of functional language may be severely limited. For all learners with ASDVI, understanding the meaning and relevance of language will be an ongoing challenge that requires ongoing and consistent instruction.

It is critical that the educational team work collaboratively to thoroughly assess the child's communication skills and to design and implement instructional interventions that enhance the child's functional communication skills. With appropriate instruction, delivered consistently across all environments, every child can learn to expand his or her communication abilities.

Social Interactions

6

B lindness and visual impairment certainly affect an individual's ability to learn incidentally through daily social interactions. Hill and Blasch (1980) suggested that nearly 85 percent of what is learned socially is mediated through the visual sense. Sacks and Silberman (Holbrook & Koenig, 2000, p. 617) stated that

> *the absence of vision or limited visual functioning may make it more diffi-cult for students with visual impairments to acquire accurate information about their social environment, the context in which social activities occur, and the interpretation of social concepts or nuances. . . . Children, partic-ularly those with congenital visual impairments, are more dependent than sighted children on others to provide valuable information about the social environment, as well as the intricacies involved in obtaining and main-taining social relationships. Perhaps of all the developmental processes, socialization is the most strongly affected by vision.*

Clearly, the development of social skills is a critical component of the cur-riculum of most children who are blind or visually impaired. Kevin is a prime example of a totally blind teenager with Asperger syndrome (see Chapter 3, Appendix A) who needs to develop his social skills.

> *Kevin had limited interests. He preferred to spend time in his room listen-ing to classical music and learning about a variety of composers. However,*

his interest in music did not match the musical interests of the other high school students. Kevin would attempt to initiate conversations with other students about classical music but ignore them when they talked about their interests. He would become upset when he was presented with rules that did not match his expectations and had little tolerance for anything other than the routines that he developed for himself. This lack of tolerance led him to have difficulty functioning in the day-to-day world. Kevin had difficulty dealing with the other people when he went to a restaurant or a grocery store, participated in leisure activities, and used public transportation. He did not know how to ask the appropriate questions to communicate effectively with other people. The team that worked with Kevin determined that targeted instruction in social skills was required to teach him to develop the skills that he needed to gain information from others, to develop conversational skills to ask his peers about their interests, and to expand his own interests, so he could be involved in the community. Through instruction, practice, and the use of braille scripts, Kevin learned to participate in groups without dominating the conversation and joined a variety of community groups, such as a fitness club, consumer organizations, and clubs at the community college. Despite these activities, Kevin still prefers to live alone and spends a great deal of time using the Internet.

IMPORTANCE OF TARGETING SOCIAL SKILLS

Students with ASDVI typically do not learn social skills incidentally, nor do they learn efficiently just by "experiencing." Consequently, a systematic, carefully planned sequence of instruction is needed to teach the many facets of social learning, including the generalization of skills. This chapter focuses on several key aspects of social development that are often the most challenging for students with ASDVI, including play skills, appropriate social behaviors, perspective taking, and problem solving. Instructional strategies and resources for each aspect are provided.

The social skills of children with ASDVI are different from those of typically developing children and from children who are visually impaired. For visually impaired children, the lack of opportunity to learn by "observation" does not mean that they cannot learn social skills; rather, they must be "taught" to understand what is happening in situations that they cannot see. These children typically do learn to comprehend and coordinate the various components of social interactions and exchanges, but the process often takes longer (Holbrook, 1996). Once they learn that there is a world beyond their reach, their solitary play will begin to emulate typical play. Children who are visually impaired typically need to learn the context and nuances of social interactions and require specific instruction to do so. Therefore, many of them will demonstrate the need for social skill development, particularly in the area of nonverbal communication (such as gestures, body language, and eye contact). Once they are taught these skills, however, they are able to generalize the information to a variety of settings and across a variety of people.

Children with ASDVI present a different set of social difficulties. Social interaction is a trademark challenge for most children with ASD, who typically have difficulty shifting attention, have weak imitation skills, and demonstrate the ritualized use of objects. At the same time, they show little interest in other people, especially other children. Their solitary play lacks the free-flowing, creative quality of play of typically developing children. For those who engage in some imaginary play, the play tends to be simple and repetitive. Furthermore, children with ASDVI often show a lack of empathy toward others and struggle to understand the intent and meaning behind another person's social, communication, and affective behavior. In addition, the issues of social cognition for a child with ASDVI are a much more complex dimension involving perspective taking (the individual's ability to understand that other people have points of view that may differ from their own), problem solving, and communicative effectiveness (the first two topics are discussed in more detail later in this chapter: social communication is discussed in Chapter 5).

Problems in social skills can lead to "overload," difficulty with critical thinking, and difficulty in changing routines. For some students, these difficulties and overload lead to frustrations that are expressed through outbursts of negative behavior. Such challenges are seen even in students who seemingly communicate well, because they have a large vocabulary or are knowledgeable about a particular topic, and can function well in a rule-based learning environment. These students still have great difficulty functioning in the day-to-day world, however, showing an imbalance in their strengths and weaknesses.

PLAY SKILLS

Although we often think of play as the fundamental activity of childhood, first as solitary play and later as a primary vehicle for interacting with their peers, many children with ASDVI need to be taught how to play. *Play* is a generic term that is applied to a wide range of activities that are satisfying to the child, are creative for the child, and are chosen by the child. Children play on their own and with others, and their play may be boisterous and energetic or quiet.

Early play skills are the stepping-stones to the eventual development of positive social interactions, and instruction in these skills has a number of components. For instance, some children need to be taught the intended purpose of a toy and how to manipulate it—how to touch and explore a toy to experience its unique tactile, auditory, and visual attributes. The case of Jeffrey is an example.

> *Jeffrey's favorite toy was his "See 'n Say." When he was given a choice of free-time activities, he consistently chose this toy and would delight in repeatedly pulling the string. Through careful observation and analysis, it became apparent to the educational team that Jeffrey would hold the toy in only one position, perseverating on the physical action of pulling the string. Jeffrey was really not playing with the toy but, rather, was focusing on the physical motor actions that were involved. His teachers helped him to expand his interest by giving him similar kinds of toys and teaching him to learn their intended purposes. By targeting the pleasures that Jeffrey gained from his See 'n Say, his teachers were able to choose similar, additional toys that expanded his play skills.*

The toys that are selected should be matched to the child's interest and primary learning medium. They should also provide stimulation through a variety of senses as long as they do not provide negative stimuli. For example, if the child with ASDVI has sensory problems with certain sounds, the toys that are used to motivate play cannot emit the sounds that the child has difficulty tolerating. Once the manipulation of toys is taught, it is important to increase the types of manipulations and to introduce a variety of play materials. Eventually, imaginative actions can be introduced with the toys to encourage creative play.

Once the child with ASDVI has developed some independent play skills with toys, it is important to introduce play with peers. This is a process that requires planful teaching. Initially, it starts with parallel play, with the peer in close proximity. Teaching parallel play begins with each child having his or her own set of materials and using toys that are of interest to him or her. The teacher takes turns interacting with the toys of interest with the child with ASDVI while they play beside another child. The focus of the interaction is on teaching the child with ASDVI to play in proximity to another child. The second step in the instructional process is to have both children have the same toys but to play side by side, with the adult interacting primarily with the child with ASDVI. After the child has learned to how to play and to interact with the adult, child-to-child play skills are then taught. Again, the adult leads the process, interacting with both children, until the child with ASDVI gains the skills to interact independently with another child.

One strategy that may be used to help teach play to children with functional vision is video modeling. Many parents have reported that children with autism spectrum disorder (even young children) have an intense interest in music and music videos. Play skills that are demonstrated through rhythmical singing may enhance a child's interest and increase the probability of learning the skill. With this strategy, play skills are demonstrated via a videotape in a variety of settings, with other children's appropriate interactions modeled for viewing. It may be possible to use descriptive video with children who are blind, although there has been no research on its effectiveness. When a video is used with a student who is blind, it needs to be orchestrated to ensure that the student can understand the concepts using only the audio component. In these situations, it is useful for the adult to role-play the interactions being demonstrated on the video. Once the child understands the skill, it is generalized with other students who demonstrate strong play skills and an interest in playing with others.

Once a child has some structured play skills, playgroups can be incorporated into instruction. In playgroups, partners are used to practice sharing, turn taking, and cooperation using multipart toys, puzzles, simple games, and snacks. Several strategies can be used to assist the student with ASDVI, including the use of visual, tactile, or auditory instruction cue cards; modeling; and prompting of correct interactions, with an immediate plan to fade the prompt. In all situations, it is important to use a reinforcement system that matches the student's skills and level of understanding.

The Play Interest Survey, which is included in *Do-Watch-Listen-Say* (Quill, 2000), can provide the team with valuable information on a wide range of play activities (see the sample Play Interest Survey in Chapter 4) that will be appropriate for the student with ASDVI. Prior to using the survey, the team may want to adjust some of the toys that are to be used to account for the primary learning media of the student with ASDVI. For example, a child who is blind will probably not enjoy blow-bubbles, but may enjoy a toy that blows air in his or her direction or a toy that emits a fun and interesting sound. Another valuable resource, *Let's Play: A Guide to Toys for Children with Special Needs,* published annually by the American Foundation for the Blind, the Toy Industry Foundation, and the Alliance for Technology Access, will assist the educational team in identifying motivating toys for children with ASDVI.

APPROPRIATE SOCIAL BEHAVIORS

Children with ASDVI have great difficulty understanding and interpreting social situations. They are often "stuck" in rigid routines that challenge their ability to make sense of and control their world. The rigid adherence to routines often causes frustration for families and other members of the educational team. It is important for all members of the team to understand the child's perception of a given situation to design appropriate interventions. Children with ASDVI need to learn what is important in a social situation and what is expected of them.

Social Stories

The use of Social Stories, a tool developed by Carol Gray, has proved effective for many students. These stories are written to describe social situations and are used by students to identify and gain a better understanding of desired social behaviors. According to Gray (The Gray Center, 2005), a Social Story "is a short story, defined by specific characteristics, [that describes] a situation, concept, or social skill using a format that is meaningful for people with ASD." Social Stories may be used to address a wide variety of topics and can provide the student with ASDVI with the social information that he or she may be missing. They are also used for acknowledging achievement.

Social Stories are designed to use four basic types of sentences: descriptive, perspective, directive, and affirmative. *Descriptive sentences* are opinion and assumption-free statements of facts (such as "I ride the bus to school every day"). They often contain answers to the "wh" questions (who, what, when, where, why). *Perspective sentences* are statements that refer to or describe the feelings, beliefs, and motivations of people other than the individual with ASDVI (for example, "Some students decide to work hard to finish assignments before recess." "Some children believe in the Easter bunny"). *Directive sentences* identify a suggested response to a situation. These sentences must be written carefully to avoid a literal interpretation by the student with ASDVI (for example, "I will try to ask for help," rather than "I will ask for help"). *Affirmative sentences* express a commonly shared value and usually follow a descriptive, perspective, or direct sentence (for instance, "I will try to keep my seatbelt fastened" (directive) and "This is very important" (affirmative).

Social Stories are different from a task analysis of a situation, scripts, or other similar strategies in that they use these four basic types of sentences in a specific ratio of frequency. A Social Story has a ratio of two to five descriptive, perspective, or affirmative sentences for every directive sentence.

Social Stories are easily adapted for use by students with ASDVI and can be transcribed into braille or enlarged for students who prefer large print. The text of the Social Story should match the learning medium (braille, large print, tangible illustrations, or audio output) and the learning characteristics of the student with ASDVI. "Sample Social Stories for Abraham" lists stories that have been used successfully with a variety of students with ASDVI, including Abraham, a middle-school student who read them in braille. (The Social Story provided to the student is included in the left column; for clarification, the type of sentence is identified in the right).

SAMPLE SOCIAL STORIES FOR ABRAHAM

Bathroom

All people need to go to the bathroom during the day.	Descriptive
Usually they need to go only one time during the morning.	Perspective
They use the bathroom quickly.	Perspective
Then they go on to the next activity.	Perspective
I will try to go to the bathroom only once during the morning.	Directive
If someone asks me if I have to go to the bathroom and I have just gone, I will say "No, thank you."	Directive

Asking for Help

Sometimes students have things to do at school that are hard for them to do.	Descriptive
The students try to do the work they are asked to do.	Perspective
Sometimes the work is just too hard.	Perspective
The students usually try and do the work themselves.	Perspective
After trying to do the work, the students ask for help from their teacher.	Affirmative
When I have tried very hard to do what I have been asked to do and cannot do it, I try to ask for help.	Directive

Group Activities

Sometimes people get into groups to talk and learn new things.	Descriptive
They pay attention to those who are talking by looking at them.	Perspective
That shows that people are interested in what they are saying.	Perspective
They will have their heads up and usually have their hands still.	Perspective
If they yawn, they cover their mouths with their hands and say "excuse me."	Perspective
It is good to pay attention to people when they are talking.	Descriptive
I will try to be interested in what people are saying by looking in their direction and by answering their questions and helping them to think of ways to solve their problems.	Directive

Source: Diane Mitchell and Jana McFerron, teachers of students with visual impairments, Salem, Oregon.

Social Stories must be introduced systematically, with data collected and analyzed to determine the effectiveness of the intervention. The Social Story should be shared just prior to the situation it supports. Reviewing the Social Story during a crisis or difficult situation may not be effective, since a student in crisis does not learn new information. Social Stories should be used one at a time; offering multiple Social Stories is likely to overwhelm a child with ASDVI with too much information at one time.

For more advanced users of Social Stories, partial sentences can be used to encourage them to guess the next step in a situation. One of the four basic sentences may be written with a portion of the sentence replaced with a blank space, and the student with ASDVI is encouraged to fill in the blank space. Doing so will help the student plan and have more control in the social situation.

Two additional types of sentences may be used in a Social Story, but not as frequently as the basic sentences. *Control sentences* are written by the student and identify personal strategies to use in a given situation to support recall and application. These sentences reflect individual interests. The student reviews the Social Story, adding the control sentences that are an appropriate facet of the interaction, as did Jeremy in the following example:

> *Jeremy, aged 10 and an expert in classical music, is irritated whenever someone says "I disagree" because he assumes that people are being critical of him if they do not agree with him. His Social Story provides information about what people mean when they disagree, helping him to understand that disagreeing with someone does not mean they are angry or do not like you. Jeremy added the following control sentence to his Social Story: "When someone says they disagree, I can think of composers improving their music after others disagreed that it sounded right the first time."*

Cooperative sentences identify what others will do to assist the student. A cooperative sentence may be used as a partial sentence to help support a student who is learning a new skill (for example, "Some people who can help me tie my shoes are ____.").

Although additional research is needed to determine the effectiveness of Social Stories, many educational teams have found that their use can be an important tool for addressing social deficits in students with ASD. Additional information about social stories can be obtained from the Gray Center for Social Learning and Understanding (see the Resources section).

Social Skills Groups

Another instructional strategy that has been implemented successfully with many students involves the use of *social skills groups*. These social groups

Since social interactions are often difficult for students with an autism spectrum disorder, appropriate interactions with peers must be specifically taught as part of the student's curriculum. Selected peers in "social skills groups" can model appropriate social behavior, affording the student opportunities for repeated practice in a variety of settings, such as this lunchroom.

give students with ASDVI an opportunity to rehearse, model, and practice appropriate social behaviors. The skills that are addressed in the group will vary, depending on the age level of the group. Key skills that are addressed through social skills groups include turn taking, getting help, following group directions, solving disagreements, using complements, and managing stress. The materials that are used will also vary, depending on the interests and age of the students and the goals to be addressed. In addition to games and other socially engaging materials, it can be helpful to use both an audio-tape recorder and a video recorder. Anecdotal reports have indicated that students improve their own social behaviors when they have an opportunity to record the expected behavior as well as to review the recordings (both audio and video).

Social skills groups support the appropriate practice and modeling of social skills. By using selected peers as models, the instructor is better able to provide direct instruction and to enhance the student's opportunities for repeated practice in using the skills in a variety of settings (at school, at home, and clubs and organizations in the community). The social skills group can be developed by following these guidelines:

1. Identify the target social behavior. At least initially, focus on one skill for an activity so the student clearly understands the skills that are being addressed.

2. Identify the social setting or settings in which the skill is used and will be taught. The educational team should identify a variety of settings throughout the day that target the skill to be practiced.

3. Identify any additional support or supports that are needed to increase the student's independent use of the skill, such as checklists, cue cards, social stories, scripts, posted rules, direction charts, and semantic maps (see Chapter 12: Classroom Supports for a description of these supports). Any of these supports can be presented in a variety of modalities, including braille, tactile symbols, pictures, auditory output devices, and large print.

4. Determine and implement the instruction (such as video modeling, audio modeling, role-playing, coaching, or direct instruction).

5. Develop reinforcement systems and a schedule for implementing them, including natural occurring reinforcements and self-reinforcement systems.

PERSPECTIVE TAKING

Perspective taking focuses on the ability to understand and ultimately to appreciate that other individuals have points of view that may differ from one's own. There are three levels of perspective taking: the ability to understand that others may perceive things differently, the ability to understand that others may have different ideas and intentions, and the ability to adjust to suit the needs of the situation and listener (Quill, 1995). The ability to take another's perspective affects the ability to derive meaning from the social world. Teaching perspective taking to the student with ASDVI must be done in small steps. For each student, the abstract concepts must be task analyzed into concrete, usable segments that the student is able to understand. Early skills for learning perspective taking can be targeted through instruction that focuses on understanding different experiences. For example, the teacher can use photographs or videotapes to describe and explain segments of events in which the student participated (such as a vacation, a day trip, or a party). Using the photographs or videoclips, the student can be taught to appreciate the event from another person's perspective. The teacher can ask whether the students and others who participated in the event enjoyed it. The student can also ask the others in the photo or video if they enjoyed the trip. He or she can be taught how one can determine if another person is enjoying a situation.

Helping students to understand that they make impressions on others can enhance their perspective-taking skills. After the teacher identifies a specific situation in which the student is involved, he or she can then break down the situation into concrete steps (such as how you look, what you say, and what you do). The teacher can then break down each of these concepts into more detailed steps (for example, *what you say* can be broken down into the words you use and the impact of these words). Once the steps are identified, the meaning and interpretations of the situation and the interactions can be explored.

For many students with ASDVI, the use of additional supports can enhance their perspective-taking abilities. For example, when identifying concrete steps, a braille user may benefit from a braille list of each of the steps involved in the task analysis. An auditory learner may benefit from an audiotape of the interaction (both role-play and real situations), using the audiotape to analyze each step. For other students, a tactile graphic demonstrating the steps and the responses may help clarify the role that each individual plays in perspective taking.

Perhaps the most difficult area for students with ASDVI to understand is the meaning gained from nonverbal communications, including body language, gestures, facial expressions, and eye contact. Again, teaching the student what these components are, when they occur, and why they are important will take careful planning. One successful strategy involves the use of an audio-described video. The video may include humor, socially inappropriate behavior, or socially appropriate behavior. The teacher and the student can pause the video to discuss and evaluate interactions and relationships. The student can then practice the gestures and nonverbal language that are used and learn how they add meaning to the situation. Students can then make videos of each other (pairing children who are sighted with the student with ASDVI) in situations that they find the most troublesome. Another strategy is to have the student with ASDVI participate in a small-group activity in which the student has to "create" something for another student on the basis of that student's likes and dislikes. Activities could include making lunch, participating in a birthday celebration, taking care of someone who is ill, or shopping for a special present. The critical component of the activity is for the student with ASDVI to find out what another person enjoys. It is essential for the teacher to assist the student to understand the relationship of the specific activity to the more global concept of perspective taking.

The Perspective Taking Game (Weiss & Harris, 2001) uses many of these strategies to build perspective-taking skills. In this game, the student with ASDVI is paired with a peer without an ASD. The student with ASDVI identifies where the peer thinks an object (such as a cup) is, on the basis of information available to the peer and the student with ASDVI. The instructor hides the cup, making sure that both students know where it is. The peer leaves the room, and the instructor and the student with ASDVI move the cup. The student with ASDVI is then asked, "Where does the peer think the cup is?" The correct response is the original location. Three questions come into play:

1. Where is the cup now?

2. Where was the cup before it was moved?

3. Where will the peer think the cup is?

Eventually, several items can be hidden but only one will be moved. The point of the game is for the student to learn that thinking and perspectives go beyond what he or she can actually see.

In teaching perspective taking, the teacher needs to be clear about what is being taught and why it is being taught. The student needs to understand how these skills help increase positive social interactions. According to Winner (2000), three steps are important to teach:

1. what concept is being taught

2. why the concept is important

3. how the concept relates back to the larger concept of social relatedness

PROBLEM-SOLVING SKILLS

Students with ASDVI often become uncomfortable and stressed and can withdraw when they are not sure what to do in a given social situation or how to respond when something unexpected occurs. These students must first learn to recognize when these situations occur and then develop a variety of problem-solving skills to help deal with them appropriately. Problem-solving skills include the ability to recognize and ask for help, self-management skills, and relaxation techniques.

Asking for Help

Knowing how and when to ask for help in a variety of ways is a critical skill both at school and at work. Before the teacher instructs the student in this skill, he or she must first assess the situation to determine how the student with ASDVI currently gets help and what others are doing in the same situation. Taking into consideration the student's preferences, the teacher develops a step-by-step sequence to teach the student what to do.

Consider, for example, a common scenario in which a student has an educational assistant or paraeducator who sits next to him or her during class periods. The teacher gives the entire class instructions and a fairly complex problem to solve. The student with ASDVI makes no attempt to do anything, because he or she does not know how to start. After a short while, the educational assistant simply tells the student what to do. Although this approach gets the work done, it does not allow the student to develop an independent strategy for getting help. One solution is to place a "reminder" on the student's desk that cues him or her to ask for help when confused. The educational assistant then uses a system to prompt the student to use the reminder. The prompt, which may be as simple as pointing to the cue, is systematically faded as the student learns the skills. A second option is to develop a list of steps to follow when one needs to ask for help. The list can be prepared in the student's primary medium, such as braille, print, or audiotape. The list may vary, depending on the environment in which it is required, but it can be used both to teach the student to know when he or she needs help and to identify the process for obtaining help. The list should give only as much information as is necessary to complete the task. For example, Tricia, a fourth-grade student, has the following list, in braille, taped to her desk to help her to ask for help appropriately:

> *If I am not sure what to do next, I*
>
> 1. *read the directions again to see if I can understand what I need to do.*
>
> 2. *If I still do not understand, I should raise my hand until the teacher calls on me.*

Self-Management Skills

Self-management skills assist the student with ASDVI to become aware of his or her behavior and to shift control of behavior to himself or herself, rather than to an adult. The components of self-management include

1. becoming aware of one's own behavior

2. selecting the target behavior or behaviors to address

3. monitoring when the behavior occurs

4. Delivering his or her own reward if the target behavior is met

These are important skills, particularly for addressing appropriate social behaviors. Self-management strategies can then be generalized in a number of environments.

Throughout the day, the student with ASDVI can use any number of self-management systems to record the behaviors that are appropriate for him or her, including checklists, tape recorders, stickers in a book, and braille cell "check-off" systems. The student uses the self-monitoring system and records data and then reviews the self-monitoring checklist with the teacher and adjusts it as needed. The use of a self-monitoring system must be designed and organized to match the student's style. The system must be easily accessible to the student and available in the appropriate medium (such as braille, print, or audiotape). The team will teach the student to recognize and record the occurrence or nonoccurrence of the behavior. Eventually, the support from the teacher will be faded, and the student will monitor and reinforce himself or herself. The following example of Kathy illustrates these points.

> *Kathy is a young adult who is blind and has Asperger syndrome. Unsure of her social interactions in a small group, she targets "appropriate conversation" (such as waiting her turn, staying on topic while talking, and asking questions about others) as her target behaviors. Kathy can identify appropriate interactions while listening to others, but is unsure and uncomfortable when she needs to implement them herself. To enhance her understanding of the situation, Kathy uses a portable tape recorder to record her conversations with adults, later reviewing the tape to determine when and where her behavior has been appropriate or inappropriate. She developed a braille list of the skills that she needs, (including "Be sure to pause so that others can speak," "Don't limit my conversation only to discussions about classical music," and "Give each person time to talk") and carries the list with her to use on the next opportunity for interaction. Kathy refers to her list to make sure that her behavior is on target and appropriate and adjusts it after each recorded session.*

Self-management may be time consuming to implement, but it has long-term benefits for the student and the team.

RELAXATION TRAINING

Relaxation training is useful for students with ASDVI who experience a high level of stress. The techniques that are taught during training can be used to establish self-control in difficult situations. One such technique is the application of deep pressure, which can calm and relax some people with ASDVI. Deep pressure can be applied through clothing (such as the use of a weighted vest); through brushing (a therapeutic technique used by occupational therapists involving brushing the skin with a therapeutic brush); and through equipment, such as Temple Grandin's "squeeze machine," which delivers deep-touch pressure that can help individuals learn to tolerate touching and reduce anxiety and nervousness (see the Resources at the back of the book). An occupational therapist should be consulted to determine if brushing or deep pressure is appropriate for an individual student, and, if so, how that pressure should be applied.

Physical exercise (like swimming, walking or running on a motorized treadmill with a steady pace, pedaling a stationary bicycle, and walking) is another a form of relaxation that is helpful for some students with ASDVI and can be performed in a variety of settings. The exercise should be available on a regular basis and be monitored to provide relaxation as well as physical benefits.

A predetermined "break area" (such as a quiet place in the classroom or another area of the school, in the community, or on the job site) can serve as a relaxation tool. Procedures should be established for using the break area. Procedures can include identification of times the break area is available, activity choices available, and length of stay while there. For some students, a particular object (like a fidget object; a "squeeze ball"; or another small, tactilely soothing object that can be held under the desk, in a coat pocket, or in a notebook) may serve as a relaxation tool. It is important to ensure that whatever object is used is used inconspicuously and does not distract the student or others.

Relaxation techniques that involve a particular set of step-by-step procedures can be helpful as well. The techniques may involve deep breathing or muscle tightening and relaxation. Cautela and Groden (1978) developed a manual for systematically teaching such techniques to students with autism spectrum disorder. The techniques are generally taught in individual sessions and are then incorporated into group situations. Individuals with ASDVI may need to be taught a technique using strategies that pair the technique with another associated movement. For example, to teach the concept of deep breathing, the instructor may need to begin by teaching the student to blow air to make a pinwheel spin or to feel air on an open palm.

SUMMARY

Social interactions are a critical gateway for success in school, at home, and in the community. The acquisition of social skills takes careful planning and instruction that reflects the team's identification of the skills that need to be taught, and why the skills are important and the team's determination of how the skills relate to the student's daily functioning. Every student has different social expectations and consequently has a different set of skills to learn. The team's goal should be to develop instruction that matches each student's goals, needs, and learning styles, so that the student learns the skills for successful social interactions with others and can use them each day.

Challenging Behaviors

Addressing challenging or problem behaviors is not a curriculum area per se, but many teams struggle to find effective strategies to address these behaviors when they exist. Because of the difficulty they have processing and conveying information, many children with an autism spectrum disorder are challenged in making the intent of their communication understood and may not easily understand the intentions of others or the workings of their environment. Consequently, many experience frustrations that are exhibited by dramatic attempts to communicate to make themselves understood or to obtain what they want. Sometimes these attempts to communicate, which can include biting, kicking, scratching, or other attempts to hurt others; temper tantrums; self-abuse; extreme noncompliance; and running, are interpreted by others as "challenging behaviors."

Many children with ASD do not respond to the usual methods of intervention that are intended to address challenging behaviors, so the educational team needs to develop a systematic plan for identifying, analyzing, and addressing these behaviors. This is also true for the student with ASDVI, who, because of the ASD, may exhibit unusual and challenging behaviors that need to be addressed on the basis of an understanding of the impact of ASD.

BEHAVIOR AND COMMUNICATION

Before the educational team begins to address the student's behavior, it is critical for them to understand behaviors in relation to ASD and the relationship between behavioral challenges and communication. In its basic form, behavior is communication, as the case of Alan illustrates:

> *Alan, a nonverbal student with ASD and significant cognitive delays, is eating lunch with several other students. Since the teachers are busy helping the other students when Alan attempts to communicate a desire for more food by making a screeching sound, they do not respond to the sound. When a staff member moves close to Alan, Alan grabs her hair and does not let go. When his initial attempt to communicate was unsuccessful, Alan attempted to communicate through hair-pulling behavior.*

When students with ASDVI do not have effective communication strategies, they rely on behaviors that they associate with getting an immediate response. Alan's case, pulling his teacher's hair gained the attention he desired. A single behavior can have more than one communicative intent, and, multiple behaviors can have the same communicative intent. Thus, the team must carefully review all relevant information to determine the critical function or functions of the behavior. Often, the intensity, duration, frequency, or persistence of the behaviors of children with ASDVI set them apart from similar behaviors of typically developing children.

The educational team and family members can learn to redirect the behavior of an individual with autism spectrum disorder and visual impairment by being patient, by taking the time to analyze the behavior carefully and thoroughly, so as to consider the link between the behavior and communication, and to teach the appropriate skills to address the function of the behavior. Research hs found that educational interventions that do not address the development of positive and pro-social behaviors will be unsuccessful in the long-term elimination of problem behaviors (Lord & McGee, 2001).

DEVELOPING A BEHAVIORAL INTERVENTION PLAN

Challenging behaviors are addressed through a functional behavior assessment and the development of a behavioral intervention plan. The functional behavior assessment, that is, the process of identifying the variables that reliably predict and maintain problem behaviors (Horner & Carr, 1997), can help the team understand the relationship of the behavior to environmental conditions and determine the needs of the student with ASDVI. The behavioral intervention plan identifies positive strategies, programs or curricular modifications, and supports that are required to address the behavior. The data collected during the functional behavior assessment will be used to determine the skills that the student needs to acquire. The instruction of these skills and the management of any environmental or instructional variables will be incorporated into the intervention plan.

Five steps can be implemented to address the behaviors through a functional behavior assessment (or six steps, if you count developing a crisis plan). To ensure consistency, it is crucial for all members of the team to participate in the identification and analysis of the behaviors and in the design and implementation of the interventions.

Step 1: Identify the Behavior

The challenging behavior must be identified in observable terms and must be defined so that everyone who works with the student will recognize it when it occurs. For example, "Peter is aggressive toward the staff and students" is an unclear definition, whereas "Peter grabs, scratches, and pinches the staff or students" is clear and specific.

It is essential that all members of the team define the behavior the same way, so when the data are collected and a plan is developed, consistent strategies can be implemented to address the behavior. It is also critical to agree that the behavior poses a problem for the entire team, including the family. Questions to ask include these:

- Is the behavior currently or potentially harmful to the student with ASDVI or others?

- Does the behavior interfere with the student's learning or the learning of others?

- Does the behavior result in avoidance by peers or adults?

As these questions are answered, it will be helpful to think not only about the present, but about a year or two in the future. Since students with ASDVI take time to learn new skills, it is better to plan ahead than to try to change a behavior that is entrenched over time, as the case of Jacob shows:

A mother was concerned about her 6-year-old son, Jacob, and the school's reaction to his behavior on the playground. As she described it, Jacob would "harmlessly slap at other students" if they got too close while playing a game. Jacob's mother observed the behavior and though it was not serious for a 6 year old, given the circumstances of the playground. A member of the team then asked her, "If the behavior is not addressed now and Jacob continues this behavior, will it be appropriate in a year or two?" After careful thought, the mother concluded that in two years, it would be a problem and much more difficult to address at that time.

Step 2: Collect Data

Once the behavior is identified and clearly defined, collect data to determine answers to the following questions:

- Where does the behavior occur?

- When does the behavior occur?

- With whom does the behavior occur?

- What happened right before the behavior occurred?

- What happened immediately after the behavior occurred?

A simple functional analysis chart can help the team collect information for these questions, as is shown in Figure 7.1.) (A blank copy of this form is provided at the end of this chapter.) Two other methods for collecting data about behavior are scatterplots and Antecedent-Behavior-Consequences (ABC) charts. Examples of forms used with both methods are provided at the end of this chapter. Each form prompts team members to collect data that will assist them in defining the behavior. (These forms, and additional information regarding their use in collecting valuable behavioral data, are available online at the Center for Effective Collaboration Web site at www.cecp.air.org/fba.)

By collecting data that allow the behavior to be clearly defined, the team members will be able to predict the times and situations when the challenging behavior will or will not be exhibited during typical daily routines t school and at home. The information will help inform the team about the functions that the challenging behavior serves for the student.

Step 3: Analyze the Data

In analyzing the data collected in Step 2, the team needs to understand that there are typically four primary functions of behavior (Janzen, 1996, 2003):

- to avoid a task or situation

- to obtain something (such as a tangible object or a social reward, for example, adult attention)

- to communicate something (for instance, a choice or an understanding)

- a combination of the pervious three functions.

The data must be analyzed to determine the function of the behavior and to develop a hypothesis about why the behavior occurs. When analyzing the data, the team needs to remember that behavior can have multiple functions

FIGURE 7.1

Sample Functional Analysis: Targeting Behavior for Change

Target behavior	Where did the behavior occur?	When did it occur?	With whom did it occur?	How long did it last?	What happened after it occurred?
Biting staff	On the way from the classroom to the gym	11/2, 8:45 am (right after student got to class and was sitting in rocker)	The instructional assistant as he was guiding the student	Tried to bite three times	The staff member moved away; the student was told to walk on his own
Biting staff	Traveling from the gym to the dining room while walking and turned on wrong path	11/3, 11:45 am	The new assistant moved close to help reorient the student physically	The student grabbed staff member's arm and bite until the staff member was able to release the grasp	The student was told to sit down on the grass and to calm down
Biting staff	In the classroom at the work table working one to one with the staff on turn taking	11/6, 2:40 pm	The classroom teacher	Attempted to bite four different times by grabbing the staff member's hand and pulling it to his mouth	The student was moved away from the table and away from the other students

Comments/issues: Student moves quickly from calm to aggressive, but change of behavior is usually preceded by high-pitched self-vocalizations.

and that the function of the behavior is not always obvious. The student may be reacting to conditions in the environment that are not immediately clear, as the case of Laurie indicates:

> *Laurie would scream, kick, and bite at various times during the day. Sometimes, she would do so during disliked activities, whereas at other times, she would do so during preferred activities. The team discovered that Laurie would exhibit these behaviors when two teachers, both female, were working with her. A continued in-depth analysis revealed that both women wore a particular perfume on their wrists. Since they were working one on one with Laurie, they came in close contact with her. Laurie had an extreme sensitivity to smells. Because she did not have the appropriate communication skills to tell anyone that the perfume was bothering her, she hit, kicked, and screamed to get the teachers away from her. Several interventions were initiated to address the problem behavior: (1) remove the smell of the perfume as much as possible, (2) slowly begin to desensitize Laurie to strong smells, (3) teach Laurie to tell a person when the smell was bothering her.*

Finding the right hypothesis to address a behavioral issue is a critical task. To do so, it is important to have team members who are experienced in analyzing data and developing a hypothesis of why the student is exhibiting the behavior. There is no simple strategy for developing a hypothesis. The team member must review the data and make an educated guess about why the student is doing what he or she is doing. Two important points will help the team develop the hypothesis. First, a student exhibits a particular behavior for specific reasons, so the team should first explore the possible reasons for the behavior. For example, is the student trying to get attention or to avoid something? Does the student have a communication system that is accessible, (that is, that matches his or her level of symbolic representation, and is the student able to use it independently? Does the student understand what is being expected of him or her?

Second, the team may need to consider if a sensory issue is affecting the student. It is important to remember that sensory issues are not always obvious. Thus, the team needs to look for hidden sensory irritants in all the sensory areas. For example, are lights emitting noises, or are there noises coming form outside the immediate environment? Are there smells coming from a different part of the building? Since there are numerous possibilities and every situation is different, the team's review of the environment is critical. The team members need to review all the information, make a decision, and then try out the hypothesis. After trying out a possible solution while continuing to collect and review the data, it may be necessary to revise the plan or perhaps develop a new hypothesis if the student's behavior does not improve.

Step 4: Develop a Written Behavioral Plan

Since challenging behaviors address a need that the student has, an effective behavioral program must be powerful enough to meet that need. Once the data are analyzed and a hypothesis is developed on why the behavior is occurring (what function it serves), the team can identify which alternative, appropriate behaviors (including specific communication skills) that serve the same functions as the challenging behaviors can be taught. The written behavioral plan will outline the instruction and strategies, any environmental considerations, and a crisis plan (if necessary), so everyone who is working with the student can use a consistent approach. The parents should be involved in the planning and have a copy of the written plan, so they can implement the same interventions at home as are being implemented in all the other settings in which the student participates. Systematic instruction and reinforcement are required to teach new skills. Programs that teach replacement behavior, on the basis of the functions of the behavior, along with the behavior itself, are more likely to produce long-term effects.

Teaching replacement skills can be a long process and requires patience and a systematic, well-planned approach. It is essential to provide differential reinforcement—the reinforcement of desirable behaviors in the absence of undesirable behaviors. Furthermore, it is important to provide instruction during times when the student is not disruptive (proactive teaching), rather than wait until a disruptive situation occurs. As part of the behavioral planning process, it is also necessary to complete or update the reinforcement assessment, so as to provide reinforcements that are specifically matched to the individual and that will have the power to stimulate a positive response.

Three major areas should be considered in designing an intervention plan:

1. **environmental alterations:** assessing for and building on the student's strengths and preferences, as well as identifying and adjusting environmental concerns (for example, changing the type or duration of an activity, the scheduling of activities, or the location in which an activity occurs)

2. **skill instruction:** teaching the student alternative behaviors that reduce impeding behaviors and teaching the ongoing appropriate communication and social skills (for instance, teaching the student to use an augmentative communication device to gain attention, rather than screaming)

3. **behavioral consequences:** reducing or eliminating inappropriate behaviors while teaching appropriate replacement behaviors (such as ignoring the student's screaming, waiting for a calm moment, and then teaching the student to use a call switch to gain attention while reinforcing the appropriate behavior)

Step 5: Evaluate the Intervention

Once the behavioral plan has been developed, a data collection system must be established to evaluate the success of the interventions. If the data demonstrate that the plan is not effective, the team needs to determine which issues have to be modified and then to provide alternative reinforcements, strategies, or communication strategies.

DEVELOPING A CRISIS PLAN

A crisis plan is needed to manage a situation involving a student who is out of control and could cause harm to himself or herself or others. This plan should be developed and implemented by the educational team. During a crisis, new learning does not occur; this is not a time to teach new skills. Rather, the goal is to keep the student and other people safe and to defuse the situation. Instruction in skills is addressed during the behavioral intervention plan, not during a crisis.

Crises can be divided into three stages of behavior or interaction immediately preceding, during, and immediately following the crisis: escalation, crisis, and de-escalation and calming. In developing a crisis plan, the team will identify for each stage the specific behaviors that identify the stage of crisis, the strategies to deal best with the behaviors or the situation, and the things to avoid during that stage (Janzen, 1996). New learning can begin once the student has calmed and the situation has returned to a state of equilibrium. The sample Crisis Intervention Plan in Figure 7.2 shows how these behaviors can be identified (a blank copy appears at the end of this chapter).

In Stage 1, escalation, the student's behaviors signal that he or she is becoming agitated. (Information can be obtained from the functional behavioral assessment). The goal of intervention during escalation is to defuse stress and return to the student to a state of equilibrium. During the crisis itself, Stage 2, intervention focuses on preventing further escalation, keeping the student and others safe, and calming the student or de-escalating of the behavior. In Stage 3, de-escalation and calming, the student's behaviors indicate his or her efforts to regain control as he or she begins to relax and calm. Intervention will support continued self-control and further calming. It is important to remember that during a crisis situation, the focus is on de-escalating the behaviors, keeping the student and others calm, and reducing demands on the student, so he or she can return to a state of equilibrium.

SUMMARY

The use of positive behavioral interventions is vital to the management of challenging behaviors of students with ASDVI. Problem behaviors are generally

FIGURE 7.2

Sample Crisis Intervention Plan

Name: _Titus (T)_

Date: _12/7/02_   Last Updated: _11/18/02_

Behavior Potential: _____ Injuring Self and Others _____

Escalation Stage	Crisis Stage	De-escalation and Calming Stage
Behavior signals ■ High-pitched vocalizations ■ Repeated requests for food ("Want treat, want treat, want treat") ■ Puffing and blowing through the mouth ■ Dropping cane ■ Slapping self on chest	**Behavior signals** ■ Biting ■ Crying and screaming ■ Throwing shoes ■ Tipping furniture over	**Behavior signals** ■ Soft crying ■ Titus vocalizing "are you calm" ■ Sitting on the floor quietly
Strategies ■ Use a calm voice ■ Reduce the demand ■ Complete the activity, if appropriate, and move to a preferred activity	**Strategies** ■ In a calm yet stern voice tell T. to sit down ■ Move children ■ Move any nearby equipment and furniture out of the way ■ Reduce noise level in setting	**Strategies** ■ Reinforce effort to calm self ■ Assist Titus to put on his shoes ■ Move to a chair or calm area ■ Show schedule
Avoid ■ Physical contact ■ Disliked activities ■ Teacher sounding stressed and raising voice ■ Using the word no	**Avoid** ■ Trying to talk to Titus ■ Any attempt at an Activity ■ Sounding upset ■ Physical proximity	**Avoid** ■ Physical contact ■ Excess talking

Additional planning: Review the data collected on crisis behavior. Review skills being taught to ensure that Titus is being taught to communicate when he needs a break. Review the schedule to ensure a good mix of preferred and nonpreferred activities. Review opportunities for choice making throughout the day.

Source: Adapted with permission from Oregon Regional Autism Services, Oregon Department of Education, Salem, OR.

not associated with the student purposely trying to hurt him self or herself or others. Rather, they are often a symptom of the student's lack of understanding, lack of communication, lack of appropriate skills, or with challenges in processing sensory information.

Teams that need additional support in identifying and analyzing behaviors, and in implementing interventions may wish to seek the help of a behavioral specialist or a school psychologist with experience and training in the design and implementation of behavioral intervention strategies. Conducting a functional behavior assessment and implementing a behavioral intervention plan will help the team to analyze the behavior and to design and implement the instruction that best supports the student. Several general instructional principles will support the successful implementation of all positive behavioral strategies:

1. Provide opportunities for making choices; teach choice making.

2. Provide instruction at an appropriate level, matched to the student's individual learning style.

3. Use symbol systems to clarify and teach new skills (pictures, braille, objects, print, or auditory output).

4. Provide opportunities for relaxation and teach relaxation strategies.

5. Use reinforcements that are meaningful to the student.

6. Teach independence and self-management skills.

Functional Analysis: Targeting Behavior for Change

Target behavior	Where did the behavior occur?	When did it occur?	With whom did it occur?	How long did it last?	What happened after it occurred?

Comments/issues:

Functional Assessment Scatterplot (1)

Student: _____ Grade: _____ School: _____

Date(s): _____ Observer(s): _____

Behavior(s) of concern: _____

Setting: _____

Activity	Time	Day of the Week					Total
		Monday	Tuesday	Wednesday	Thursday	Friday	
Total							

Source: Reprinted from "Addressing Student Problem Behavior: Part II—An IEP Team's Introduction to Functional Behavioral Assessment and Behavior Intervention Plans," Appendix A, Center for Effective Collaboration and Practice, Washington, D.C., May 12, 1998. Retrieved from http://cecp.air.org/fba/problembehavior2/main2.htm.

Functional Assessment Scatterplot (2)

Student _____ Setting _____ Observer(s) _____

Activity _____ Date _____

No. of Students _____ Start Time _____ End Time _____ Total _____

Observation
Internal: 10 sec ____ 15 sec ____ 20 sec ____

Time Sampling
Procedure: 1. Continuous
Recording: ____

2. Noncontinuous
Recording: ____
(every ____ min)

3. Other ____

Phase		Appropriate Responses					Total	Consequences of Appropriate Responses	Inappropriate Responses					Total	Consequences of Inappropriate Responses
		Peer interaction	Alone	Adult Interaction	Organized games	Parallel play			Peer interaction	Alone	Adult Interaction	Organized games	Parallel play		
Activity															
Other															
Total															

Comments:

Source: Reprinted from "Addressing Student Problem Behavior: Part II—An IEP Team's Introduction to Functional Behavioral Assessment and Behavior Intervention Plans," Appendix A, Center for Effective Collaboration and Practice, Washington, D.C., May 12, 1998. Retrieved from http://cecp.air.org/fba/problembehavior2/main2.htm.

ABC Checklist

Student Name (D.O.B): _____   School / Building: _____

Time	Date	Antecedent What was happening *just prior* to the behavior occurring?	Behavior	Consequence What happened after the behavior to resolve the problem?	Duration How long did the behavior last?	Intensity
		___ Alone ___ With peers ___ Riding in a bus/van ___ Preparing for an outing ___ Participating in a group ___ Asked to do something ___ Asked/told "not to" ___ Transitioning ___ Working on academics (which one(s)? ___) ___ At recess ___ Being ignored ___ At lunch ___ Given a warning ___ About to begin a new activity ___ Other (describe)	___ Refusing to follow instructions ___ Disrupting class (describe) ___ Making verbal threats ___ Hurting self ___ Destroying property ___ Screaming/yelling ___ Biting ___ Throwing ___ Kicking ___ Running away ___ Grabbing/pulling ___ Crying loudly ___ Other (describe)	___ Student ignored ___ Used proximity control ___ Gave a nonverbal cue ___ Gave a verbal warning ___ Changed assignment ___ Redirected ___ Student lost privilege ___ Sent to office ___ Suspended ___ Gave detention ___ Physical assist/prompt ___ Physical escort ___ Physical management ___ Other	___ < 1 minute ___ 1–5 minutes ___ 5–10 minutes ___ 10–30 minutes ___ ½–1 hour ___ 1–2 hours ___ 2–3 hours ___ 3+ hours	1 Low 2 3 4 5 High

NOTES:

Source: Reprinted from "Addressing Student Problem Behavior: Part II—An IEP Team's Introduction to Functional Behavioral Assessment and Behavior Intervention Plans," Appendix B, Center for Effective Collaboration and Practice, Washington, D.C., May 12, 1998. Retrieved from http://cecp.air.org/fba/problembehavior2/main2.htm.

ABC Observation Form

Student Name (D.O.B): _____ School / Building: _____

Time	Date	Antecedent What was happening *just* prior to the behavior occurring?	Behavior	Consequence What happened after the behavior to resolve the problem?	Duration How long did the behavior last?	Intensity
					___ < 1 minute ___ 1–5 minutes ___ 5–10 minutes ___ 10–30 minutes ___ ½–1 hour ___ 1–2 hours ___ 2–3 hours ___ 3+ hours	1 Low 2 3 4 5 High

NOTES:

Source: Reprinted from "Addressing Student Problem Behavior: Part II—An IEP Team's Introduction to Functional Behavioral Assessment and Behavior Intervention Plans," Appendix B, Center for Effective Collaboration and Practice, Washington, D.C., May 12, 1998. Retrieved from http://cecp.air.org/fba/problembehavior2/main2.htm.

Crisis Intervention Plan

Name: _____

Date: _____   Last Updated: _____

Behavior Potential: _____

Escalation Stage	Crisis Stage	Calming Stage
Behavior signals	Behavior signals	Behavior signals
Strategies	Strategies	Strategies
Avoid	Avoid	Avoid

Additional planning: Review the data that were collected on crisis behavior. Review the skills being taught to ensure that the student is being taught to communicate when he or she needs a break. Review the schedule to ensure that there is a good mix of preferred and nonpreferred activities. Review the student opportunities for choice making throughout day.

Source: Adapted with permission from Oregon Regional Autism Services, Oregon Department of Education, Salem OR.

Orientation and Mobility

Typically developing children use their vision and hearing to gather information about their environment and use this information to move safely and efficiently through it, learning as they do so to understand the environment. Children who are visually impaired must learn to organize their environment with minimal, distorted, or no visual feedback. Orientation and mobility (O&M) instruction teaches them skills for using their residual vision, if any, and information from their own senses to accomplish the same safe, efficient movement that sighted children learn incidentally. The ability to move about the environment leads to self-control, and enhances access to and participation in an expanding, interactive world. An O&M instructor, a professional who has completed a university course of instruction in O&M, is a valuable and ongoing member of the educational team who conducts assessments of and provides instruction to the student and works with other team members to help ensure that each member knows and implements appropriate O&M strategies and techniques with the student.

O&M instruction is one of the areas of the expanded core curriculum for students with visual impairment. Most children who are visually impaired require assessment of, and instruction in, O&M skills. Similarly, O&M instruction is an important instructional component for students with ASDVI. However, students with ASDVI often face additional challenges in learning to move safely and efficiently with little or no vision. This chapter addresses these issues and can be used by all members of the educational team, including parents, caregivers, teachers, O&M instructors, and other service providers, to augment the O&M instructional program.

Orientation begins with an understanding and knowledge of one's body, its parts and their movement capabilities and its spatial relationships to the environment and to objects in the environment. Orientation involves knowing where you are and being able to think about and plan your movement. At a foundational level, it begins with the ability to understand that things exist even when they may not be in the immediate environment. Mobility is actual movement from place to place. It begins with the most simple of purposeful movement, or movement with *intent*. O&M instruction provides the student with the skills that he or she needs to move safely in the environment and typically encompasses

- sensory awareness (teaching skills that allow the student to gain information about the world through his or her senses)

- body image or body awareness (teaching about the parts of the body and how they move)

- environmental and spatial concepts (such as the realization that objects exist even if they are not heard or felt and understanding the relationships between objects (like up or down, close or far, and concepts that are related to distance)

- skills and strategies that allow safe and independent movement, including

  ◆ early purposeful movement (reaching, rolling, crawling, and walking)

  ◆ guided travel (using another person to assist in travel but actively participating in this travel, also referred to as "sighted guide travel")

  ◆ protective techniques (specific strategies that can be used to provide protection while traveling without the use of a mobility tool, such as a cane)

  ◆ the use of mobility "tools" (skills that are used in specific situations allow for added protection and a better understanding of the travel environment, including instruction in cane travel and in the use of other mobility devices)

  ◆ travel in specific environments (skills that are used to travel in known and unknown neighborhoods, business areas, work environments, and so forth)

  ◆ the use of public transportation systems (skills that are necessary to use public bus systems, trains, subways, and the like).

Orientation and mobility instruction teaches the skills students need to move safely in the environment, including the use of mobility devices such as the long cane.

O&M assessment and curricula that are used for students who are visually impaired can also be used for students with ASDVI. This chapter does not reiterate a sequence of instruction in O&M, since several high-quality curricula exist that identify an O&M sequence of instruction and skills (see Resources section at the back of this book). Each student needs to be taught how to understand his or her environment and how to move about in it to an appropriate extent. These O&M resources can help guide the team consider the "typical" development of O&M skills. However, the unique learning needs of a student with is ASDVI necessitate more than consideration of the typical O&M scope and sequence; they require adjustments that address key differences in the approach to and the planning, sequencing, and delivery of O&M instruction.

ASSESSMENT

As with any good O&M program, high-quality instruction is founded on high-quality assessment. All students whose visual impairment affects their ability to move purposefully in the environment and to understand the environment as they move about it, should be assessed for O&M skills. The process of planning a program of instruction in O&M requires keen observations, careful consideration of long-range needs, and an ongoing analysis of the environments in which the student is expected to travel now and in the future.

An O&M assessment of a student with ASDVI is best conducted by the educational team. Because O&M skills are incorporated throughout the student's day, assessment should reflect each team member's discipline. Furthermore, for a student with ASDVI, it is essential to include an evaluation of the student's communication and social interactions in an O&M assessment because these abilities must be reflected in the instruction and in the expectations regarding the student's travel in the environment. The importance of assessing factors related to communication and social interaction is illustrated in the following example:

> Kim was learning to go to the mall and was motivated to do so by the opportunity to purchase a Coke from a fast-food restaurant in the food court of the mall. Kim is nonverbal and is dependent on an adult who is accompanying her to communicate with the public. As part of O&M instruction, a symbolic card system was introduced so she could engage the public herself. Using the cards to communicate her desire to the salesperson at the restaurant (for example, one card says "I would like a small Coke please), she is learning to manage her purchase independently. Without the incorporation of communication skills into Kim's O&M instruction, her travel would have neither meaning nor function.

It is helpful to consider O&M assessment for students with ASDVI as a two-step process. The initial step is comparable to the O&M assessment that is conducted with any student who is visually impaired and should be designed to provide the team with information regarding the student's:

- ability to move about in the environment

- conceptual understanding of the environment

- travel demands at home, at school, and in the community

- sensory skills and abilities

- student's cognitive skills

- physical abilities and any specific limitations in them

The team can use many of the resources that are available to assess these areas (see the Resources section at the back of this book). In particular, *Teaching Age-Appropriate Purposeful Skills (TAPS)* (Pogrund et al., 1993) is a commercially available tool that supports assessment in five general travel environments:

- home or living environment

- campus environment

- residential environment

- commercial environment

- public transportation

TAPS begins with a list of functional mobility tasks (e.g., initiating any movement, purposefully searching for an object, or locating specific rooms) that are related to the specific environment. These tasks can be adapted for use in a variety of natural environments.

The second step is to conduct an assessment to gather information on the unique characteristics that are associated with an autism spectrum disorder, since manifestations of these characteristics can have a profound impact on the student's ability to learn from, be motivated by, and move about and feel safe in the environment and, consequently, can have profound implications for O&M instruction and the development of O&M skills. Therefore, it is important for the team to consider these behaviors and characteristics when planning O&M instruction and to determine how these characteristics may affect the student's ability to move efficiently from place to place. These behaviors and characteristics frequently include

- a poor understanding of spatial relationships

- general spatial disorientation

- problem-solving difficulties

- difficulty understanding abstract concepts and processing information abstractly

- limited or unique motivators

- a strong need for structure and predictability

- hypersensitive or hyposensitive responses to specific sounds, textures, and smells

- a gestalt learning style—the ability to learn in "whole chunks" but difficulty breaking down information into separate pieces and organizing it

- unique and highly exaggerated interests in specific objects and perseverative behaviors

The educational team can use the following six questions to augment information that is gathered through the use of more traditional O&M assessment tools,

1. How does the student process and manage sensory information?

2. What are the student's primary motivators, preferences, and interests?

3. What is the student's attention span?

4. How does the student manage and deal with change?

5. What are the student's primary strengths and challenges and primary learning styles?

6. What are the student's current and future travel needs?

The team can use a form to gather the information for each question and to consider potential implications and instructional strategies. The entire O&M Questionnaire form appears in Appendix 8A, while completed examples of various sections appear in the text. The forms O&M Instruction and Collaboration and Task Analysis of Skills Needed (also included at the end of this chapter) can then be used to guide the development of the O&M program on the basis of the information that is obtained in the assessment.

As the O&M instructor, with support from the other team members, prepares to conduct the assessment and to provide instruction, she or he needs to determine how best to communicate with the student. Initially, the O&M instructor may have to communicate through a staff member who is experienced in working with the student. This is a short-term solution for the O&M instructor to get a feel for how the student processes information and how to present information in a way that makes sense to the student. For example, if an O&M instructor is trying either to assess a student for or to instruct a student in traveling from point A to point B and provides information verbally to a student who communicates best using objects, the student will probably not understand what is expected and hence the O&M instructor will not get a clear picture of the student's O&M skills and limitations; rather, the only skills that may be assessed may be the student's communication skills. Therefore, in planning for the assessment and for subsequent instruction, the O&M instructor must be able to identify the difference between communication skills and O&M skills and ensure that the appropriate communication tools are provided so the student understands what is being requested. If the student is using an object system, a picture system, or a braille system, the O&M instructor will need to bring appropriately matched items related to the mobility task, so she can communicate with the student. For example, if a student uses objects to represent various rooms, when the O&M instructor is assessing the student's ability to travel from Room A to Room B, she needs to have the appropriate symbolic representation of Room B to help the student understand that he is being asked to travel to Room B. Once the communication systems are established, the O&M instructor is ready to proceed with the assessment issues.

Sensory Information

Many students with autism spectrum disorder have unusual reactions to sensory information and are hypersensitive or hyposensitive to sounds, odors, textures, sights, or situations. These hyper- and hyposensitivities often lead to fear and avoidance. Identifying the student's ability to process and manage sensory information is critical for O&M instruction. For example, a student may strongly resist traveling down a specific hallway in the school building, but does not appear to have the same reaction to other hallways. The assessment identifies that the student is hypersensitive to the sound of the school bell and hence may be particularly afraid to travel down the hallway of the school knowing that the bell is located there. Simply discussing the schedule for the bell may calm the student, so he or she knows when the bell will sound, may give the student the confidence to travel down that hallway. Of course, additional strategies may be needed, depending on the severity of the sensory intrusion.

Because sensory training is often a critical component of O&M instruction, the team must be knowledgeable about and responsive to, the student's ability to process sensory information. For students who have difficulty processing sensory information, it is necessary to break down instructional tasks into segments that allow the students slowly to increase their tolerance to sensory input. Information on the assessment of sensory processing and establishing a sensory profile is included in Chapter 4: Assessment. This information is applicable to O&M assessments as well (see the information on the Sensory Profile and the Sensory Profile Observation Form at the end of Chapter 4). This information can be used to complete Part 1 of the O&M Questionnaire form (see Figure 8.1) and to generate appropriate strategies for instruction.

Motivators, Preferences, and Interests

One way in which a student can be motivated to move in his or her environment is to use the objects, activities, or people in the environment that are the most motivating as goals or destinations to move or travel *to*. Once identified, the environment can be arranged so that movement to desired objects is required. For higher functioning students, this concept also applies. For example, if a student is particularly interested in "Disney movies," he or she may be highly motivated to learn how to travel to the local video store. The skills that she or he learns on this route can then be generalized to other situations.

Information about the student's motivators, preferences, and interests, (discussed in Chapter 2) is critical to O&M assessment. Information that is gathered through the use of the Reinforcer Development, Learner Interests, Play Interest Survey, and Preference Checklist forms (included at the end of Chapter 4) can be incorporated when assessing and planning for O&M instruction. Figure 8.2 gives an example of how this information can be applied to O&M instructional strategies.

Creative O&M instruction can take advantage of even unusual motivators. For example, Jane, a student with ASDVI, had a unique perseveration with the number 6. O&M instruction successfully used this interest by planning routes and teaching appropriate skills in traveling to each room in the school building that had a 6 in its number (such as Room 26 and Room 64). Jane was highly motivated to travel to these destinations, with skills learned during travel to these destinations later generalized to other destinations.

Attention Span

Many students with ASD are easily distracted, which hampers their ability to maintain attention when necessary. Individual students' abilities to use previously learned skills may vary dramatically, depending on the environment, stresses, distractions, scheduling, and other factors. Because of these factors, previously learned and demonstrated skills may not be "available" to the student, and his or her ability to use learned skills may change from day to day, as the case of Tony illustrates:

FIGURE 8.1

O&M Questionnaire, Part 1

1. How does the student process and manage sensory information? What are the student's primary distracters?

Sensory Information	Implications for movement and travel; strategies for O&M instruction
Vision Bryan is totally blind; he does not use vision to gain information	Bryan cannot rely on visual information to orient to the environment. Thus, instruction needs to be provided that is not dependent on visual interpretation.
Auditory This is Bryan's primary learning modality. He can repeat any sound and inflection that he hears. He can discriminate the make and model of cars from their sounds. He tends to walk from side to side in the hall as he gets auditory feedback.	The sequence of instruction must be based verbal direction. Bryan tends to repeat the same questions over and over. He may benefit from using audiotaped instruction that is broken down into a step-by-step process to learn a new skill or to locate a specific destination. Auditory discrimination may be difficult at times because Bryan gets fixated on certain auditory feedback like cars or music and cannot discriminate the essential auditory elements that are needed to travel.
Touch Although totally blind, Bryan has difficulty with tactile interpretation and with reading braille. He does not like any light touch on his hands, arms, shoulders, or back.	Bryan may not be able to read braille directions or follow tactile maps. Using hand-over-hand instruction may cause some defenseiveness.
Taste Bryan is highly motivated by some food (candy, sweets, and chips) but is hesitant to try any new food.	The O&M instructor may be able to teach functional routines and locations that are favorite places to eat or to get snacks. Bryan may be motivated to travel by earning snacks.
Smell Bryan can discriminate smells but not always orient to the location of a smell.	Bryan may be inconsistent in locating landmarks on the basis of discriminating smells. Therefore, a smell must always be paired with another, more concrete, landmark.
Movement Bryan's gait and general movement are not fluid. Bryan has difficulty adjusting to changes in the environment (steps and changes in surfaces).	Bryan may need a cane that allows for extra time to react and that provides maximum feedback without giving uncomfortable tactile feedback to his hands. Consider the length of the cane, cane materials, the type of tip, and the type of grip.

Import information from the Sensory Profile Observation Form.

FIGURE 8.2

O&M Questionnaire, Part 2

2. What are the student's primary motivators, preferences, and interests? How can these motivators be incorporated into O&M instruction?

Student's motivators, preferences, and interests	Strategies for incorporating motivators, preferences, and interests into O&M instruction
Bryan likes anything to do with cars and car parts. He likes to ride and "drive" cars that are parked.	Use the opportunity to explore cars as reinforcement for completing lessons. Teach traffic patterns using toy cars.
Bryan likes to sing and play country music.	Make up country songs that teach directions to specific locations. Use the opportunity to earn music time as Bryan learns skills or completes lessons. Teach destinations that include music stores.
Bryan likes to play the same videotape repeatedly.	Audiotape directions to destinations. Use different people's voices that Bryan likes and is motivated to record each step.
Bryan likes most junk food.	Use food to reinforce correct skills. Teach a variety of locations to shop and eat out. Teach Bryan to find a variety of locations that offer similar kinds of food.
Bryan likes to imitate other people's voices.	Bryan can record directions to destinations to be played back on a tape or CD player.

Import information from the Reinforcer Development, Learner Interests, Play Interest Survey, and Preference Checklist forms.

Tony, a high school freshman with Asperger syndrome, has learned to cross two-way lighted intersections independently by interpreting traffic sounds and identifying the "parallel surge" of traffic. On most days, he can consistently demonstrate his ability to cross streets safely. However, Tony often has days when something is "bothering him" to the point that it consumes his thoughts (which he calls his "concerns"). His parents and teachers indicate that while the concerns may seem "trivial," to Tony, they are overwhelming. Recently, he was concerned about misplacing a favorite videotape. He has difficulty expressing his frustrations and is not able to concentrate on anything other than his "concerns."

On days when he is preoccupied with his concerns, Tony is not able to cross the street safely, because he is not able to concentrate on the traffic sounds long enough to make appropriate judgments about safe street crossings. His O&M instruction incorporated strategies to teach Tony to identify the days when his concerns were impeding his judgment, and he was taught to use alternate routes on these days.

The O&M instructor (and other staff) must be skilled in developing an awareness of the subtle ways in which a student who is experiencing frustration may give that message. For example, a student may repeat the same question over and over even when the question has been answered. Or, he or she may insist on talking about a situation that may seem irrelevant to the current events. A nonverbal student may make frequent high-pitched sounds, twirl, or appear not to hear a request. Careful assessment and consideration of distractions must be incorporated into lesson planning, as is illustrated in Figure 8.3. The lessons must be developed and implemented with flexibility and an expectation that modifications that are based on information from the assessment will be required. The O&M curriculum may have to include instruction in "alternate" strategies (such as using alternate routes or "hiring" a guide to assist with the street crossing) to be used in these situations.

Change

Students with ASD often struggle with change. Unanticipated changes in the environment or in scheduling can be traumatic. The team needs to know the extent to which the student can handle change and what the student's behavior is when the student is struggling with change. This information serves a twofold purpose. First, it informs the team of the need to maintain consistency across environments, particularly among team members, and between the home and the school environments. Second, it provides information on the need to teach the student to manage change appropriately. Figure 8.4

FIGURE 8.3

O&M Questionnaire, Part 3

3. What is the student's attention span? Does the student have particular issues or situations that challenge his or her ability to maintain attention? What strategies help increase abilities to maintain attention?

Issues or situations that challenge the student's ability to maintain attention	Strategies for increasing the student's ability to maintain attention and focus
Jo Anne is teased by other students about her areas of interest. Teasing may have occurred just before the lesson or days before the lesson, but she is still perseverating about it.	Allow Jo Anne several minutes to talk about the teasing, set the timer, and then do not allow her to talk about it during the rest of the lesson. Write down the teasing issue on a piece of paper and have her throw it away, making the issue "physically gone" during the lesson. Encourage Jo Anne to earn points for not focusing on the teasing during the lesson that can be turned in for treats, prizes, activities.
Jo Anne does not want to wear shoes or socks, regardless of the weather conditions.	Agree ahead of the lesson time what Jo Anne will wear during the lesson. Make sure that the socks fit without bunching up and are made of a material that the student can tolerate. Find shoes that she will tolerate for short periods and reinforce her for keeping them on.

FIGURE 8.4 · O&M Questionnaire, Part 4

4. How does the student manage and deal with "change"?

Does the student have difficulty dealing with change?	Strategies to assist the student to cope with change or to understand that change will occur
☐ Yes ☐ No If yes, what changes are difficult for Steve: ☑ Change in daily schedule ☐ Change in steps/sequences of a routine ☐ Change in adults working with the student ☑ Prefers working with women; has difficulty when changing from a female to a male teacher. The teacher's tone of voice affects Steve's performance.	Notify Steve of a change as far in advance as possible. Use a system to notify him that a change is coming (for example, use a "change" card and insert it into the schedule). Build change into the lesson plan, so he does not become dependent on the same thing every time. Use a calm, even voice when working with Steve. Try not to be loud or overexcited about either positive or negative events.

presents an example of how such information can be applied to instruction. To the extent possible, the student needs to learn how to handle change.

The O&M program needs to reflect appropriate instructional timing and pace. Sometimes team members will think that the O&M instructional program must be changed because the student's progress is limited when, in fact, the program is appropriate but the delivery of instruction is simply too fast or too slow, and the student is not able to manage the constant change in instruction.

Strengths, Challenges, and Learning Style

Information on a student's strengths and challenges is critical for the development of all the components of any student's IEP because this information highlights the impact of the disability. However, it is often overlooked in developing an O&M program. The team needs to identify the general teaching style that is the most conducive to a student's learning and to develop O&M instruction that accepts and respects the student's strengths and challenges. Information about assessing a student's learning style and primary

FIGURE 8.5	**O&M Questionnaire, Part 5**

5. What are the student's primary strengths and primary challenges? What is the student's primary learning style?

Student's learning style and primary learning medium	Ideas to incorporate the student's learning style and primary learning medium into O&M instruction
Meagan is an auditory learner with a limited ability to use tactile information. If the tactile information is unique, easy to locate, and concrete, then she may be able to use the information to confirm directions being followed or the location of destinations. Meagan has difficulty generalizing skills to different settings. Meagan tries hard to please her parents and teachers, and enjoys spending free time listening to music with friends.	To instruct Meagan, the best approach is to pair auditory learning with functional routes. She is not a student who will learn new destinations independently. The use of specific mobility techniques will be taught as part of the instruction of functional routes. Each route she needs to use will be broken down into step-by-step tasks (such as, Walk to the end of the hall, turn right, and walk to the double doors). Once the steps are determined, they will be recorded on a tape or CD. Meagan will be taught the sequence by listening to each step one at a time and following the directions using prompts that the instructor provides. At each step, there will be a concrete landmark to assist her in following the directions.

Import information from the Profile of Student Learning, Use of Sensory Channels, and General Learning Media Checklist forms.

learning medium appears in Chapter 3 (see Profile of Student Learning, Use of Sensory Channels, and General Learning Media Checklist. Figure 8.5 shows how this information can be applied to O&M instruction.

Successful teaching strategies are developed, in part, by responding to the student's primary learning style and strengths and challenges. For example, many students with ASDVI learn best when they are provided with instruction that is repetitive and allows for errorless learning (ensuring that the student does not make mistakes while initially learning a skill). Many students benefit from structure and consistency. Some may respond best by always having abstract concepts paired with concrete symbols (for example, the concept of traveling to the cafeteria can be reinforced by pairing this activity with an object cue, such as a bowl). Others may respond best to instruction that has minimal verbage or that is presented with a limited vocabulary.

The generalized teaching strategies that have proved successful must be incorporated into O&M instruction as well. For example, if the assessment identifies that the student has a strong ability to memorize, O&M routes can be presented by having the student memorize a series of steps that are involved in finding a desired location. Additional information on this area is presented in *Imagining the Possibilities* (Fazzi & Petersmeyer, 2001), which includes examples of ways to develop functional lessons to support the generalization of information.

Travel Needs

Information on the student's current and future travel needs is included in any high-quality O&M assessment of a student who is visually impaired. It is mentioned here to highlight the need to develop an O&M program that is based on the functional application of movement and travel needs of students with ASDVI. Clearly identifying present and future travel needs is paramount in this regard (see Figure 8.6 for an example).

Observe the student in both natural, familiar environments and unfamiliar environments. How the student responds to and interacts with objects and people in familiar and unfamiliar environments can be particularly telling when one considers the student's O&M needs. Talk to the student's parents, to other teachers and service providers, and to the student. Observe typical children in the school environment to identify movement and travel expectations for students of any given age. A careful analysis of the student's present and future travel needs will ensure that the O&M program of instruction is functional, rather than arbitrary.

DEVELOPING THE O&M PROGRAM

Each student with ASDVI requires an individualized O&M curriculum, and the information assessment obtained in the guides the team in developing a program that is designed to accommodate the student's unique needs. As was mentioned earlier, the skills and travel needs of students with ASDVI are often similar to those of visually impaired students, so the sequence of instruction for any student who is visually impaired is applicable to a student with ASDVI. However, the team needs to weigh a "traditional" approach to O&M instruction against a more functionally based approach. For most students with ASDVI, the functional application of O&M skills is the application of choice. Specifically, it is preferable to teach O&M skills in the student's usual environment and in naturally occurring situations. Students who are challenged in using sensory input and natural cues to learn about their environment and to understand the purpose of their movements learn best through instruction in natural environments, with an emphasis on functional routines. Using the natural environments, the team is better able to teach the student

FIGURE 8.6 — O&M Questionnaire, Part 6

6. What are the student's current and future travel needs?

Daily Routines and Anticipated Routines	Current Methods of Travel	Strengths and Difficulties	Instructional Strategies Needed
Classroom to cafeteria	Carlita uses a cane but relies on listening and following the crowd of other students	Carlita can miss finding the doors if the other students are quiet or during travel at non-meal times.	Teach a functional routine using recorded directions, so the student can locate the cafeteria at any time.
Cafeteria to music class	Carlita uses a cane with a ball tip but generally wanders through the hall following auditory sounds	She is inconsistent with coverage and training with cane. If no music is coming from the music class, will overshoot the door and wander until rescued by the music teacher or a staff person.	Using a CD with a headset and a cane, the student will follow a recorded set of directions that identify landmarks at each step until the music room is located.
Classroom to city bus stop	Guided travel	Finds the stop in a timely manner. Requires a staff member to travel except during lesson time. From the classroom to the bus stop, does not require a street crossing.	On the return, the student may need to ride around to avoid the street crossing. Using a CD with a headset and a cane, the student will follow a recorded set of directions to identify landmarks at each step until the bus stop is located.
Bus stop to job site	Guided travel	Carlita requires a staff member to be available to go to and from the job site every day. Gets to the job in a timely manner.	Carlita may need to consider hiring a guide or learning the route systematically following a step-by-step auditory tape. The student may need to use alternate transportation or go to the job site with a work partner.

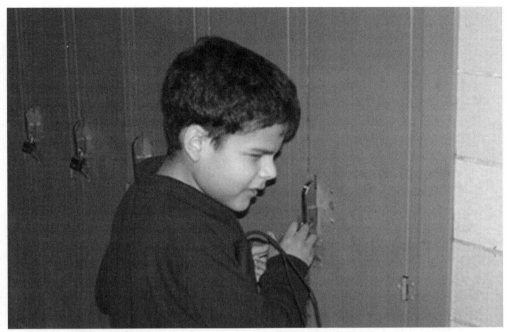

Students with ASDVI typically have difficulty in using sensory input to learn about their environment and the purpose of their movements. These students learn best in their usual environment, including at school, and in naturally occurring situations with functional goals.

skills that can later be generalized, thus enhancing the student's understanding of his or her world and its expectations thereof. Fazzi (1998, p. 452) highlighted the importance of functional application for students with multiple disabilities:

> *Traditional instruction in O&M follows a sequence of skill building that assists the student who is blind to travel independently in increasingly complex environments. The hierarchy of skills is sequenced along a continuum, which suggests prerequisite status for many skills. . . . Skill areas include human guide, protective techniques, and trailing; cane skills, including diagonal, two-point touch technique, and touch and drag; indoor travel, including negotiating doors, stairs, escalators, and elevators; travel in residential areas; travel in light-business areas; use of public transportation systems; travel in urban or downtown areas; and travel in rural areas. . . . Although students with multiple disabilities may benefit from instruction in many of these areas, a strictly hierarchical approach to sequencing may be inappropriate.*

These principles also apply to students with ASDVI.

For students with ASDVI, the skills that are the most relevant, and that best address their unique learning needs are founded on O&M goals that are

- functional, with application occurring in natural environments and implemented and supported by all team members

- reflective of chronologically age-appropriate skills weighed against functional-age abilities and expectations (for example, learning to cross streets independently versus hiring a guide to assist with crossings and using a typical cane and arc for walking versus using a modified grip on a cane and allowing the use of constant contact when the student lacks physical coordination)

- reflective of the student's and family's priorities for movement and travel

- implemented with ample frequency to support ongoing repetition and practice

To establish instructional priorities and develop appropriate O&M goals, the following steps can be used to identify the student's immediate and long-range areas of need:

1. Identify the student's current travel demands at home, at school, and in the community and those for each in the next two to three years (see Figure 8.6).

2. Task analyze the mobility skills that are needed to travel in these environments. (See Figure 8.7 for an example. This form can be used for orientation and communication skills as well.)

3. Task analyze the orientation skills that are needed in these environments.

4. Task analyze the communication skills that are needed in these environments.

5. Identify the discrepancies between the student's current abilities and the skills identified in items 1–4.

6. Establish priorities among the travel needs and identify the immediate functional goals as well as the anticipated "next steps."

Once goals are identified, Figure 8.8 offers an example of a simple O&M instruction and collaboration plan that identifies a specific strategy, necessary materials and adaptations, and the people who will implement it.

O&M instruction, with a focus on providing the student with skills to move safely and with intent, encompasses all developmental areas and provides a functional means to incorporate other curricular areas into its appli-

FIGURE 8.7

Task Analysis of Skills Needed

☐ Mobility Skills   ☐ Orientation Skills   ☐ Communication Skills

Steps	Additional Information
The watch timer indicates to the student it is time for lunch	Student wears an auditory timer
Move to the schedule area to check the schedule	Auditory tape with the directions to cafeteria and headphones in schedule area
Locate the tape, player, and headphones	
Put in the tape, put on the headphones, rewind the tape to the beginning	
Listen to Direction 1 and pause the tape	
Follow Direction 1 (locate the cane at the door)	
Listen to Direction 2 and pause the tape	
Follow Direction 2 (locate the door with the cane, turn right, locate the steps with the cane)	
Listen to Direction 3 and pause the tape	
Follow Direction 3 (walk down steps, locate the door with the cane, push the door open, and walk through the door)	
Listen to Direction 4 and pause the tape	
Follow Direction 4 (locate the sidewalk with the cane, turn left, locate the right-side shoreline	
Listen to Direction 5 and pause the tape	
Follow Direction 5 (shoreline with the cane until the building is located, find the door open on the right)	
Listen to Direction 6 and pause the tape	
Follow Direction 6 (enter the door, turn left, hand up the cane)	
Listen to Direction 7 and pause the tape	
Follow Direction 7 (square off at cane hook wall, walk forward to table)	
Listen to Direction 8 and pause the tape	
Follow Direction 8 (locate the chair, sit down, put the tape and headphone in the hip pack)	

FIGURE 8.8	O&M Instruction and Collaboration Plan
Strategy	**Materials and Equipment Needed**
Locate destinations using an audio recording of step-by-step directions.	A cane with a mushroom tip and weight added

Audiotape or CD player

Headphones (one set for the instructor and one set for the student)

An adapter for a double headphone attachment

A hip pack or backpack |
| **Environmental Adaptation Needed** | **Persons Responsible** |
| Preview the route and then prerecord a step-by-step task analysis of the routine | The O&M instructor, for the setup and weekly review

The teacher, for daily practice as the student goes to the dining room |

cation. It supports motor development and improves fitness, strength, energy, stamina, and coordination. It also supports the functional application of communication and social skills and the development of life skills for foundational (basic-level) students (for example, independent toileting skills are supported by travel to and from the bathroom) as well as more advanced students (for instance, work skills are supported by travel to and from the job site). Toward this end, it is critical that the entire team, including the parents, know and understand the goals that are associated with O&M instruction and are clear about the techniques that the student is learning and the strategies that are being used to implement the instruction.

O&M INSTRUCTIONAL STRATEGIES

For situations in which traditional skills or approaches are not appropriate or they are not successful, a skill or instructional modification or support can be implemented by adapting or enhancing equipment, modifying the instructional strategy or approach, or changing the technique entirely. Sauerberger (1993) discussed the importance of considering alternate options for many students, emphasizing that if a student is able to use a technique that is safe, even if unorthodox, there is no reason not to use the technique. The O&M instructor must consider the principles and rationale behind the techniques being taught and then adapt them, if appropriate, on the basis of the individual student's needs. Sauerberger was referring specifically to students who are deaf-blind, but this principle certainly applies to the O&M needs of students with ASDVI.

In the following sections examples of three critical skill areas are presented that should be incorporated into each student's program. For each area, strategies that have been successful with a variety of students with ASDVI are provided, along with a discussion of the relevance for each. These ideas are meant not to be incorporated into each student's program of instruction but rather, to serve as a basis for thinking "outside the box" when developing O&M instruction.

Understanding Spatial Relationships

Many students with ASDVI struggle to understand the environment, even a familiar environment, because they are overwhelmed by the ongoing and ever-changing events and activities and by auditory, tactile, or visual stimuli. Thus, O&M instruction that teaches them skills for gaining a better understanding of and for organizing space helps them to "make sense" of the environment. The goal of O&M instruction in this regard is for the student to understand that spatial relationships exist between objects (such as up or down and close or far) and between environments and to enhance the student's spatial perceptions of the environments (for example, from anywhere in the classroom, does the student know where the door leading to the hallway is, or upon leaving the classroom, does the student know what she or he will encounter in turning right or turning left?).

Most students with ASDVI must be specifically taught to organize the environment in a meaningful way. For many, their natural perspective of the environment may be spatially "disorganized." Therefore, the processes and strategies that a student with ADVI uses to organize the environment may be different from what may be considered to be "typical" for a student with visual impairment who does not have ASD. The goal is to assist the

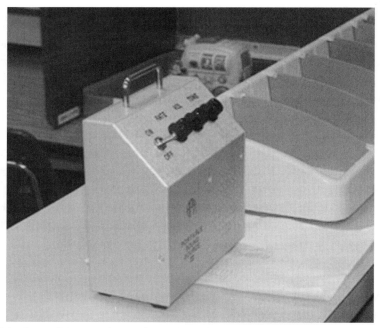

This Portable Sound Source is used as an auditory reference point to help a student locate his object calendar box.

student with ASDVI to organize from a perspective that makes sense to him or her, but not necessarily to others.

The following are some instructional strategies for teaching an understanding of spatial relationships and organizing space that may be especially useful with students who have ASDVI:

- Use reference points. Teach the student to orient himself or herself using reference points. A reference point is a stationary object or environmental feature (such as the entry door to the classroom) that can be used as "ground zero"—the point from which everything else is judged.

- Use identifiers (such as personal identifiers or room and building identifiers). The identifiers should be designed using the student's learning medium (braille, large print, pictures, and object cues), and can help the student to feel "centered," to understand better where he or she is, and to understand environmental and spatial relationships. Identifiers need to be used consistently in the home and school environments and by every member of the educational team, including the parents. For example, Rosa's object calendar system uses a small bowl to identify "time for lunch." As part of O&M instruction, the bowl is used as an anticipation cue for communicating that Rosa will be traveling to the cafeteria; this object cue also helps Rosa "imagine" where she is going before she starts, helping to build her awareness of her environment. This cue or identifier gives Rosa the motivation to travel down the hallway, despite distractions along the way.

- Practice full participation in activities, particularly if the student does not have enough vision to see different environments. Only by fully participating can the student come to understand spatial perspectives and relationships. For instance, during snack time, Jason fully participates with his classmates by helping the teacher get the supplies from the cabinet, taking them to the table, getting the food items from the refrigerator and cupboard, having the snack with his classmates, and helping to put everything away and to clean up. This full participation allows him to build his understanding of the various physical attributes of the classroom and of the specific locations of various items.

- Teach and use the skill of pointing (pointing with a finger or hand or through body positioning). This skill will enhance the student's spatial awareness.

- Strive for "errorless learning." Many students struggle if they initially orient to an environment or learn a specific route incorrectly. Some students remember exactly how they learned or performed a task. For example, when Tina is going to be learning a new skill or routine, it is critical that she perform the skill correctly the first time. Thus, she must receive additional support and instruction to ensure that the way she performs the skill initially is the way the skill needs to be performed. Unless Tina performs the skill correctly, her teachers need to spend weeks teaching her to "unlearn" the behavior.

- Be conscious of body placement—the student's body placement as well as the teacher's. Some students with ASDVI are conscious of body placement and have a need for defined personal body space. A student may be uncomfortable, for example, if the teacher stands "too close" or stands behind him or her when providing instruction. It is critical that all members of the educational team who work with the student know these preferences and make accommodations as appropriate.

- Use transition times as teaching times. Teachers often feel the need to hurry to get to the next location in which instruction will occur (for instance, when the next class is music, the entire class is hurried to travel down the hallway to the music room). For many students with ASDVI, the transition time is as critical as the class itself, and hurrying only exacerbates their anxieties and frustrations. In these instances, it is better either to allow extra time or to "rethink" the primary goal of the lesson; the main objective may, in fact, be successful travel down the hallway.

- Be sequential and concrete in teaching strategies. Many students with ASDVI, including more advanced learners, may not be able to process abstract "spatial" information. For example, Anton, a bright student, is able to travel independently throughout his high school. He memorizes each of his routes and carefully follows the sequence of steps that are required to travel from point A to B. However, Anton is not able to comprehend that the route from point B to point A is just a reversal of the route from point A to point B; he sees the two as completely separate routes. His instructors know that they must approach all his routes from the perspective that point B to point A is a separate route, not a reversal of point A to point B.

- Provide space for personal possessions. Each student should have a place for his or her "things," and know how to travel to and from this location as appropriate for his or her ability.

- Teach the student about environmental consistencies and inconsistencies. Many students with ASDVI do not incidentally learn the similarities and differences among environments. It is important, for example, to specifically teach that the cafeteria and the gymnasium are both large rooms, shaped like a square, with walls made of cement block, *but* that the cafeteria has tables and chairs and a kitchen located on the north wall, while the gymnasium has bleachers made of wood, with a locker room for girls located on the west wall and a locker room for boys located on the east wall.

- Use boundaries or borders to define space. Many students will enhance their understanding of their spatial environment through the use of clearly defined space; boundaries and borders can help the student differentiate among various spaces in a room. Vertical borders and boundaries (such as wall dividers, bookshelves, desks, and study carrels) and horizontal boundaries (like different flooring textures, and high-contrast rugs) can be used to define space more clearly.

- Be conscious of environmental distractions. Sometimes a student with ASDVI seems distracted and becomes disoriented for "no apparent reason" when, the student is actually distracted by something in the environment that the teachers and other students ignore (such as a noise coming from the adjoining classroom or the smell of a nonpreferred food cooking in the cafeteria). The team must constantly be alert to these environmental distractions.

- Be conscious of the layout of a room and changes in the layout, limit distractions, and teach the student strategies to manage distractions to the extent possible.

Boundaries and borders can help students differentiate among various spaces in a room. This mat provides a clear boundary that students can easily perceive, creating a space for motor activities that is separate from the rest of the classroom.

Maintaining Orientation

Many students with ASDVI also struggle with their ability to maintain orientation in both familiar and unfamiliar environments. Information that most individuals who are visually impaired typically use to organize and define space and maintain their orientation in the environment is often overwhelming or overlooked by students with ASDVI. When considering how best to teach orientation skills in familiar and unfamiliar environments, the O&M instructor needs to apply information that has been obtained in the assessment to the broad question, What information can the student use to understand the environment that he or she is in? For example, how does the student know that he or she is in the classroom, not in the cafeteria? What skills does the student need to use appropriate sensory and environmental information to maintain his or her orientation? Of course, these questions are important for all visually impaired students, but this critical skill area often needs to be emphasized in the instruction of students with ASDVI. The following are some instructional strategies for teaching students with ASDVI to maintain orientation.

- Use boundaries and borders to define space.

- Establish areas for personal possessions. For example, provide each student with a place to keep his or her personal items. This place can be a locker, a cabinet in the classroom, a foot locker, or a box located under the coat rack. It can become a reference point for the student and helps to support the development of basic organizational skills and a feeling of "self."

- Use clearly marked environmental identifiers; do not limit the identifiers to only tactile ones. For example, a student may primarily use object symbols to identify various locations in his or her environment. Auditory identifiers can be incorporated by using any of the portable auditory output devices that are on the market; the team can also use inexpensive recordable "talking picture frames" that are available at most discount and drug stores. A talking picture frame can be mounted, for example, outside a door and programmed to say "Mr. Johnson's office" when located and activated.

■ Consider environmental inconsistencies and possibilities for distractions and teach ways to "handle" them. For example, many students with ASDVI struggle with anything in the environment that is "different" from what they previously experienced (for instance, the grass is higher because it has not been mowed, the sidewalk has puddles because of a recent rainstorm, or loud sounds are heard at a particular intersection because of nearby construction). It is important to teach the student about environmental inconsistencies and to teach him or her strategies to deal with them.

■ Make use of consistent reference points.

■ Maintain consistency in the use of communication systems across environments and throughout the student's day. For example, it is critical for all members of the educational team to work together to ensure that the communication system and instructional strategies that are used with the student are applied consistently across all environments. If the student is using a tangible symbol system in the classroom, that the system should be portable, be used in all other environments and be incorporated into O&M instruction.

■ Teach and use natural environmental cues; pointing out environmental consistencies can be calming and help the student to orient more fully. For example, many students with ASDVI do not incidentally learn about natural environmental cues and need to be specifically taught them. A student may not pick up on the fact that it tends to be noisier and more hectic near places where many people gather in a group (such as the school office or a checkout area of a grocery store.) Specifically teaching this concept will assist the student to use this information to help maintain orientation.

■ Carefully consider the layout of a room; avoid confusion and "environmental clutter."

■ Consider the use of auditory maps and tactile maps. The maps may be simple or complex, depending on the student's level of understanding.

■ Teach strategies that allow the student to deal with "change," including environmental changes.

■ Teach problem-solving skills; include specific, sequential strategies that allow the student to discern information from the environment. For example, because many students with ASDVI struggle with problem-solving skills, they can benefit from instruction that teaches a sequence to follow to help solve problems (for example, "If I am lost in the school, I can either listen for the noise coming from the office and go there to ask for help or stop and wait until another student walks by, so I can ask him or her for help").

Moving Independently

Instruction should enhance the student's ability to learn from the environment. The best way to learn from the environment is to move through it. Many students with ASDVI may not be motivated to move because of fears, because they are afraid, have limited interests, or simply do not know or understand the concept of space. It is the team's responsibility to provide the skills that allow the student not to be afraid of moving within the environment, providing opportunities for the student to continually increase his or her understanding of the environment. Her are some instructional strategies to help a student with ASDVI to move independently through the environment, to have expectations for movement and travel, and to follow through on these expectations:

■ Use schedules (such as concrete or object schedules or braille calendars) to reinforce the student's expectations.

■ Consider an alternate, perhaps "unconventional," means to an end. Sometimes it is best to consider the end goal and apply alternate strategies to achieve the goal if something is impeding the student's progress. For example, a student may be capable of independent travel using the city bus system, but not be able safely to cross the street that is the most direct route to his or her workplace. As an alternate route, the student learns to stay on the bus until the route "loops back" to the other side of the street. This alternate strategy adds about 30 minutes to the route, but allows the student to achieve the goal independently. Similarly, the student could learn the skills that are necessary to "hire" a guide to assist with the street crossing. The guide could be another student or an employee in a nearby store who is available at a given time each day to assist with the crossing.

■ Incorporate the need for movement and travel into the student's routine. It is critical for the team to work collaboratively to ensure that the student's day is structured so the student has the *need* to travel. The student will never learn to travel (at a level of appropriate independence) unless opportunities and expectations for such travel are developed and implemented consistently.

- Make sure to incorporate appropriate breaks into the student's schedule after a careful assessment of the student's ability to maintain attention.

- Allow for and teach choice making during O&M instruction. A student will be more willing and motivated to learn and explore if he or she is given choices about where and when he or she will move.

- Use "high-interest" objects and areas to stimulate the student's motivation to move.

- Teach strategies that allow the student to explore the environment safely. Ensure that a student's movement is not limited because of a fear of the unknown.

- Consider the use of mobility devices and orientation tools (see the next section); for students who are not capable of using a cane, consider the use of adapted mobility devices to serve the same purpose.

MOBILITY TOOLS AND DEVICES

All mobility tools and devices, including the long white cane, are designed to provide the user who is visually impaired with information about and feedback from the environment; they offer protection during travel by allowing a student to detect or verify the presence of obstacles and drop-offs. Although the long white cane is appropriate for many students with ASDVI, and instruction in its use is critical, some students are better served through the use of alternate mobility devices. For many, an alternate mobility device may be a precursor to the long cane, whereas for others, its use will be appropriate in the long term.

Many mobility devices are constructed of PVC pipe and include various adaptations of curved tips, rollers, grips, and wheels. Some are designed for use with one hand, while others require the use of both hands. Other commercially available toys and objects can be used as is, including devices and toys with handles (such as push toys and play lawn mowers), pushcarts, and toy cars. Some students will benefit from adaptations made to wheelchairs, walkers, and crutches to be used as mobility devices. Pogrund et al. (1993) suggested four questions to ask when considering an adaptive mobility device:

- Does the device motivate the student to move?

- Does the student have a severe physical or cognitive disability that interferes with his or her ability to protect himself or herself?

- Does the student have deficits in proprioception and kinesthesia that interfere with his or her ability to protect himself or herself with a cane?

- Is the device socially appropriate for the student's age and environments?

Many students with ASDVI benefit from the use of adapted mobility devices. For information about the design of these devices and instruction in their use, see the Resources and Additional Readings at the back of this book. When contemplating the best design for an adapted mobility device, the team needs to be sure to consider the student's tactile and auditory preferences and sensitivities.

SUMMARY

O&M instruction helps a child with ASDVI to become more independent as he or she learns to understand the world better by moving, exploring, and learning to use sensory information. The O&M instructor works with the student and the team to provide instruction that supports the student's ability to gain access to and move independently and safely in his or her environment, providing the positive experiences and fostering the development of skills that are necessary to encourage independent, purposeful movement. Although the O&M specialist will assume primary responsibility for O&M instruction, all members of the educational team need to be actively involved in the design and implementation of an O&M curriculum, since each member has a vital and important role to play. Consistency among team members is critical.

The O&M curriculum that is developed for individual students with ASDVI is as varied as the students themselves. The instructional emphasis areas differ among students, and instruction itself must remain flexible. Furthermore, ongoing assessment is critical. Students' needs, environments, and learning strengths and challenges change. The O&M curriculum must be compatible with the student's present needs and skills and provide for future travel and movement needs. The curriculum itself is *dynamic*, not static.

The child needs to be stimulated to explore his or her surroundings without such advantages as watching movement, lights, interesting sights, or colors that go with daily movement. O&M instruction can give the student with ASDVI the opportunity to have the positive experiences that are necessary to encourage independent movement. Each student needs to learn to interact with his or her environment in order to understand it.

O&M Questionnaire

1. How does the student process and manage sensory information? What are the student's primary distracters?

Sensory Information	Implications for movement and travel; strategies for O&M instruction
Vision	
Auditory	
Touch	
Taste	
Smell	
Movement	

Import information from the Sensory Profile Observation.

2. What are the student's primary motivators, preferences, and interests? How can these motivators be incorporated into O&M instruction?

Student's motivators, preferences, and interests	Strategies for incorporating motivators, preferences, and interests into O&M instruction

Import information from *Reinforcer Development, Learner Interests, Play Interest Survey,* and *Preference Checklist.*

3. What is the student's attention span? Does the student have particular issues or situations that challenge his or her ability to maintain attention? What strategies help increase abilities to maintain attention?

Issues or situations that challenge the student's ability to maintain attention	Strategies for increasing the student's ability to maintain attention and focus

4. How does the student manage and deal with "change"?

Does the student have difficulty dealing with change?	Strategies to assist the student to cope with change or to understand that change will occur
☐ Yes ☐ No If yes, what changes are difficult for the student: ☐ Change in daily schedule ☐ Change in steps/sequences of a routine ☐ Change in adults working with the student ☐ _____ ☐ _____ ☐ _____ ☐ _____ ☐ _____	

5. What are the student's primary strengths and primary challenges? What is the student's primary learning style?

Student's learning style and primary learning medium	Ideas to incorporate the student's learning style and primary learning medium into O&M instruction

Import information from the Profile of Student Learning, Use of Sensory Channels, and General Learning Media Checklist.

6. What are the student's current and future travel needs?

Daily Routines and Anticipated Routines	Current Methods of Travel	Strengths and Difficulties	Instructional Strategies Needed

Task Analysis of Skills Needed

☐ Mobility Skills   ☐ Orientation Skills   ☐ Communication Skills

Steps	Additional Information

O&M Instruction and Collaboration Plan

Strategy	Materials and Equipment Needed
Environmental Adaptation Needed	**Persons Responsible**

Autism Spectrum Disorders and Visual Impairments: Meeting Students' Learning Needs, by Marilyn H. Gense and D. Jay Gense, Copyright © 2005, AFB Press. All rights reserved. This page may be copied for educational use only.

Independent Living Skills

Independent living skills encompass the skills that an individual needs to function as independently as possible, including eating, dressing, toileting, grooming, and personal and home management skills. These skills often pose challenges for students with visual impairments because it can be difficult for them to learn all they need to know without the incidental learning that comes from observing others in day-to-day situations. Most children who are visually impaired need to receive direct instruction in independent living skills using a variety of multisensory approaches. For children with ASDVI, certain areas of living skills have presented particular difficulty—perhaps because of the sensory deficits and sensory overload presented by these areas. In addition, the lack of development in these areas may make school placements more difficult.

With regard to eating, sensitivity to smell, taste, and the texture of food may affect the students' interest in eating and willingness to try a new food, and some children may eat items that are not food (pica). Eating problems may be present at birth or be the result of an experience focused on eating. Sleeping problems or the lack of sleep are another area that has long been associated with ASD. Many children wake up in the middle of the night and wander about the house or wake other members of the household, attempt to open doors and leave, or put themselves in unsafe situations. The threat to safety and the lack of adequate sleep make this a critical issue for students with ASDVI. Similarly, many young children with ASDVI have difficulty learning the toileting routine, perhaps because they have sensory issues;

do not understand the routine, since they have not observed it; or do not respond to the need to go to the bathroom interests in or perseverate on other issues.

These three problems are important to address and may require different strategies from those that are used and to teach other living-skill routines. This chapter focuses on general approaches to addressing skills and instructional strategies for eating, sleeping, and toileting. Additional information on other living skills is included in the Resources section at the back of this book.

GENERAL STRATEGIES FOR APPROACHING INDEPENDENT LIVING SKILLS

The first step in addressing living skills is to assess the individual student to identify his or her current skills and to determine behaviors and skills to be targeted for instruction. It is also important to assess the immediate and future environments in which the student will be interacting. The six questions presented in Chapter 8 for augmenting the assessment of O&M skills also apply to an assessment of independent living skills.

The results of an assessment will provide guidance to the team about where to start. The assessment may be conducted through the following activity offered by Kelly and Smith (2000, p. 575):

> One useful technique for determining a student's level of functioning in activities of independent living is to conduct a comprehensive analysis of a student's daily schedule or an ecological inventory, and in doing so, examine skills that are developmentally appropriate and a natural part of a student's activities. Such an analysis involves observing the environments in which the activities are performed, identifying usual activities, and observing sighted peers to determine the skills needed for participation. . . . The next step is for the teacher of students with visual impairments to conduct a discrepancy analysis of the activities to determine those typically done by children of the same age as the student with a visual impairment and what the student can currently do.

For students with ASDVI, it is essential to provide instruction in the natural environment in which the skills will be used. If the skill is not taught in the naturally occurring setting, a plan must be implemented to ensure that the student is taught to generalize the skills to the settings in which the skill will be used. It is also important for the parents and other members of the educational team to provide opportunities for the student to practice new skills. Assessment must also consider the student's preferred learning medium, since instruction and supports need to reflect these preferences.

SAMPLE TASK ANALYSIS OF EATING SKILLS

Eating Skills (Basic)	Eating Skills (Refined)
1. Locates the spoon on the table	1. Holds the bowl with the left hand
2. Locates the bowl	2. Locates the spoon on the table with the right hand
3. Scoops the food	3. Locates solid food in the bowl with the spoon
4. Eats a bite	4. Scoops the food on the spoon
5. Returns the spoon to the bowl	5. Brings the food to the mouth
6. Scoops the food	6. Puts the food in the mouth
	7. Chews the food
	8. Locates the bowl with the spoon
	9. Locates the solid food in the bowl
	10. Scoops the food on the spoon

Once the target behaviors and skills are identified and the learning medium is established, the team task analyzes the skills and routines to be taught. The extent to which the skills need to be broken down will depend on the student. Begin by breaking the task into reasonable components. As instruction is provided, an analysis of data will help determine if the steps need to be more refined. An example of a simple task analysis that shows basic eating skills and a more refined list of skills appears in the accompanying "Sample Task Analysis of Eating Skills."

For a student with ASDVI, instruction begins by prompting him or her to complete the task correctly. A variety of prompts can be considered, and it is important for the instructor to provide the least amount of prompting required to complete the task correctly and to begin immediately to plan for systematically fading the prompts. When working with a student with ASDVI, it is critical to understand that verbal prompting is the most difficult to fade. Thus, care must be taken to acknowledge when verbal prompts are being used and to fade them as you would any other prompts. As was discussed in Chapter 3, levels of prompts include

- *physical prompts* (such as hand under hand, hand over hand, full or partial prompts, touch prompts, and blocking prompts)

- *verbal prompts* (including restating a verbal direction, making a statement, and reminding the student)

- *modeling prompts* (demonstrating the requested behavior)

- *gestural prompts* (like pointing, tapping, and placing the student's hand beside material)

- *positional prompts* (such as moving a target object closer to the student)

The effective use of prompts helps support a correct response; prevents errors; and ensures that the request, the response, and the consequence are closely aligned. Initial instruction focuses on shaping rough attempts and systematically reinforcing appropriate responses. As the student progresses, more will be expected of him or her before reinforcements are given.

For many students with ASDVI who are developing independent living skills, additional supports (such as include objects, written text, or other reinforcing materials) may be necessary to help them to learn and maintain skills. As was discussed in Chapter 3, the supports for students with autism spectrum disorder are typically referred to as visual supports. For students with ASDVI, it is helpful to consider the supports to be *symbolic,* rather than visual. The symbolic supports are used as prompts during instruction to help to clarify instruction and assist the student to attend, organize, and understand concepts. These supports include the use of objects, tactile graphics, photographs, written language (including large print and braille), videotapes, and audiotapes. The difference between symbolic supports and other prompts is that symbolic supports are not faded, although they may change form (such as moving from an object support to a picture support) and become more refined as skills are learned. The type of symbolic support being used should match the student's primary learning medium. For example, for a student who uses braille, instruction in a morning routine may involve a checklist of steps written in braille that support the teaching. The student with ASDVI will read the first step (one or two keywords or a sentence, depending on the student); the instructor then prompts the student to complete the step correctly.

The instructional strategies discussed in Chapter 3 can be used to teach individual skills (such as tying shoes laces or cooking an egg) or a functional routine (a morning routine for school, cooking breakfast, and cleaning up). A functional routine is the performance of more than one skill in the proper

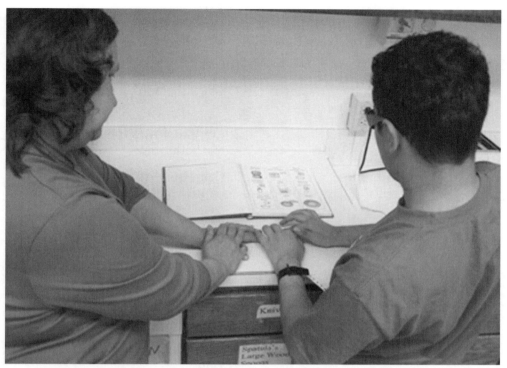

In teaching independent living skills such as cooking, the visual supports typically used for students with autism spectrum disorders may be replaced with symbolic supports for students who are also visually impaired. Here, the steps in making oatmeal are presented in large print, tactile graphics, and braille.

order. The accompanying "Sample Functional Routine: Using the Bathroom" illustrates the activities and steps involved in a typical routine.

EATING

One characteristic that is associated with ASD is the excesses and deficits in sensory responses. This characteristic may be manifest in the area of eating. It is not clear if the difficulty that some students have with eating (such as a hesitancy to touch or taste unfamiliar foods) is a result of tactile defensiveness (an aversion to the textures of food), olfactory infusion (an aversion to strong smells), a combination of the two, or motor problems that are associated with chewing and swallowing.

For students with ASDVI, mealtime and eating can be stressful for both them and their family members. Many children exhibit extreme preferences for one food or refuse foods altogether. As they grow older, they may have difficulty scooping, spearing, and cutting food, perhaps because of tactile

SAMPLE FUNCTIONAL ROUTINE: USING THE BATHROOM

Activities	Steps
1. Notifies the adult of the need to use the bathroom	1. Gains the adult's attention
2. Locates the bathroom	2. Communicates the need to use the bathroom
3. Uses the bathroom appropriately	3. Gains permission to go to the bathroom
4. Washes the hands	4. Locates the bathroom
5. Exits the bathroom	5. Enters through the door
6. Returns to the previous or next location	6. Locates the stall
	7. Unfastens clothing
	8. Pulls clothing down
	9. Voids
	10. Uses toilet paper
	11. Pulls up clothing
	12. Fastens clothing
	13. Flushes the toilet
	14. Exits the stall
	15. Washes hands
	16. Dries hands
	17. Locates the door
	18. Exits the bathroom
	19. Locates the next location

defensiveness with the utensils, difficulty with fine motor manipulations, the lack of a visual model, or a combination of all these factors.

Before the members of the educational team determine which intervention strategies are to be used, they need to collect data on the student's eating patterns, including food preferences, the times the day when the food is eaten, and the types of utensils and dishes that are used (such as metal, plastic, glass, or rubber). Sometimes, the texture of the utensil, rather than the food itself, can be the cause of eating difficulties. It is important to note if the child reacts differently when he or she is given the opportunity to smell or touch the food before he or she puts it in his or her mouth. In addition, it is vital to rule out food allergies, other allergies, dental problems, sore throats, or other potential health-related problems. A great deal of information is available on diet and autism spectrum disorder. (Refer to the Resources section at the back of this book for current information on dietary issues for children with ASD).

Once the information on the student's eating patterns is collected, the team can begin to collaborate on interventions. An occupational therapist who is knowledgeable about feeding issues may be an important part of the team if there are concerns about oral-motor problems. The occupational therapist can also provide recommendations about a variety of strategies that may assist the student in the feeding process. When the eating difficulties are associated with textures and smells, a systematic program must be developed to introduce new foods. In this program, new foods that are similar to preferred foods are introduced first; then slight variations in textures, flavor, odors, and color can be introduced over time. When new foods are introduced, it is important to keep portions small (one or two small bites). New foods can be paired with preferred foods to provide reinforcement for eating. For students with ASDVI, it is far more important to end the meal on a positive note than to force them to stay at the table until everyone else is finished.

If the team determines that some of the eating problems are a result of defensiveness about the eating utensils, a variety of options are available. For example, some students with ASDVI have an aversion to hard plastic. If a food is presented on a utensil that is made of plastic or if a drink is given in a hard plastic cup, these students act like they do not want the food or exhibit challenging behaviors, but when a utensil is changed to metal or the plastic cup is changed to a glass, the students are more cooperative in the eating process. Once a student has established success in the process, plastic utensils and dishes can be systematically introduced, using small steps and small amounts. It is important to include a plan to teach a student to eat in a variety of environments using a variety of utensils, so he or she will be successful at school, at home, and in the community.

It is critical to include the student with ASDVI in the entire meal process because his or her incidental learning will be limited. As is developmentally appropriate, the student should be involved in purchasing food (initially, one or two favorite items) and given an opportunity to have hands-on experience handling and preparing the food. A symbolic support reference (braille, print, large print, tactile symbols, objects, photographs, or audio) can be developed to help the student to understand the concepts that are being taught. For example, a reference can be used for showing a menu of food items that are available, for making choices, for grocery shopping, and for cooking, to name a few. Social Stories (see Chapter 6) and symantic maps or other graphic representations (see Chapter 12) can be used to teach concepts that are related to the eating experiences.

SLEEPING

Children who are visually impaired may have difficulty sleeping because they may be confused between day and night or have not had enough physical activity during the day. Students with ASD may also have trouble sleeping. Some children with ASD are "night roamers," others require less sleep than most typical children, and still others may have undetermined sensory difficulties that impair their ability to sleep. Often, the sleeping problems reflect a combination of factors.

First, the family must address the potential dangers to the child's safety that are involved in the child being awake or awakened during the night. To prevent problems that are associated with wandering the house, modifications can be made to the child's bedroom to ensure the child's safety; even if he or she remains awake in the bedroom, he or she will be in a safe environment. The modifications that are needed will depend on the child's age, vision, skills, and interests. The Autism Society of America (www.autism-society .org/site/PageServer?pagename=livingsafety) offers a number of safety tips to consider, including these:

1. Identify priority areas that require modification (such as the child's bedroom or kitchen).

2. Use locks when appropriate.

3. Safeguard windows.

4. Make electrical outlets and appliances safe (use child safety plugs and cover the outlet).

5. Lock dangerous items away.

6. Safeguard the bath area.

7. Provide identification in case the child gets lost or runs off and is unable to communicate effectively.

If the student with ASDVI has difficulty sleeping because of sensory issues, a number of solutions are possible. It has been noted that individuals with ASD and ASDVI have difficulty with light pressure and with textures of some

FIGURE 9.1	**Nighttime Routine Checklist**
Check as Completed	**Nighttime Routine**
✓	Awake: Stay in room
	Awake: Turn on music
	Awake: Pull up weighted covers
	Awake: Look at a book
	Awake: Play with toys
	Bathroom: Call for help (intercom system)
	Do not leave the room until _7:00_ A.M.

materials and surfaces. Changes in the textures and pressure of bedroom furniture, bedding, and clothing may help these children develop better sleeping patterns. A different bed (such as a waterbed, large beanbag chair, or a hammock) may make a significant difference for some children. Bedding changes include the use of different sheet material, sleeping bags, weighted comforters, and heavy blankets. Sleeping garments that match the child's preference for clothing and weight can be explored. For many children, pajamas that are lightweight may be uncomfortable. Clothes that fit tightly, creating a sense of deep pressure (such as those made of Lycra) may be helpful.

For a child with ASDVI who is calmed by music or sounds, a system that plays music or sounds throughout the night may prove beneficial. However, the parents need to ensure that the child will not become increasingly engaged by the music or become fixated on parts of a song, to the point that he or she loses more sleep or exhibits a behavioral challenge when the parents try to interrupt the behavior. Furthermore, the parents need to make sure that the child does not have access to the system until he or she can appropriately use the equipment.

It may be helpful to develop a nighttime routine that is supported by symbolic references in the child's primary reading medium. The reference can be a checklist of activities and expectations, such as the one presented in Figure 9.1. A talking alarm clock or a large-print clock may be used to help the child understand when it is time to get up. The child can match the time on the checklist to the time on the clock. It is also important to ensure that the child has a mechanism for communicating his or her need for adult assistance during the night and when it is appropriate to request assistance. The mechanism or system that is used will depend on the child's age, skills, and communications systems.

TOILETING

Toilet training can be an area of difficulty for many students with ASDVI. It is often a time-consuming task and requires instructional consistency among all the members of the educational team. A number of skills are involved in the toileting routine, including recognizing the need to go to the toilet, entering the bathroom, pulling down one's pants and underwear, sitting on the toilet, waiting to eliminate, eliminating in the toilet, using toilet paper, pulling one's pants and underwear back up, flushing the toilet, washing one's hands, and drying one's hands. The initial goal may be only to teach eliminating in the toilet. Gradually, instruction in the entire toileting routine can begin. If the student can complete some of the steps already, he or she should be given the opportunity to complete these steps independently.

Children are ready for toilet training at different ages, but whatever the age, a child with ASDVI needs some basic skills (such as the ability to follow simple directions and to sit for five minutes) before toilet training begins. Once it is established that the child is ready to begin training, the child's elimination pattern needs to be established by tracking the times each day that the child wets and soils himself or herself. Typically, it takes a minimum of two weeks to establish the child's pattern. A form, such as the one presented in Figure 9.2, can be used to establish an elimination pattern.

Schedule training is the easiest approach to assist children with ASDVI to eliminate in the toilet. In schedule training, a child is told when to go to the bathroom and goes when he or she is placed on the toilet. Typically, the child is taught to go every 90 minutes or at intervals that are suggested by the elimination pattern. In this training, the child is taught to wait until he or she is taken to the toilet. Schedule training still involves the child being dependent on the adult to send him or her to the bathroom, on the basis of the data that have been collected on the child's pattern of elimination. If the child starts going to the bathroom independently during this process, the behavior should be immediately reinforced.

For many children, another step in the routine is required to develop independence: They must be able to move from locations throughout the house or classroom to the bathroom. Thus, it may be helpful for the O&M instructor to be involved in teaching a child various routes to the bathroom. When it is time for a scheduled visit, take the child to the toilet. Reinforce

FIGURE 9.2 Toileting/Elimination Schedule

Student _____ Date _____

Time of Check	Monday	Tuesday	Wednesday	Thursday	Friday	Saturday	Sunday

the child for good sitting and voiding. If the child has not voided after 5 minutes, remove the child from the toilet and take him or her back to the toilet 30 minutes sooner than is scheduled. If the child has an accident, have him or her help clean it up and then practice going from the accident point to the toilet. It is important to remain calm. It is recommended that once schedule training begins, diapers should no longer be used when the child is awake.

Once the child is schedule trained, begin to increase the time between trips to the toilet. Instead of placing the child on the toilet, put a chair near the toilet at the scheduled time, show the child the relationship between the toilet and the chair, and have the child sit on the chair. The goal is for the child to move to the toilet independently. If it is necessary to prompt the child, immediately work to fade the prompt. As the child becomes successful, move the chair farther and farther from the toilet.

There are other options for more intensive toilet training. One process requires an extreme commitment because it is time consuming. In this intensive training procedure, the child is placed on the toilet, given favorite liquids, and reinforced for sitting and heavily reinforced for eliminating. Once the child is successful, the child is moved to a chair that is place farther and farther from the toilet. For a child who is blind, it is essential to show him or her the relationship between the toilet and the chair. It is also important to ensure that the child has the independent mobility skills to move from the chair to the toilet.

Another approach is to use symbolic supports to help the child with ASDVI understand all the steps that are needed to learn the skill. To use this approach, the steps in the toileting process must be analyzed (generically or specifically, depending on the child's skills). The next step is to match the steps to a system to let the child know the sequence for completing the task. The system will reflect the child's primary learning medium (a braille list, an object/tactile system, an auditory output device, or pictures). In addition to the system for teaching the task, a symbol (braille, print, picture, object, or auditory) can be placed on the child's schedule to initiate the routine.

As with all tasks, it is important to teach a communication system to indicate the need to go to the bathroom and to ensure that the child has sufficient mobility skills to move from various locations to the bathroom independently. The O&M instructor can work with the team and the student to plan routes that are efficient and that promote independence.

SUMMARY

In this chapter, three critical living skills for students with ASDVI were highlighted. These are by no means all the living skills that need to be addressed. Students need instruction in dressing, bathing, grooming, and eventually cooking and cleaning. The key to addressing these areas is to break down each skill into concrete, teachable steps that match the student's level of functioning. For example, a higher-level student may need a checklist of the different chores that need to be completed each day, whereas low-level student may need step-by-step instructions for each chore. The key is to make sure that the instruction matches the student's learning style.

Career Education

10

Career education, career exploration, and career development should be a vital part of the curriculum of students with ASDVI from an early age. Unemployment and underemployment are significant problems for adults with visual impairments, as well as adults with autism spectrum disorder. For students with the dual impairment of autism spectrum disorder and visual impairment, the challenges are exacerbated.

Career education and career exploration for students with ASDVI should begin in preschool and continue throughout the school years. These students must have direct, hands-on experience with all facets of productive living and employment skills that are needed in adulthood.

Temple Grandin, an associate professor of animal science at Colorado State University, is a renowned author and speaker. She also is an individual with ASD, and writes about what it takes for an individual with ASD to be successful in the world of work (see Grandin & Duffy, 2004; Grandin & Scariano, 1994). Grandin believes that there should be a gradual transition from the educational setting to the employment setting for people with ASD. She also thinks that career planning can, and should, begin early and can begin by considering the student's childhood fixations, obsessions, and interests. Many people with ASD, such as Gaby, have used such an interest as the basis for a career.

Gaby, a 14 year old with ASDVI, loves paper. As a child, she would find small pieces of paper and flick them against her skin or her lips and sometimes in front of her eyes. These behaviors continued throughout her adolescence. The educational team who worked with Gaby brainstormed various jobs that could incorporate her unique fascination with paper. Eventually, Gaby obtained supported employment in a county government office, where she shreds documents. She learned her job quickly and enjoys her work.

Career education is not limited to employment. It must also include instruction in the skills that are necessary to function at levels of independence and interdependence that match the individual's strengths, interests, and skills. As was discussed in previous chapters, students with ASDVI are particularly challenged in the areas of communication and social skills. Therefore, in addition to specific job-related skills, it is imperative that these students are taught the communication, social relationship, and organizational skills that are necessary to function in a work environment. The individualized career education curricula must also incorporate the daily living, problem-solving, and O&M skills that are necessary for success in adulthood. The failure to acquire these skills can lead to difficulties on the job, as the case of Joe illustrates.

Joe, a young man with Asperger syndrome and limited vision, had a strong interest in computers and video technology since childhood. After he graduated from high school, he completed a two-year course of study to obtain certification in the development of software for computer games. His expertise in software design quickly led to his full-time employment with a technology firm. Despite his talents, Joe had a difficult time at work. His limited communication and social skills led to daily frustrations. Joe was not interested in interacting with his colleagues and wanted to talk only about his limited interests. He assumed that his skills surpassed those of his colleagues and he did not understand why he was not immediately promoted to a management-level position. Joe also did not understand why he could not maintain his "typical sleep patterns" and report for work whenever he wished. His rationale was based on his limited perspective that he knew he was more productive when he was not awakened by an alarm clock and that he should sleep until he awoke naturally, regardless of the time. Although Joe had the technical skills required for his job, his communication and social challenges ultimately led to his decision to resign after three months of employment.

As the team begins long-range planning, it will be important to consider the level of *independence* and *interdependence* that the student seeks. Independence suggests that an individual is the only person responsible for all aspects of daily life, while interdependence defines situations in which the individual does some things independently but requires support and assistance with others (Wolffe, 1998).

A student's interests and skills can be used to support career education. This student, who enjoys using his proficient braille skills, is gaining work-related experience by creating braille overlays for certificates given to the players in a goal ball tournament.

In preschool, career education activities are incorporated as children learn to be responsible for their basic care, to follow directions, to perform basic organizational tasks, and to "pretend-play" adult situations. All these skills are precursors to the development of the skills that are necessary for adult living. During the elementary school years, students continue to learn to follow more complex directions, to work individually and in a group, and to organize materials, to engage with peers and adults, to manage simple household chores, to develop communication skills, to identify workers in the community, and to develop problem-solving strategies and skills.

Middle school and high school students with ASDVI must learn to become increasingly more responsible for themselves and should begin to pursue more formal career-related activities. Skills that are addressed at this level include the organization of time; participation in volunteer and paid work activities; the development of specific career interests; and the generalized skills that are associated with understanding work duties, refining of social skills and building social relationships, expanding communication skills, engaging in job-shadowing experiences, acquiring interviewing skills, and writing résumés.

TRANSITION PLANNING

Students with ASDVI typically need extended time to develop the skills that are needed to be successful in adulthood. Thus, it is critical to begin early to teach these skills and to continue to evaluate and refine instruction as the students gain new skills. In the United States, the Individuals with Disabilities Education Act requires educational teams to begin transition planning activities for students by age 14. For most students with ASDVI, the transition planning and instruction should begin much earlier. Indeed, a team would be wise to consider transition planning at the time of the initial evaluation of the student, as the student's interests and learning styles are being identified. This information will be vital for building a foundation of planning activities and instruction that will used from that point forward.

In planning for the transition from school to work, the team needs to assess the student's potential career interests. Several tools can provide additional information to help the team, including the Career Assessment Inventory (Johansson, 2002), the McCarron-Dial Evaluation System (1986), and the Career Occupational Preference System (Knapp & Knapp, 1995) (contact information for each is included in the Resources section at the back of this book). Each of these tools can provide valuable information to the team.

PERSON-CENTERED PLANNING AND MAPS

Additional information can be obtained through what has been termed person-centered planning, a process for helping the student and the team plan for the future (Garner & Dietz, 1996). Person-centered planning addresses an individual's strengths, interests, and hopes for the future in the areas of work, leisure activities, residence, and social skills and relationships.

One tool that has been used successfully as part of person-centered planning is McGill Action Planning System (MAPS) (Forest & Lusthaus, 1989; Forest & Pearpoint, 1992). MAPS is a problem-solving collaborative team approach to the design of an IEP that addresses postschool outcomes for the student, including career planning, through the implementation of an action plan. Although there are variations of MAPS, at least four questions each team members has to consider during the MAPS process:

1. What are the student's strengths?

2. What are the student's needs?

3. What dreams do you have for the student?

4. What are your fears for the student?

Using the MAPS process, all the team members respond to these questions. Each team member's response is important because it helps to portray the student to the best advantage and brings the student's abilities, rather than deficits, into focus. Ultimately, the team uses the information obtained from the responses to these questions to develop specific follow-up plans that address the student's needs, and fears identified while building on the student's strengths and dreams. Each plan identifies who will do what, when, and where in a specific area.

Figure 10.1 presents an example of one team's responses to these four questions about Garth, a high school student with ASDVI. The responses were used to identify goals for Garth's IEP that addressed the identified needs and fears and targeted strengths and dreams.

Students with ASDVI and their families will need the support of the community to assist in the transition from school to adulthood. For students who are not ready to manage all aspects of adult living by themselves, a "Friends of" club may be of great assistance. A "Friends of" club is comprised of individuals (such as family members, former teachers, friends, college students, or community volunteers), identified by the student and his or her parents, who are interested in providing some level of support to the student. The "Friends of" club ideas can be incorporated into the student's IEP, with the areas in which the student may need assistance (such as grocery shopping, budgeting, bill paying, leisure outings, house cleaning, and transportation) and the "Friends of" the student who can provide the necessary support identified. Using a monthly calendar, the "Friends of" the student gather to determine what level of help they can provide. Some may volunteer for a weekly project, others may volunteer for once-a-month activities, and still others may simply fill in occasionally when another friend cannot help out. The student and his or her parents fill in the calendar (using the student's primary learning mode). The student can then follow the schedule noted on the calendar. The following case example depicts Dan's experience with his "Friends of" club.

FIGURE 10.1

Educational Team's Responses During a MAPS Process for Garth

Student's Strengths

- Likes anything to do with music
- Can learn to imitate any song or passage
- Is friendly
- Likes to be around others
- Loves cars
- Identifies car models by the sound
- Is a good auditory learner
- Has a supportive family

Student's Needs

- Needs to find work involving music
- Needs to learn to travel on the bus to the community leisure center
- Needs to develop a "Friends of Garth" support group
- Needs to learn to hire a driver
- Needs to locate a supported apartment setting in which to live
- Needs to learn to plan for and cook simple meals
- Needs assistance with money management

Dreams

- Wants to be a singer
- Wants to live in his own home close to his family
- Wants to have friends
- Wants to have support to manage money
- Wants to have public transportation available
- Wants to have a place to go every day, even if not a job

Fears

- Will not find work
- Will be isolated
- Will need to live at home even as an adult
- Will not be safe in the community
- Will miss appropriate leisure activities

After he completed his school program, Dan continued to live at home. His parents wanted to change their role in Dan's life as Dan entered adulthood even though he was living at home. Dan had his own bedroom, living room, and bathroom and shared the family kitchen. He was responsible for preparing his own meal and for performing his daily routines and exercise routine. Dan's parents assisted him with transportation (either drove him or made arrangements for other transportation) to and from the community college that he attended and the grocery store. The Commission for the Blind assisted in developing a volunteer work-social experience. Other members of the "Friends of Dan" club, which included adults in his neighborhood, former teachers, extended family members, and friends, arranged for the following activities for Dan:

- *swimming (once a week)*

- *participation in an evening community activity (once a month)*

- *workout sessions at the local fitness center (three times a week)*

- *transportation to piano lessons (twice a month)*

- *reading mail (once a week)*

- *telephone calls to "chat" (twice a week)*

Dan's calendar is updated each month. Through this process, Dan has a variety of community contacts that provide the support he needs to continue and expand his rich and fulfilling life as active adult.

A "Friends of" club can be as creative as it needs to be to meet the student's individual needs. The needs certainly will change as the student continues to settle into adulthood.

Because many students have difficulty with social and communication skills, it may be difficult to demonstrate their skills. In these instances, a video résumé may be particularly beneficial because it can provide a mechanism to illustrate the student's skills to potential employers and landlords. The video résumé can depict the student functioning in a variety of environments and situations and performing specific tasks.

SETTING REALISTIC EXPECTATIONS

In career planning for students with ASDVI, it is critical for the educational team to set realistic expectations and demands. Not every student will work full time, and some may not even have paid jobs; whatever level of employment is appropriate, however, it still is important to state clearly to both the student and the potential employer how the student is currently functioning.

For example, if a student can maintain focus on a task for only 15 minutes at a time without a break, the student should not be put in a situation in which he or she is expected to work for several hours without a break. At the same time, care must be taken to ensure that the employer gives the student clear, honest, and accurate feedback on the work that he or she has completed. A student with ASDVI who is repeatedly told that he or she is doing a "great job" at a particular skill may interpret this statement to mean that his or her skills are better than those of other employees when the employer actually means that the student is merely doing the job in the expected manner. Because many students with ASDVI are very literal in their interpretation of language, it is important to be clear and honest about performance. As is the case in all the other areas of instruction, the student may need a concrete system to identify what is expected, such as a checklist of tasks, a timer to signify breaks, or a schedule for each segment of the day.

The members of the educational team need to observe potential jobs to identify all the skills that are required to be successful in any given situation. During the observation, they need to note both the specific skills of the job and the types of social interactions that are needed to be successful. For example, if employees are expected to leave the work area during lunchtime and breaks, the student will need to be taught the skill and be given an opportunity to practice it. The O&M instructor may be involved to ensure that the student is able to navigate the work environment.

SUMMARY

The most vital component of career education is planning. The team needs to help make sure that each student enters the job situation with all the skills that he or she needs to be successful, not just the ability to perform a particular task. Career planning is a partnership among the student; the teachers and family members, who have in-depth knowledge of the student; the transition specialist, who knows the potential jobs; and the employer, who knows which tasks need to be performed. Together, these partners identify all the skills that are required for a job, break down the job into manageable teaching steps, and teach the student the steps on the job.

Recreation and Leisure 11

Recreational and leisure activities include physical, cultural, artistic, and social interests in which an individual engages during his or her free time. Typically, people tend to select such activities by viewing them, exploring options, trying different activities, and determining those they would like to pursue. Many students with ASDVI have limited skills in this area, limited or narrow areas of interest, and often little interest in trying new activities. Thus, the educational team will be challenged to explore and expand a student's skills.

For students with ASDVI, a wide array of experiences in leisure and recreational activities must be provided. As with all individuals, it is important to remember that not everyone enjoys the same things or wants to participate in the same way. Understanding the individual with ASDVI and providing experiences that match, and ultimately expand, his or her interests are the keys to developing appropriate recreational and leisure interests. It requires creativity and flexibility on everyone's part to make it happen.

Students should be exposed to a wide variety of recreational and leisure skills to help them select activities that are of the greatest interest to them, and to identify activities that can be shaped to match the students' interests. To begin, the educational team needs to complete an assessment of a student's use of free-time activities and recreational and leisure skills. These skills bring together several areas of the curriculum for students with ASDVI, including communication skills, social skills, O&M skills, organizational skills, and independent living skills, so the student's abilities and strengths in each will need to be considered. Careful planning is required to orchestrate and coordinate recreational and leisure activities so that the student can be involved in the selection, planning, and implementation of the activities.

EXAMINING INTERESTS AND SKILLS

For many students with ASDVI, preferred recreational and leisure interests may not be apparent. In this case, family members may have interests and participate in activities that they would like to pursue with or for the child. Therefore, in assessing a student's interests, the team may find it helpful also to assess the family members' interests.

Leisure activities may include

- listening to the radio, records, audiotapes, and CDs
- reading books and magazines
- watching movies and descriptive videos
- engaging in hobbies or crafts
- playing board games (including tactile and enlarged-format games)
- attending sporting events
- attending cultural events
- attending social events
- playing card games
- playing electronic games
- playing musical instruments
- playing with toys

Recreational activities may include

- gardening
- ball games (including beep ball and goal ball)
- skating
- bowling
- playing golf, miniature and regular
- cycling (on a tricycle, tandem bike, side-by-side bike, stationary bicycle, or regular bicycle)

Students will benefit from systematic introduction of new leisure activities when instruction provides enough support to allow them to overcome their fears of new experiences. This student has learned to enjoy the tactile sensations of playing with clay.

- running (with a guide or on a treadmill)

- hiking

- swimming

- skiing

Organizations with appropriate recreational activities include

- YMCA (www.ymca.net)

- YWCA (www.ywca.org)

- The ARC (www.thearc.org)

- United States Association of Blind Athletes (www.usaba.org)

- Easter Seals (www.easterseals.com)

- Special Olympics (www.specialolympics.org)

Local fitness clubs are another good resource.

The options are seemingly endless, and the members of the team can be creative in considering the student's and family's interests to develop recreational and leisure activities. It may be necessary to modify or adapt a game or activity to accommodate the student's visual impairment. For example, it is important to give the student an opportunity to learn the preliminary skills that are needed to perform a recreational or leisure activity before the student participates in a group. These points are illustrated in the following case examples of Derek and Julie:

> *Derek wants to learn to play goal ball, but he has difficulty following the sound of the rolling ball when other students are present during instruction. Derek's teacher breaks down the steps that are needed to catch and roll the ball and then systematically teaches Derek all these steps. Once Derek learns these preliminary skills, the teacher instructs him in the group aspects of the game.*

> *Julie wants to participate with the group but is not interested in actually playing goal ball. She can still learn to participate by being involved in other aspects of the game. For example, Julie likes time, numbers, and keeping things organized, so instead of being taught to play the game, she is taught to run the time clock and keep score. Julie's interests and perseverations serve as an opportunity to participate in the game.*

The student may need opportunities to be oriented to the materials and the environment (such as the boundaries for a game of kickball). Rules for games can be written in the student's primary learning medium (such as braille or large print). In addition, checklists or other accommodations can be made if the student needs a symbol system (such as a raised-line spinner or large-print pictures of the steps to follow when playing Uno to support his or her learning.

Students with ASDVI may not be naturally motivated to participate in recreational and leisure activities other than the activities that have become a focus for them (for example, a student who has an extreme interest in trains does not want to talk about or try other activities). Thus, the educational team, including the family members, need to determine the components of the student's interests and explore other recreational and leisure activities that have similar components, so the student's interests and options for activities can be expanded, as was done with Mike:

> *Mike, a braille reader with an autism spectrum disorder, enjoyed the facts listed on baseball and basketball cards. In his free time, he would work with*

a peer to braille the information on each card. Mike would then read the information and share it with adults he encountered because many of his peers were not as interested in the information as he was. To expand his leisure activities beyond the cards, the team decided to braille the directions to several board games that students his age enjoyed. Mike did not enjoy playing games, but he actively participated by reading the rules, keeping track of the participants' score, and conversing with the students who were playing the game. Mike's enjoyment of reading facts allowed him to participate in his own way in a leisure activity with others.

ASSESSMENT OF INTERESTS

Two helpful assessment and planning tools are included in *Developing Leisure Time Skills for Persons with Autism: A Practical Approach for Home, School, and Community* (Coyne, Nyberg, & Vandenburg, 1999). First, using the Leisure Observation Sheet (see Figure 11.1 and the blank version at the end of the chapter), the evaluator sets up the recreational area using at least six items that provide for different types of use and interaction. Interactions can include table activities (table games or card games), physical activities, and solitary activities. The evaluator begins by orienting the student with ASDVI to the setting and to the location of the materials and activities. The student is then told that during this free time, she or he may choose how to use the time and the materials within this environment. The evaluator observes the student's behavior and records the results using the Leisure Observation Sheet. Three areas are coded: social level, social interactions, and involvement in the activity. Observations of the student continue for two to six days to obtain a clear picture of the student's abilities and levels of involvement. Using the information from the Leisure Observation Sheet, the team can plan the appropriate level to begin instruction and offer opportunities for participation.

Second, the tool Natural Settings and Resources for Activities (see Figure 11.2 and the blank version at the end of this chapter) can be used to provide a community-referenced list of age-appropriate activities and to identify natural settings in which the activities are performed. The team begins by identifying potential age-appropriate activities for the individual and then investigates where activities may be available in different settings within the school, home, and community. This form and ensuing activities assist the team members, including the family, to collaborate in an effort to identify, provide opportunities for, and teach leisure and recreational skills.

The team will need to task analyze the activity to identify all the skills that the student will need to learn to participate in the activity successfully.

FIGURE 11.1

DIRECTIONS FOR LEISURE OBSERVATION SHEET

Preparation

Set up a recreational area with at least six items that provide an opportunity for different types of use and interaction. For example, a magazine would provide an opportunity for solitary activity, whereas a ball would provide an opportunity for social interaction. The area should be arranged so that different types of activities, such as table activities and physical activity, can occur.

Explain that this is free time and that the individual can do what she or he wants in that area. Avoid direct participation in an activity unless involvement is requested by the individual.

Recording Information

After an adjustment period of at least five minutes, observations of behaviors are recorded on the Leisure Observation Sheet in four consecutive five-minute periods. A timer can signal the five-minute intervals. Initially, four to six days of observations are often necessary to get adequate information. Three areas are covered in coding: social level, social interactions, and activity involvement.

Place a mark under the appropriate social level during each five-minute interval using the following coding system.

Watches Others: Exhibits no behavior other than as an onlooker, is aware of others and is observing them

No Activity: "unengaged" behaviors, such as staring into space, or self-stimulation, such as rocking; no contact with an external object or another person

Plays Alone: Plays alone with an object that is different from those used by peers within close proximity

Plays Beside Peers: Approximates the action of one or more peers, but does not interact

Interacts with Peers: Interacts with peers doing the same or a similar activity; includes borrowing or lending equipment

Engages in Cooperative Play: Mutually interacts with peers in doing an activity; activity can not continue without cooperation (such as playing catch or checkers)

Record all social interactions during each five-minute interval under the Social Interactions section of the Leisure Observation Sheet. Describe the materials that were selected and how they are used.

FIGURE 11.1 continued

Sample Leisure Observation Sheet for Chris

Code Behaviors for Four Consecutive Five-Minute Periods during Unstructured Time

Name: Chris

Date: January 2004

Time: 2:00

School: Bush Elementary

Observer: R. Jackson

	Social Level							Social Interactions								Describe activity (object involved, other people involved, place, behavior, etc.)
	Watches Others	No Activity	Plays Alone	Plays Beside Peers	Interacts with Peers in Play	Engages in Cooperative Activity	Interacts with Adults Only	No Response to Adult	No Response to Peers	Responds to Adult	Responds to Peer	Initiates to Adult	Initiates to Peer	Continues to Interact with Adult	Continues to Interact with Peer	
	X		X	X			X			X		X		X		Ran over to Music area, picked up CD player, wanted to know how it worked. Repeatedly asked questions about how it worked. Turned it on and off.
	X			X			X					X				Moved to area where other peers were playing a game of Connect Four. He watched from the periphery but didn't attempt to interact.
	X			X		X				X	X	X		X		Put on roller skates with other students. Skated around with others but was constantly talking about how to skate rather than just skating. Has excellent balance.
	X			X		X				X	X	X				Continued to skate, didn't want to stop. Talked to adults but not to other students.

(continued on next page)

Source: Reprinted with permission from P. Coyne, C. Nyberg, and M. L. Vandenburg, *Developing Leisure Time Skills for Persons with Autism.* Copyright © 1999, Future Horizons, Arlington, TX.

FIGURE 11.1 continued

Sample Leisure Observation Sheet for Tommy

Code Behaviors for Four Consecutive Five-Minute Periods during Unstructured Time

Name: Tommy
Date: May 17, 2004
Time: 10:00 am
School: OSB
Observer: R. Jackson

Social Level							Social Interactions								Describe activity (object involved, other people involved, place, behavior, etc.)
Watches Others	No Activity	Plays Alone	Plays Beside Peers	Interacts with Peers in Play	Engages in Cooperative Activity	Interacts with Adults Only	No Response to Adult	No Response to Peers	Responds to Adult	Responds to Peer	Initiates to Adult	Initiates to Peer	Continues to Interact with Adult	Continues to Interact with Peer	
NA		X							X						Swing, rocking chair, board game, CD player, and balls available. Three students and two staff are in the room. Student was oriented to all options and then told to play. Student is totally blind. He finds a rocking chair and immediately sits and rocks.
NA		X													Continues rocking without any acknowledgment that others are present.
NA		X													Rocking and vocalizing; not interested in trying anything else.
NA		X													Continues to rock, vocalizing.

Source: Reprinted with permission from P. Coyne, C. Nyberg, and M. L. Vandenburg, *Developing Leisure Time Skills for Persons with Autism.* Copyright © 1999, Future Horizons, Arlington, TX.

FIGURE 11.2 — Sample Natural Settings and Resources for Activities Form

Leisure Activities	School				Community						Home	
	Break/Between Classes	Recess	Extracurricular	Elective Classes/Specials	Parks/Playgrounds	Recreation Programs	Community Pool	Community Colleges	Clubs/Organizations	Commercial Recreation	Outside	Inside
Swinging	X	X			X						X	
Bike riding				X	X	X			X	X	X	X
Walking	X	X		X	X	X			X		X	
Swimming			X	X	X	X	X	X		X	X	X
Bowling				X		X		X		X		X
Listen to music	X	X	X		X						X	X
Table games		X			X	X			X		X	
Treadmill		X		X				X		X		X
Roller skating		X		X	X	X				X	X	X
Concerts			X					X		X	X	X

Source: Reprinted with permission from P. Coyne, C. Nyberg, and M. L. Vandenburg, *Developing Leisure Time Skills for Persons with Autism.* Copyright © 1995, Future Horizons, Arlington, TX.

An example of a task-analysis form for this purpose is included in Figure 11.3 (a blank Task Analysis Data Sheet appears at the end of this chapter). The individual skills then need to be taught systematically.

BENEFITS OF RECREATION

Recreational and leisure skills are an important part of any curriculum for students with ASDVI. With careful and creative planning, the development of a student's skills in this core curriculum area and many of the other areas can be enhanced and can provide opportunities for the functional application of many of the student's skills. By breaking skills down into small components, the team can convert a leisure activity into an enjoyable recreational pursuit. As each component is mastered, a new skill develops that can be used to enhance the day-to-day life of a student with ASDVI. Project Autism of the University of North Carolina's Department of Recreation and Leisure Studies, has developed the *Project Autism Guidelines Manual* (2001). The following is a partial list of the benefits that people with autism spectrum disorder can derive from participating in recreational activities, derived from that manual and from Coyle, Kinney, Riley, and Shank (1991).

- to expand interests (to learn new activities and try new things)

- to develop/improve communication skills (to increase skills in conversation, assertion, cooperation, and competition using recreation)

- to explore or expand knowledge (to learn more and be more aware of what is available)

- to improve cognitive functioning (to increase skills, such as decision making, problem solving, attention span, and strategy)

- to be with, interact with, and build friendships with others (to be able to meet new people and learn the skills to interact with them)

- to be able to make leisure choices (to learn to select which activity the individual would like to do)

- to help others and be able to contribute to the home and community (to volunteer or engage in other activities to provide for others)

- to enhance self-control (to learn how to participate in favorite activities and perhaps use them to help calm)

- to follow rules, directions, and procedures (to learn how to get along within specific boundaries)

FIGURE 11.3

Task Analysis Data Sheet

Student: Jacob

Skill/Activity: Working out at Jerry's Gym fitness club

Steps	Date			
	2/12	2/19	3/1	
Travel to corner of 5th and Main to catch bus #4	I	I	I	
Travel on bus to Jerry's Gym	I	I	I	
Travel from bus stop to gym location	V	V	I	
Locate locker room	V	V	V	
Change into workout clothes	I	I	I	
Travel from locker room to weight room	PP	PP	V	
Complete weight circuit—2 reps on each of 5 machines	V	M	V	
Travel to treadmill; use for 20 minutes	V	M	M	
Return to locker room to shower and change	V	V	V	
Travel from gym to bus stop	V	V	I	
Catch bus #4 return route	I	I	I	
Get off bus at 5th and Main	I	I	I	
Walk home	I	I	I	

PROMPT CODE:

I — Independent
P — Total physical
PP — Partial physical
V — Verbal
M — Model
O — Other

- to gain others' respect (to gain positive reinforcement from performing new activities)

- to enjoy completing and mastering things (to provide a sense of accomplishment)

- to improve physical functioning (to refine gross and fine motor skills through recreational activities)

- to keep in shape physically (to increase physical fitness through physical recreation activities)

- to relax physically and emotionally (to use the recreational activities to help calm and relax during times of anxiety)

- to learn and improve coping skills (to relieve anxiety, stress, and tension using recreational activities)

- to heighten self-awareness and self-esteem (to feel a sense of accomplishment, independence, and pride)

- to promote integration in the community (to increase age-appropriate choices, behavior, and participation in the community)

- to increase satisfaction with life

SUMMARY

Educators, parents, and members of the community must assist students with ASDVI to identify opportunities for engaging in recreational and leisure activities in their areas of interest; to locate where these opportunities exist at home, at school, and in the community; to break down the skills that are needed to participate in each leisure activity; to teach the student systematically how to perform the activity; to incorporate other essential skills into the leisure activity (communication, independent living skills, and O&M skills); and to provide the support necessary to participate on a regular basis.

Leisure Observation Sheet

Code Behaviors for Four Consecutive Five-Minute Periods during Unstructured Time

Name:

Date:

Time:

School:

Observer:

Describe activity (object involved, other people involved, place, behavior, etc.)

Social Level							Social Interactions											
Watches Others	No Activity	Plays Alone	Plays Beside Peers	Interacts with Peers in Play	Engages in Cooperative Activity	Interacts with Adults Only	No Response to Adult	No Response to Peers	Responds to Adult	Responds to Peer	Initiates to Adult	Initiates to Peer	Continues to Interact with Adult	Continues to Interact with Peer			

Source: Reprinted with permission from P. Coyne, C. Nyberg, and M. L. Vandenburg, *Developing Leisure Time Skills for Persons with Autism*. Copyright © 1999, Future Horizons, Arlington, TX.

Natural Settings and Resources for Activities

Leisure Activities	School				Community						Home	
	Break/Between Classes	Recess	Extracurricular	Elective Classes/Specials	Parks Development			Community Colleges	Clubs/Organizations	Commercial Recreation	Outside	Inside
					Parks/Playgrounds	Recreation Programs						

Task Analysis Data Sheet

Student: _____

Skill/Activity: _____

Steps	Date			

PROMPT CODE:

I   — Independent
P   — Total physical
PP — Partial physical
V   — Verbal
M — Model
O — Other

Classroom Supports

12

The members of the educational teams, including parents, are responsible not only for *what* services are incorporated into each student's IEP, but *where* these services are provided. Many students with ASDVI participate in the typical academic curriculum and receive specialized instruction and supports in the regular classroom environment, alongside their classmates without disabilities. Other students may be served in the regular education classroom, but work only partially on typical academic course work and receive instruction that is designed to meet their special needs. Still other students' programs focus on an adaptive, life skills curriculum; academic course work is provided at a more fundamental or basic level, if at all.

Students with ASD are often challenged in participating successfully in a general education classroom, not because they are not capable to do the work, but because some of their unique learning characteristics make it difficult for them to understand what is expected of them, to apply the information they have learned, and to deal with the pace of instruction as most children do. Successful inclusion in the general education classroom is often dependent on a student's ability to understand what is happening in the classroom and what is expected of him or her, and to know what to do next.

Students with ASD, including those with ASDVI, can and do learn to succeed in environments alongside their nondisabled peers. Given that students with autism spectrum disorder obtain, retain, and use information in unique and seemingly unusual ways, it is easy to understand why they often struggle with typical classroom instruction and the methods that are used to deliver that instruction. Supports and strategies must be developed and implemented to assist the educational team in including these students to the maximum extent possible. All types of students will benefit from the use of the supports and strategies discussed here—supports that will help them to make sense of the classroom environment and to understand the changing activities, lessons, and events. Successful, active participation is possible with appropriate instruction and support.

IDENTIFYING CHALLENGES

With regard to the appropriate use of classroom support, the team needs to begin by considering and identifying the learning characteristics that can impede success in the classroom environment. By understanding these characteristics and identifying the specific characteristics that apply to a given student, the team will be better able to implement strategies and supports that help the student to compensate for the disability. Understanding and identifying "why" a behavior exists is critical to developing strategies for addressing it. Some of the more common behaviors or learning characteristics that may be seen in students with ASD include

- a focus on extraneous or insignificant details (such as difficulty perceiving what is relevant and what is not when reading or listening to "lecture" material)

- not knowing where to start a task or when a task is completed and hence appearing not to be paying attention

- not knowing when to ask for help, how to ask for help, or what to do when "stuck"

- being overwhelmed with the fast-paced flow of instruction in a typical classroom environment and hence experiencing "sensory overload" and "shutting down"

- being highly distractible (for example, being side-tracked by various sensory stimuli or off-task because of an intrusive thought or a remark by another person)

- having difficulty generalizing information

- exhibiting an extraordinary ability to learn or memorize some information quickly (such facts and written materials) but having great difficulty applying the information functionally—an ability that may be deceiving if the assumption of understanding is based solely on the ability to repeat or verbalize the information

- exhibiting seemingly contradictory levels of abilities across the curriculum (for example, being a mathematics wiz but not being able to make sense of the simplest story problems in math, or to compute simple change when making a purchase or being able to recite verbatim a short story read days ago but not being able to identify the main character in the story or explain the plot)

- having difficulty with incidental learning (being unable to "pick up on" concepts or issues that are being discussed)

- struggling with or being unable to perceive the social nuances of peers and adults

- needing a longer time to process directions or guidelines and additional supports to do so

These challenges are often exaggerated in students who are also visually impaired, since these students may easily miss the visual and social cues on which most students rely to provide important and ongoing information related to the content and flow of instruction. A careful assessment of a student's learning style and learning challenges is essential because as misinterpretations of these learning characteristics can lead to a misunderstanding of the student's abilities and intentions. Consider the following examples:

Simon is assigned a task, but sits quietly and appears inattentive or uninterested. The teacher may assume that he is not paying attention or is ignoring the assignment. In reality, Simon is paying attention and is ready to begin, but simply does not know where to start, He does not have a strategy to ask for help, and he does not understand what to do to begin.

Melissa never turns in her homework. The teacher assumes that she simply is not completing her work. In fact, Melissa completed all her homework and has it in her backpack, but because she interprets language literally, she believes that she has met the teacher's expectations because the teacher said, "Do all your homework," not "Do all your homework and turn it in tomorrow."

Without the provision of simple but necessary support systems, a student may fail, may experience frustration, or may simply "shut down." The team must try to understand how the student perceives a situation and interprets the others' expectations of him or her through an ongoing assessment of the student's ability to process, sequence, and implement a given set of instructions. This information will allow the team to develop and implement appropriate educational programs and supports for the student that help the student better manage the environment, to relieve potential stress and anxiety, and facilitate learning.

ORGANIZING THE ENVIRONMENT

Students with ASDVI will benefit from the team's consideration of three broad areas of organization in designing a program that best facilitates learning:

- organization of space

- organization of activities

- organizational supports and strategies

Organization of Space

When objects, materials, supplies, and utensils magically "appear" and "disappear" to a student with ASDVI without accompanying explanations, the opportunity to understand and make sense of the world is drastically reduced. The location in which a task is performed, as well as all the materials that are associated with the task, need to be organized so that the student can find them easily. It is important for the team to design places for performing different kinds of tasks and to organize the materials that are needed for each task organized and clearly mark them in the student's preferred learning medium (print, braille objects, pictures or auditory device). In addition, the student must have clear access to the materials and be able to move easily around the materials in the locations. All these considerations will depend on the student's age, needs, and level of functional vision. As the environment becomes more organized, the student's understanding will increase, his or her anxiety will be reduced, and his or her ability to have some control of the environment will be enhanced.

Organization of Activities

The ability to predict and prepare for activities helps the student with ASDVI deal with ever-changing situations. An individually designed schedule is a valuable tool for sequencing events and tasks throughout the day that provides the student with concrete information that can be referred to frequently. Schedules need to be flexible. The development of the schedule is guided by considerations of the difficulty of the activity, liked versus disliked tasks, the duration of an activity, and active versus inactive activities. As with all other facets of a program, the medium that is used to demonstrate the schedule should match the student's primary learning medium (braille, print, objects,

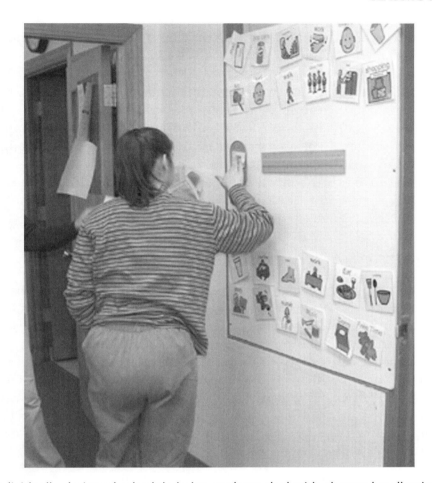

An individually designed schedule helps students deal with change by allowing them to predict and prepare for activities. The medium used should match the student's primary learning medium. This schedule uses large print and pictures.

pictures, or auditory devices). The schedule is refined over time as the student acquires skills, expands his or her preferences, and adjusts to changes.

Organizational Supports and Strategies

For all children at an early age the development of organizational skills is critical to their overall independence and success in gaining access to a variety of environments. For students with ASD, including students with ASDVI, deficits in executive functioning (the ability to organize thoughts and work and to create plans and successfully execute them) often challenge their ability to organize and complete tasks. Shopping and homework assignments, for example, often require help to organize and complete. Most students with

ASDVI who participate in an academic curriculum have great difficulty developing a concrete, step-by-step plan for effectively managing the open-ended assignments that are given in their classes (Klin, Volkmar, & Sparrow, 2000). These deficits may also cause problems in vocational environments, where there are few, if any, concrete instructions and rules. Organizational systems and skills help individuals to elicit meaning and purpose from the often-overwhelming details of and stimuli in the environment. Students with ASDVI cannot scan a room to locate an object or people or conceptually organize the environment and hence need organizational skills to understand and manage their world. These skills assist them to focus on relevant information, reducing the need for constant verbal directions.

INSTRUCTIONAL SUPPORTS AND STRATEGIES

Instructional supports and strategies augment instruction in a way that provides information that a student uses to help organize, sequence, and understand what is expected of him or her. Supports and strategies can range from a braille calendar that shows the activities that a student will participate in that day to a cue card in large print to help a student remember what to say when he or she needs help. The successful use of these supports and strategies can provide a framework for understanding what is happening, what is going to happen, and how it all "fits together." Used appropriately, supports can help minimize the frustration and anxiety that many students experience and increase their level of participation and independence by

- helping the student establish and maintain attention

- giving the student information in a form that she or he can quickly and easily interpret

- clarifying verbal information

- providing a concrete way to teach concepts, such as time, sequence, and cause and effect

- providing a structure for understanding and accepting change

- supporting the successful transition between activities or locations (Hodgdon, 1995)

Modifying Supports for Students with ASDVI

Numerous resources are available in the field of ASD that can help the team develop and implement supports and instructional strategies to assist the student to gain a better understanding of classroom activities (see the Resources at the back of this book). Many of the supports that are beneficial to students with ASD are termed "visual" supports, since they typically refer to visual representations or cues that are given to students to reinforce instruction or to serve as instructional aids. The educational team may assume that these supports will not be effective with a student with ASD who is impaired. In fact, the concept of the support or strategy will be equally beneficial to a visually impaired student with ASD; the challenge for the team is to analyze the *purpose* of the visual support and to provide the necessary modification that accommodates both the purpose of the support (addressing the ASD) *and* the visual impairment. The *need* for the support does not change, but the *medium* through which it is delivered may. For students with ASDVI, the visual supports can be adapted or modified by teachers of students who are visually impaired who are adept at designing or developing adaptations that accommodate a student's visual impairment. This chapter presents strategies and supports that will be useful for many students with ASDVI. It also provides strategies for and adapting these supports for use by students who are braille readers and students who use tangible symbols or pictures and examples of adapted supports.

To begin, it is critical that the team use the information from a learning media assessment (see Chapter 4) to determine the appropriate format through which supports are delivered—whether in braille, in large print, or auditorily. In addition, the team must ensure that any supports that are provided match the level of symbolic representation that the individual understands (see Chapters 4 and 5 for more detail).

Once the team has determined the student's preferred learning medium and level of communication, the team can consider the student's needs for organizational support. Of course, the needs must be determined individually, and not all students require all supports. The team must ensure that the supports are clear, literal, and organized. In general, the team will want to provide supports that help the student understand

- when to begin

- how to begin

- what to do (what the task involves)

- when the task or activity is done

- what to do when the task or activity is completed

- how to ask for help, if needed

A student with low vision uses this weekly large-print calendar. He has noted that on Tuesday he will learn to make a "vampire shake," a blood-red drink with berries and strawberry ice cream.

Types of Supports

This section presents examples of specific supports and general strategies that can be used to foster the student's meaningful participation in the classroom and ability to organize and comprehend short- and long-term expectations. With the discussion of each support are examples of adaptations for students who are visually impaired.

Calendars provide information about activities that will occur over days, weeks, or months. Much like a calendar that is used by adults, an individualized calendar can help a student better understand the concepts of time and organize his or her life. A calendar can help a student understand "what's next" and alleviate the student's anxiety about the unknown future. The case of José, a student with ASDVI, is an example.

> *José's favorite activity is cooking, so much so that he often refuses to do anything else. José starts every Monday morning reviewing the weekly large-print calendar schedule (see Figure 12.1). He is particularly excited to review all his "favorite" activities of the week, including cooking, with his teacher. When José becomes "agitated" because he is not going to his cooking class, the teacher returns to the calendar and reviews the sequence of events, point-*

FIGURE 12.1 José's Weekly Schedule of Favorite Activities

Monday	Tuesday	Wednesday	Thursday	Friday	Saturday	Sunday
Morning Swimming	Morning Art	Morning Classroom activities	Morning Art	Morning Shopping	No School	No School
Afternoon Music	Afternoon Gym	Afternoon Music	Afternoon Gym	Afternoon Cooking		

ing out when the cooking class is scheduled and what will happen before the cooking class. José is more comfortable knowing that the cooking class is, in fact, on his schedule—that it will be held on Friday afternoon after he goes shopping. Knowing this schedule, he is able to maintain his concentration during other times.

This type of weekly schedule is easily accommodated for a student who reads braille, as is shown in Figure 12.2.

A calendar schedule is also important for students who are not formal readers. In this case, an *object calendar* will allow the student to know what will happen next, provide the student with a structure through which she or he can anticipate activities, be alert to unexpected changes in her or his routine or schedule, and make decisions about the daily activities.

Many of the resources targeting the fields of deaf-blindness and visual impairment/multiple disabilities will be beneficial to teams who work with students with ASDVI. In particular, three resources will be useful when considering an object calendar system: *Calendars for Students with Multiple Impairments Including Deafblindness* (Blaha, 2001), *Communication: A Guide for*

FIGURE 12.2 José's Weekly Schedule in Braille

An object calendar allows students who are not formal readers to know what will happen next. The tactile items in this object calendar represent a student's next three activities: a spoon for snack, a ball for playtime, and a book for reading.

Teaching Students with Visual and Multiple Impairments (Hagood, 1997), and *Visual Supports: Helping Your Child Understand and Communicate* (*Center for Autism and Related Disabilities* 1998).

Daily Schedules (see Figure 12.3) outline the day's events in sequential fashion. Reviewing the daily schedule each morning and referring to it throughout the day, as necessary, will help the student understand when his or her favorite and less-favored activities will be occurring.

Some students benefit from tracking the day's events by using a pencil to check off activities as they are completed. Such tracking gives the student a sense of control and provides an additional reference marker for the completion of a task and a cue to initiate the next task. Similar tools can assist the braille reader, as is shown in Figure 12.4. In this example, braille full cells are placed in front of each line. The student can use the full cells to scratch off completed items. Braille readers can also track their completion of tasks by placing removable "sticky dots" in front of completed items.

FIGURE 12.3

Sample Daily Schedule

Today is: _Monday_____   _November 17, 2002_____
          Day   Date

9:00	Reading
10:00	Spelling
10:30	BREAK
11:30	Swimming
12:30	Lunch
1:00	Group work in classroom
2:00	Music
3:00	FREE-CHOICE ACTIVITY
3:15	Bus

FIGURE 12.4

Sample Daily Schedule in Braille

Task lists and task organizers serve as a supplement to the daily schedule and are used to identify the steps or sequence of steps that are involved in a single activity, as in the following sample task list:

When it's time for swimming, I need to

1. get my swimsuit and towel from my backpack

2. come back to class and sit quietly at my desk until the teacher tells me it's time to go

3. walk quietly to the gymnasium pool; don't run or shout

4. go to the locker room and find my locker

5. change into my swimsuit

6. wait quietly until the teacher tells me it's OK to walk to the pool

Usually developed in a checklist fashion, these supports can provide the student with a reference system and a way to track the steps to be completed in an activity. Again, the task list can be implemented using objects, pictures, or audiotapes. For students who are nonreaders, picture task organizers can be used.

Choice boards and choice lists provide a student with available options, and a mechanism for identifying his or her preferences. A student can also use choice boards and lists to choose among the options that are available to him or her, and hence to have some control over them. In its simplest form, a choice board gives the student the choice between two items (toys for play time, activities, and so forth.)

Cue cards can be used to help a student recall a word or options that are available to him or her, especially during stressful situations; to remember to use a newly learned skill to complete a routine; and to support the successful transition between activities or locations. For example, the cue card for obtaining help, which is taped to the top of Jeremy's desk, says this:

When I need help, I can

1. raise my hand until the teacher comes to help

2. go to the teacher's desk and wait until he says "Jeremy, do you need help?"

The team can easily accommodate the needs of a student who reads braille or large print when designing cue cards, choice boards, and choice lists. These simple tools give a student some control over his or her life by providing enhanced decision-making responsibilities and options.

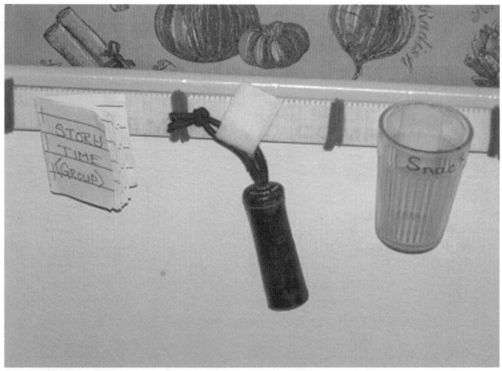

Choice boards provide students with a mechanism for identifying their preferences and thus a way to exert control over their activities. In this instance, a student has used a piece of Velcro to choose jump rope over story time or snack.

Calendars, schedules, lists, and organizer supports can be used concurrently to provide structure and organization for the student, as is illustrated in Figure 12.5.

ADDITIONAL INSTRUCTIONAL STRATEGIES AND SUPPORTS

Numerous other supports are available to assist the student with ASDVI to organize and structure his or her environment, to schedule, and to understand which choices are available. This section describes strategies and instructional supports that are relevant for most students with ASDVI. Additional information about supports is included in the Resources at the back of this book.

SEMANTIC MAPS

Many students with ASD struggle with reading comprehension skills; they may be able to read fluently but comprehend little of what they have read.

	FIGURE 12.5	Classroom Supports Used by Jonah, with Adaptations for His Visual Impairments	
Support provided	The support allows the student to know	How the support is used	Supplementary information
Daily schedule	When to begin What to do	Jonah uses his daily schedule to identify what events or tasks are scheduled throughout the day and to identify what he will be doing that day. By knowing the sequence of the day, his anxieties are reduced (For students not capable of a "full-day schedule," a schedule developed for shorter lengths of time is appropriate.)	Use a braille or large-print schedule system. For students who are nonreaders, use an object schedule system. Audiotapes may be used with either group
Task list for individual activities	How to begin When the task or activity is done	Jonah uses a task list for individual activities; the list identifies how to start, and the steps involved in each activity. The final step in the activity is identified as the last step through color-coded, bolded print. Jonah uses red, bold print to indicate the last step in the activity he's working on	For braille users, the final step could be placed beneath a single raised line; alternately, several full cells could precede the last step.
Choice list	What to do when the task is done	Each activity has a choice list after the last step. Jonah uses the choice list to identify the options available to him at that time (for example, the list may offer a free choice activity or moving on to the next activity).	Use a braille or large-print choice list or menu board. For students who are non-readers, use an object system. Audiotapes may be used with either group.

FIGURE 12.5 continued			
Support provided	**The support allows the student to know**	**How the support is used**	**Supplementary information**
Cue cards	How to ask for help	Jonah keeps a "Help" cue card taped to his desk. He refers to it when he needs help. It identifies appropriate ways he can ask for help, including "Raise my hand until the teacher comes to help; or go to the teacher's desk and wait until he says 'Jonah, do you need help?'"	

Semantic maps, also called semantic organizers and graphic organizers, support comprehension and understanding by summarizing and illustrating concepts and interrelationships among concepts in a text through the use of diagrams or other pictorial devices. Semantic maps look like a spider web in which lines connect a central concept to a variety of related ideas and events. The examples in Figure 12.6 show the relationships among some simple concepts—types of breakfast food and types of dogs. Semantic maps can help a student to

- organize and simplify information

- view important relationships

- reinforce his or her conceptual understanding of written information

Semantic maps can be presented in braille as well, as is illustrated in Figure 12.7.

KEY-POINT HIGHLIGHTING

Many students struggle with identifying key points in written text. Highlighting the critical concepts is a simple but effective strategy to help them understand the critical information they are reading. This strategy supports a student's ability to comprehend what she or he reads. Using a favorite colored highlighter will assist the student to "target" important information.

For students who are visually impaired, the concept of highlighting can be easily accommodated. Those with low vision can use high-contrast colored

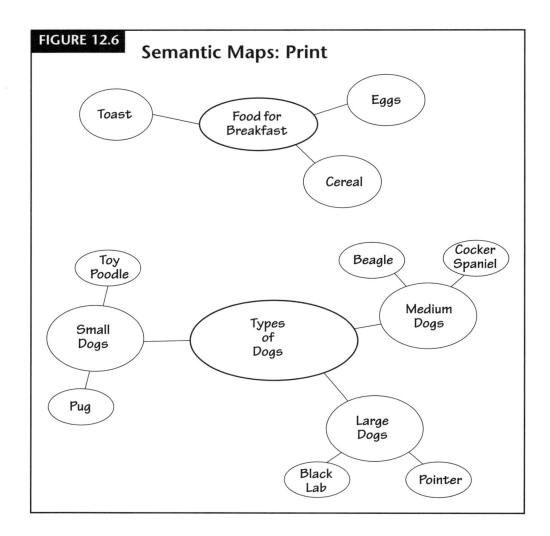

FIGURE 12.6

Semantic Maps: Print

highlight pens or fluorescent highlighters, and those who are blind and need braille can use full cells in front of rows or double space the braille and add a line underneath targeted words using several dot 2-5 cells.

OUTLINES

Simple outlines will help a student to focus on the critical concepts, to focus on important information, rather than to become overwhelmed with detail. Much like highlighting, outlines can provide structure and organization, as in the case of Pamela:

Pamela is assigned to read a chapter in her textbook with information on China's Yangtze River. Before she starts to read the chapter, her teacher pro-

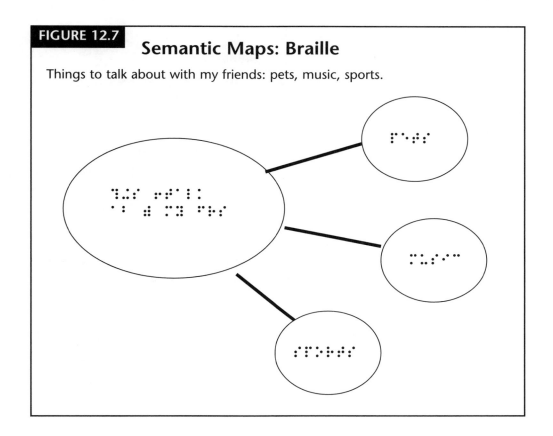

FIGURE 12.7

Semantic Maps: Braille

Things to talk about with my friends: pets, music, sports.

vides the following outline to help her focus on the most important information in the chapter:

    I. Yangtze River

        A. Description

            1. China's longest river

            2. runs from the East China Sea to the mountains of Tibet

        B. Benefits for people

            1. supplies good soil and water

            2. supplies food

            3. provides a means of transportation and communication

Outlines can easily be transcribed into braille or large print.

FUNCTIONAL CURRICULUM

Not every student will participate fully in a typical academic curriculum. This is true for some students who are high functioning, as well for those who have more basic learning needs. Many students with ASDVI are gifted in one academic area yet struggle in another, and some students do not benefit from an academically focused curriculum. When a student is having difficulty learning academic skills that are presented in the typical manner, the team should consider a functional curriculum to augment or replace academic instruction, as appropriate. A functional curriculum is founded on activities that the student will need to live, work, and engage in recreational activities in his or her community The functional activities may include balancing a checkbook, clipping coupons, joining a fitness club, ordering and paying in a restaurant, and reading newspaper advertisements. The team can use a simple chart (see the sample Functional Curriculum Ideas at the end of Chapter 3) to stimulate creative ideas for designing a functional curriculum. The list of skills is endless, and it is the team's responsibility to determine the skills that the student will need and the level of independence that he or she may attain.

ADDITIONAL GENERAL STRATEGIES

In addition to the supports and strategies that have been discussed, there are several general strategies that can be considered. The specific uses of these strategies will vary, depending on a student's needs. General strategies for consideration include these:

- Teach tolerance and acceptance of "change"; the student must learn that schedules, activities, and the people with whom he or she works change and must have a way to understand that change is going to occur, as in the example of Tommy:

Tommy had difficulty understanding any change in his daily schedule. He quickly grew accustomed to the voice of a particular staff member who worked with him and would hit, bite, and throw things when either the staff member or the schedule changed. Two strategies were implemented to address changes. First, because Tommy was using a tactile schedule, an object cue called "Oops" was introduced. Whenever the "Oops" object was placed in the schedule, it meant that a change was going to occur. Tommy was reinforced positively for adjusting appropriately to the change.

Second, Tommy was taught to tolerate staff changes better. The class-room staffing pattern was established so that the staff members who worked with Tommy were rotated at least every half day. This change helped ensure that Tommy did not learn to react to and follow the directions of only one staff member.

■ Recognize that you may need to "add to" or enhance most, if not all, information; do not assume that the student can understand simply because she or he can recite, as was the case with Jackie:

Jackie learned to read braille by first learning the contractions and then using the contractions in words. She was eventually able to read words in the context of a story. When Jackie was asked questions about a story, however, she could not answer them—she was able to decode words but was unable to apply meaning to them. One approach to help supply meaning was to develop experience stories that were based on real-life activities that Jackie was interested in and understood. Another was to assign Jackie stories to read on topics that interested her. Since Jackie was interested in music, stories about music or with musical themes increased her understanding of what she was reading.

■ Support instruction through the use of "preteaching" strategies. Preteaching helps a student to understand new concepts and vocabulary and to establish organizational structure and can lessen his or her anxiety. This strategy was used with Jared.

Jared is in the fourth grade. Before he began social studies instruction with the entire class, Ms. Johnson spent about 15 minutes with him, preteaching the main concepts that would be discussed in class and reviewing new vocabulary that would be introduced. In addition, semantic maps helped Jared understand the relationships between the new countries that he and his classmates were studying and the related information for each country, such as population, size, and economy. These preteaching strategies greatly enhanced Jared's ability to understand the lesson presented to the entire class.

■ Be conscious of transitions times because transitions between activities and between environments can be difficult for many students with ASDVI. Provide cues or other information that allow the student to anticipate and prepare for transitions and to know when, in fact, transitions have occurred.

■ Recognize the importance of frequent, ongoing, and accurate communication between the teacher(s) and the parents. Design a system to ensure that this communication will occur regularly.

- Understand that many students with ASDVI require a longer time to process directions or guidelines than do their typical classmates. Many need additional supports to do so (such as information presented through one sense paired with information presented through another (using, for example, both braille and an auditory device). Supports should not be dependent on the teacher's presence or input, and the educational team must plan for the fading of supports so the student does not learn to be completely dependent on them. The team needs to think about and plan for supports that allow independent functioning without ongoing intervention or instruction by adults

- Schedule breaks throughout the student's day. Make sure that the student has a way of knowing when a break will occur (by, for example, listing "break time" in the student's print, braille, or object schedule).

USE OF INSTRUCTIONAL ASSISTANTS

Educational placement allows for and supports individual instruction, small-group instruction, and instruction provided in an inclusive classroom. A school district will often place a student in a regular classroom and provide an instructional assistant or paraeducator to support the student's individualized needs. An instructional assistant, a member of the educational team, works under the direction of the teacher and implements the program of instruction that the teacher has systematically designed, teaching skills, implementing the behavioral plan, helping to teach functional routines, and expecting and encouraging communication and movement. He or she must be prepared to provide consistent instruction so the student is able to make sense of the world. This provision can be successful, but *only* if there is an infrastructure that provides for the instructional assistant's ongoing supervision, support, and training. The instructional assistant must endorse or buy in to the implementation of an educational program that encourages and teaches the student to think and function independently, when appropriate. The skills that the student must learn have to be available beyond the immediate presence of the assistant. Without appropriate training and support and a clearly defined job description, the instructional assistant may actually impede the student's functional independence. Rather than support the student's ongoing learning, the assistant can, in effect, help maintain the student's isolation by serving as a constant go-between among other service providers, peers, family members, and the student. Although the educational team can identify the need for support provided by an instructional assistant, the implementation of this service must be carefully considered and constantly managed and evaluated.

SUMMARY

Successful inclusion in a typical classroom environment depends on the ability of the student with ASDVI to gain access to information in a way that is personally meaningful. Supports can help the student organize information and clarify expectations. Members of the educational team need to assess the environment and the classroom expectations carefully and consider the student's abilities and challenges before they decide which supports are necessary.

Successful inclusion of students with ASDVI in a general classroom environment can be complex. It is critical that the team members use their collective expertise and input to identify the unique challenges that a student may experience and to use the information they have gathered through an ongoing assessment to identify, create, and implement classroom supports that assist the student to participate to his or her maximum potential. As was noted at the beginning of this chapter, students with ASDVI can and do learn to succeed in environments alongside their nondisabled peers. Successful, active participation is possible for them with appropriate instruction and support.

REFERENCES

American Psychiatric Association. (1994). *Diagnostic and statistical manual of mental disorders, fourth edition.* Arlington, VA: American Psychiatric Press.

American Psychiatric Association. (2000). *Diagnostic and statistical manual of mental disorders, fourth edition, text revisions.* Arlington, VA: American Psychiatric Press.

Anderson, S., Boigon, S., Brown, D., Davis, K., Methvin J., & Simmons, V. (1991). *Oregon Project for Visually Impaired and Blind Preschoolers* (5th ed.). Medford: Southern Oregon Education Service District.

Arick, J. R., Loos, L., Falco, R., & Krug, D. A. (2004). *The Star Program: Strategies for teaching based on autism research.* Austin, TX. Pro-Ed.

Baker, J. (2003). *Social skills training for children and adolescents with asperger syndrome and social-communication problems.* Shawnee Mission, KS: Autism Asperger Publishing Co.

Barth, R. S. (2001). *Learning by heart.* San Francisco: Jossey-Bass.

Bayley, N. (1993). *Bayley Scales for Infant Development.* San Antonio, TX: Psychological Corp.

Blaha, R. (2001). *Calendars for students with multiple impairments including deaf-blindness.* Austin: Texas School for the Blind and Visually Impaired.

Bondy, A., & Frost, L. (2001). *A picture's worth: PECS and other visual communication strategies in autism.* Bethesda, MD: Woodbine House.

Brown, C., & Bours, B. (1986). *A resource manual for the development and evaluation of special programs for exceptional students: Volume V-K. Movement analysis and curriculum for visually impaired preschoolers.* Tallahassee, Florida: Department of Education.

Brown, C., & Dunn, W. (2002). *Adolescent/Adult sensory profile.* San Antonio, TX: Harcourt Assessment.

Bruininks, R. H., Woodcock, R. W., Weatherman, R. E., & Hill, B. K. (1996). *Scales of Independent Behavior–Revised.* Itasca, IL: Riverside.

Cass, H. (1996, March 27). *Visual impairment and autism—What we know about causation and early identification.* Paper presented at the Autism and Visual Impairment Conference, Edinburgh. Available: www.ssc.mhie.ac.uk/ archive/proceedings/hcass.html.

Cautela, J. R., & Groden, J. (1978). *Relaxation: A comprehensive manual for adults, children, and children with special needs.* Champaign, IL: Research Press.

Center for Autism and Related Disorders. (1998). *Visual supports: Helping your child understand and communicate* [Online]. Available: http://card.ufl.edu/ visual/html

Chen, D., & Dote-Kwan, J. (1995). *Starting points: Instructional practices for young children whose multiple disabilities include visual impairment.* Los Angeles: Blind Children's Center.

Chess, S., Korn, S., & Fernandez, P. B. (1971). *Psychiatric disorders in children with congenital rubella.* New York: Bruner/Mazel.

Corn, A. L., & Koenig, A. (Eds.). (1996). *Foundations of low vision: Clinical and functional perspectives.* New York: AFB Press.

Coyle, C. P., Kinney, W. B., Riley, B., & Shank, J. W. (Eds.). (1991). *Benefits of therapeutic recreation: A consensus view.* Philadelphia: Temple University Recreation Program.

Coyne, P., Nyberg, C., & Vandenburg, M. L. (1999). *Developing leisure time skills for persons with autism: A practical approach for home, school and community.* Arlington, TX: Future Horizons.

Davidson, J., & O'Meara, P. (1997). *Guide to help establish your student's level of representation.* Unpublished paper. Oregon Regional Program Services, Oregon Department of Education, Portland, OR.

DiLavore, P., Lord, C. & Rutter, M. (1995). The pre-linguistic autism diagnostic observation schedule. *Journal of Autism and Developmental Disorders, 25,* 355–379.

Dunn, W., Saiter, J., & Rinner, L. (2002). Asperger syndrome and sensory processing: A conceptual model and guidance for intervention planning. *Focus on Autism & Other Developmental Disabilities, 17,* 172–186.

Fazzi, D. L. (1998). Facilitating independent travel for students who have visual impairments and other disabilities. In S. L. Sacks & R. K. Silberman (Eds.), *Educating students who have visual impairments with other disabilities* (pp. 441–468). Baltimore, MD: Paul H. Brookes.

Fazzi, D. L., & Petersmeyer, B. A., (2001). *Imagining the possibilities: Creative approaches to orientation and mobility instruction for persons who are visually impaired.* New York: AFB Press.

Ferrell, K. A. (1985). *Reach out and teach: Meeting the training needs of parents of visually/multiply handicapped young children.* New York: American Foundation for the Blind.

Ferrell, K. A. (2000). Growth and development of young children. In M. C. Holbrook & A. Koenig (Eds.), *Foundations of education: Vol. 1. History and theory of teaching children and youths with visual impairments* (2nd ed., pp. 111–134). New York: AFB Press.

Ferrell, K. A., Shaw, A. R., & Deitz, S. J. (1998). *Project PRISM: A longitudinal study of developmental patterns of children who are visually impaired.* Greeley: Division of Special Education, University of Northern Colorado.

Forest, M., & Lusthaus, E. (1989). Promoting educational equality for all students: Circles and MAPS. In S. Stainback, W. Stainback, & M. Forest (Eds.), *Educating all students in the mainstream of regular education* (pp. 43–58). Baltimore, MD: Paul H. Brookes.

Forest, M., & Pearpoint, J. (1992). MAPS: Action planning. In J. Pearpoint, M. Forest, & J. Snow (Eds.), *The inclusion papers: Strategies to make inclusion work* (pp. 52–56). Toronto: Inclusion Press.

Fraiberg, S., & Freedman, D. (1964). Studies in the ego development of the congenitally blind. *Psychoanalytic Study of the Child, 19,* 113–169.

Freeman, S., & Drake, L. (1996). *Teach me language: A language manual for children with autism, Asperger's syndrome, and related developmental disorders.* Langley, BC, Canada: SKF Books.

Gamel-McCormick, M., & Dymond, S. (1994). *Augmentative communication assessment protocol for symbolic augmentative systems.* Richmond, VA: Virginia Commonwealth University. Available: www.ttac.odu.edu/Articles/Game/.html.

Garner, H., & Dietz, L. (1996). Person-centered planning: Maps and paths to the future. *Four Runner, 11*(2), 1–2. Available: www.ttac.odu.edu/Articles/person.html.

Gense, M., & Gense, D. J. (1994). Identifying autism in children with blindness and visual impairment. *RE:view, 26,* 56–62.

Gilliam, J. E. (1995). *Gilliam Autism Rating Scale.* Austin, TX: Pro-Ed.

Gilliam, J. E. (2000). *The Gilliam Asperger's Disorder Scale.* Austin, TX: Pro-Ed.

Grandin, T., & Duffy, K. (2004). *Developing talents: Careers for individuals with Asperger syndrome and high-functioning autism.* Shawnee Mission, KS: Autism Asperger Publishing Co.

Grandin, T., & Scariano, M. M. *Emergence: Labeled autistic.* New York: Warner Books.

Gray, C. (1994). *Comic strip conversations.* Jenison, MI: Jenison Public Schools.

Gray, C. (2000). *The new social story book.* Arlington, TX: Future Horizons, Inc.

The Gray Center. (2005). *Social Stories.* Kentwood, MI: The Gray Center for Social Learning and Understanding [Online]. Available: www.thegraycenter.org/Social_Stories.htm.

Hagood, L. (1997). *Communication: A guide for teaching students with visual and multiple impairments.* Austin: Texas School for the Blind and Visually Impaired.

Hagood, L. (n.d.). *A standard tactile symbol system: Graphic language for individuals who are blind and unable to learn braille.* Austin: Texas School for the Blind and Visually Impaired. Available: www.tsbvi.edu/Outreach/seehear/archive/tactile.html.

Hawaii Early Learning Profile. (1988). Palo Alto, CA: VORT Corp.

Heffner, G. (2000). *Treating echolalia* [Online]. Available: http://communities.msn.com/TheAutismHomePage/educationampspeech.msnw.

Hill, E. W., & Blasch, B. B. (1980). *Concept development.* In R. L. Welsch & B. B. Blasch (Eds.), *Foundations of orientation and mobility* (pp. 265–290). New York: American Foundation for the Blind Press.

Hobson, R. P., & Bishop, M. (2003). The pathogenesis of autism: Insights from congenital blindness. *Philosophical Transactions: Biological Sciences, 358,* 335–344.

Hobson R. P., Lee, A., & Brown R. (1999). Autism and congenital blindness. *Journal of Autism and Developmental Disorders, 29,* 45–56.

Hodgdon, L. A. (1995). *Visual strategies for improving communication: Practical supports for school and home* (Vol. 1). Troy, MI: Quirk Roberts Publishing.

Hodgdon, L. A. (1999). *Solving behavior problems in autism: Improving communication with visual strategies*. Troy, MI: Quirk Roberts Publishing.

Holbrook, M. C. (1996). *Children with visual impairments: A parents' guide*. Bethesda, MD: Woodbine House.

Holbrook, M. C., & Koenig, A. (Eds.). (2000). *Foundations of education, Vol. 2. Instructional strategies for teaching children and youths with visual impairments* (2nd ed.). New York: AFB Press.

Horner, R. H., & Carr, E. G., (1997). Behavioral supports for students with severe disabilities: Functional assessment and comprehensive intervention. *Journal of Special Education, 31,* 84–104.

Jamieson, S. (2004) Creating an educational program for young children who are blind and who have autism. *RE:view, 35,* 165–177.

Janzen, J. (1996). *Understanding the nature of autism: A practical guide*. San Antonio, TX: Therapy Skill Builders.

Janzen, J. (2003). *Understanding the nature of autism: A guide to the autism spectrum disorders* (2nd ed.). San Antonio, TX: Therapy Skill Builders.

Johansson, C. B. (1986). *Career Assessment Inventory: The enhanced version*. Minneapolis, MN: National Computer Systems.

Johnson-Martin, N. M., Attermeier, S. M., & Hacker, B. J. (2004). *The Carolina curriculum for infants and toddlers with special needs* (3rd ed.). Baltimore, MD: Paul H. Brookes.

Jordan, R. (1996, March 27) *Educational implications of autism and visual impairment*. Paper presented at the Autism and Visual Impairment Conference, Edinburgh. Available: www.ssc.mhie.ac.uk/archives/proceedings/jordan.html.

Jose, R. (Ed.). (1993). *Understanding low vision*. New York: American Foundation for the Blind.

Kanner, L. (1943). Autistic disturbances of affective contact. *Nervous Child, 2,* 217–250.

Kelly, P., & Smith, P. (2000). *Independent living*. In M. C. Holbrook & A. Koenig (Eds.), *Foundations of education, Vol. 2. Instructional strategies for teaching children and youths with visual impairments* (2nd ed., pp. 569–616). New York: AFB Press.

Klin, A., Volkmar, F. R., & Sparrow, S. S. (Eds.). (2000). *Asperger syndrome*. New York: Guilford Press.

Knapp, R. R., & Knapp, L. (1995). *Career occupational preference system.* San Diego, CA: Edits.

Koenig, A., & Holbrook, C. (1995). *Learning media assessment of students with visual impairments* (2nd ed.). Austin: Texas School for the Blind and Visually Impaired.

Kranowitz, C., Sava, D., Haber, E., Balzer-Martin, L., & Szklut, S. (2001). *Answers to questions teachers ask about sensory integration.* Las Vegas: Sensory Resources.

Krug, D., Arick, J. R., & Almond, P. (1993). *Autism screening instrument for educational planning* (2nd ed.). Austin, TX: Pro-Ed.

Leaf, R., McEachin, J., Harsh, J. D., & Boehm, M. (1999). *A work in progress: Behavior management strategies and a curriculum for intensive behavioral treatment of autism.* New York: DLR Books.

Lord, C. (1997) Diagnostic instruments in autism spectrum disorders. In D. J. Cohen & F. R. Volkmar (Eds.), *Handbook of autism and pervasive developmental disorders* (pp. 460–483). New York: John Wiley & Sons.

Lord, C., & McGee, J. (Eds.). (2001) *Educating children with autism.* Washington, DC: National Academy Press.

Lord, C., Rutter, M., Di Lavore, P. C., & Risi, S. (2000). *Autism Diagnostic Observation Schedule (ADOS).* Los Angeles: Western Psychological Services.

Lowscence, L. (1994, July 7). *Techniques and suggestions for evaluating students with autism.* Paper presented at the Autism Society of America convention, Kansas City, MO.

Marriner, N. (2001). *Visually cued instruction* [Online]. Available: www.talklc.com/handout/Visually_Cued_Instruction.html.

Maurice, C., Green, G., & Luce, S. (1996). *Behavioral intervention for young children with autism.* Austin, TX: Pro-Ed.

McCarron-Dial Evaluation System. (1986). Dallas: McCarron-Dial Systems.

McCart, A., & Turnbull, A. (2004). *The issues: Behavioral concerns within inclusive classrooms* [Online]. Available: www.pbs.org/teachersource/prek2/issues/602issue.shtm.

Morse, M., Pawletko, T., & Rocissano, L. (2000). *Autistic spectrum disorders and cortical visual impairment: Two worlds on parallel courses—Part 2* [Online]. Available: www.tsbvi.edu/Education/vmi/autism-cvi.htm.

Myles, B. S., Bock, S. J., & Simpson, R. L. (2001). *Asperger syndrome diagnostic scale.* Austin, TX: Pro-Ed.

National Agenda for the education of children and youths with visual impairments, including those with multiple disabilities, Revised (2004). New York: AFB Press.

National Center on Birth Defects and Developmental Disabilities, Autism Information Center. (2004). *About Autism* [Online]. Available: www.cdc.gov/ ncbddd/aic/about/default.htm.

National Institute of Child Health and Human Development. (2001). *Autism and Genes—Autism Research at the NICHD* (01-4961). Washington, DC: U.S. Government Printing Office.

National Institute of Mental Health. (2003). *Autism* [Online]. Available: www.nimh.nih.gov/publicat/autism.cfm.

National Research Council. (2001). *Educating children with autism.* Washington, DC: National Academy Press.

Newborg, J., Stock, J. R., Wnek, L., Guidubaldi, J., & Svinick, J. (1984). *Battelle Developmental Inventory.* Allen, TX: Teaching Resources. [Available from Riverside Publishing Co.]

New York State Department of Health. (1999). *Clinical practice guideline: Report of the recommendations: Autism/pervasive developmental disorders, assessment and intervention for young children (age 0–3 years)* [Online]. Available: www.health.state.ny.us/nysdoh/eip/autism/index.htm.

O'Hare, A. (1996, March 27). *Autism and visual impairment: Taking the issues forward in the context of multi-disciplinary working.* Unpublished paper presented at the Autism and Visual Impairment Conference, Edinburgh.

Ozonoff, S. & Dawson, G. (2002). *A parent's guide to Asperger syndrome and high-functioning autism.* New York: Guilford Press.

Pawletko, T., & Rocissano, L. (2000). *Autism in the visually impaired child* [Online]. Available: www.tsbvi.edu/Education/vmi/autism-vi.htm.

Pogrund, R., Fazzi, D. (Eds.). (2002). *Early focus: Working with young blind and visually impaired children and their families* (2nd ed.). New York: AFB Press.

Pogrund, R., Healy, G., Jones, K., Levack, N., Martin-Curry, S., Martinez, C., Marz, J., Roberson-Smith, B., & Vrba, A. (1993). *TAPS comprehensive assessment and on-going evaluation.* Austin: Texas School for the Blind and Visually Impaired.

Pogrund, R., Healy, G., Jones, K., Levack, N. Martin-Curry, S., Martinez, C., Marz, J., Roberson-Smith, B., Vrba, A. (1995). *Teaching Age-Appropriate Purposeful Skills (TAPS): An orientation and mobility curriculum for students with visual impairment* (2nd ed.). Austin: Texas School for the Blind and Visually Impaired.

Pring, L. P. (Ed.). (2005). Autism and blindness: Research and reflections. London: Whurr Publishers.

Project Autism guidelines manual. (2001). Chapel Hill: Department of Recreation and Leisure Studies, University of North Carolina. Available: www.unc.edu/depts/recreate/crds/autism.

Quill, K. A. (1995). *Teaching children with autism: Strategies to enhance communication and socialization.* Florence, KY: Thomson Learning, Delmar Publishers.

Quill, K. A. (2000). *Do-watch-listen-say: Social and communication intervention for children with autism.* Baltimore, MD. Paul H. Brookes.

Reed, H., Thomas, E., Sprague, J. R., & Horner, R. H. (1997). Student guided functional assessment interview: An analysis of student and teacher agreement. *Journal of Behavioral Education, 7,* 33–49.

Reisman, J., & Hanschu, B. (1992). *Sensory integration inventory revised—For individuals with developmental disabilities.* Hugo, MN: PDP Press.

Rowland, C., & Schweigert, P. (1996). *Analyzing the Communication Environment (ACE): An inventory of ways to encourage communication in functional activities.* Portland: Center on Self-Determination, Oregon Health Sciences University.

Rowland, C., & Schweigert, P. (2000). *Tangible symbol systems* (rev. ed.). Portland: Center on Self-Determination, Oregon Health Sciences University.

Sacks, S. & Silberman, R. (Eds.). (1998) *Educating students who have visual impairments with other disabilities.* Baltimore, MD: Paul H. Brookes.

Sacks, S. & Silberman, R. (2000). Social Skills. In A. Koening & M. C. Holbrook (Eds.), *Foundations of education, Volume 2. Instructional Strategies for teaching children and youths with visual impairments* (2nd ed., pp. 616–652). New York: AFB Press.

Sattler, J. (2004). *Assessment of children: Cognitive applications and behavioral and clinical applications.* Circle Pines, MN: AGS.

Sauerburger, D. (1993). *Independence without sight or sound: Suggestions for practitioners working with deaf-blind adults.* New York: AFB Press.

Schoen, A. A. (2003). What potential does the applied behavior approach have for the treatment of children and youth with autism? *Journal of Instructional Psychology, 30,* 125–130.

Schopler, E., Reichler, R. J., & Rochen Renner, B. (1986). *Childhood autism rating scale.* Circle Piens, MN: AGS.

Sparrow, S. S., Cicchetti, D. V., & Balla, D. A. (2005). *Vineland adaptive behavior scales* (2nd ed.). Circle Pines, MN: AGS.

Sundberg, M. L., & Partington, J. W. (1998). *Teaching language to children with autism.* Pleasant Hill, CA: Behavior Analysts.

Warren, D. H. (1994). *Blindness and children: An individual differences approach.* New York: Cambridge University Press.

Weiss, M. J., & Harris, S. (2001). *Reaching out, joining in: Teaching social skills to young children with autism.* Bethesda, MD: Woodbine House.

Wetherby, A., & Prizant, B. (1997). *Communication enhancement for young children with pervasive developmental disorders.* Paper presented at the national conference of the Autism Society of America, Orlando, FL.

Wing, L. (1997). The history of ideas on autism: Legends, myths, and reality. *Autism: The International Journal of Research and Practice, 1*(1), 13–23.

Winner, M. G. (2000). *Inside out: What makes the person with social-cognitive deficits tick?* Arlington, TX: Future Horizons.

Wolffe, K. (1998). Transition planning and employment outcomes for students who have visual impairments with other disabilities. In S. Sacks & R. Silberman (Eds.), *Educating students with visual impairments and other disabilities* (pp 339–365). Baltimore, MD: Paul H. Brookes.

Yack, E., Sutton, S., & Aquilla, P. (2001). *Building bridges through sensory integration: Occupational therapy for children with autism and other pervasive developmental disorders.* Toronto: Parentbooks.

ADDITIONAL REFERENCES

Allen, J. (1999). *Words, words, words: Teaching vocabulary in grades 4–12.* Portland, ME: Stenhouse Publishers.

Attwood, T., & Gray, C. (1999). *Understanding and teaching friendship skills.* Retrieved 11/19/02 from: www.tonyattwood.com/paper3htm.

Baker, B., & Brightman, A. (1997). *Steps to independence.* Baltimore, MD: Paul H. Brookes.

Benoff, K., Lang, M. A., & Beck-Viisola, M. (2001). *Compendium of instruments for assessing the skills and interests of individuals with visual impairments or multiple disabilities.* New York: Lighthouse International.

Blakely, K., Lang, M. A., & Hart, R. (1991). *Getting in touch with play: Creating playing environments for children with visual impairments.* New York: Lighthouse International.

Blasch, B., Weiner, W., & Welsh, R. L. (1998). *Foundations of orientation and mobility* (2nd ed.). New York: American Foundation for the Blind.

Boswell, S. (2002). *Building communication around routines.* Retrieved 12/15/02 from Division TEACCH Web site: www.teacch.com/teacchco.htm.

Boyce, F., & Hammond, F. (1996). *Autism and visual impairment—Making sense.* From Proceedings of Autism and Visual Impairment Conference. Retrieved 4/4/03 from Scottish Sensory Centre Web site: www.ssc.mhie.ac.uk/archive/proceedings/boyce.html.

Bregman, J. D., & Gerdtz, J. (1997). Behavioural Interventions. In D. J. Cohen & F. R. Volkmar (Eds.), *Handbook of autism and pervasive developmental disorders* (2nd ed.). New York: Wiley & Sons.

Buckman, S. (2002). *Don't forget about self-management.* Retrieved 12/24/02 from Indiana Resource Center for Autism Web site: www.iidc.indiana.edu/irca/behavior/selfmgt.html.

Center for Quality Special Education, Michigan Department of Education. (1989). *Special education program outcomes guide: Visual impairment.* Lansing, MI: Michigan Department of Education.

Chen, D., Friedman, C. T., & Calvello, G. (1989). *Parents and visually impaired infants (PAVII).* Louisville, KY: American Printing House for the Blind.

Coyle, C. P., Kinney, W. B., Riley, B., & Shank, J. W. (Eds.). (1991). *Benefits of therapeutic recreation: A consensus view.* Ravensdale, WA: Idyll Arbor, Inc.

Cvach, P. (1989). *Time management strategies for achieving success.* Sponsored by the National Institute on Disability in Rehabilitation Research (ED/OSERS); McLean, VA: Learning Disabilities Project. (ERIC document reproduction number ED 329076).

Dodson-Burk, B., & Hill, E. W. (1989). *An orientation and mobility primer for families and young children.* New York: American Foundation for the Blind.

Dodson-Burke, B. & Hill, E. W. (1989). *Preschool orientation and mobility screening.* Alexandria, VA: AER.

Dunn, W. (1999). *Sensory profile: User's manual.* San Antonio, TX: Psychological Corporation.

Edgar, S., & Shepherd, M. (1983). *The use of advanced organizers to aid learning and recall. Technical report no. 34.* Sponsored by Special Education Program (ED/OSERS), New York, NY: Columbia University Teachers' College (ERIC Document Reproduction Number ED 308649).

Ek, U., Fernell, E., Jacobson, L., & Gillberg, C. (1998). Relation between blindness due to retinopathy of prematurity and autistic spectrum disorders: A population-based study. *Developmental Medicine and Child Neurology, 40,* 297–301.

Fraiberg, S. (1977). *Insights from the blind.* New York: Basic Books.

Fullerton, A., Stratton, J., Coyne, P., & Gray, C. L. (1996). *Higher functioning adolescents and young adults with autism: A teacher's guide.* Austin, TX: Pro-Ed.

Gense, D. J., & Gense, M. (2000). *The importance of orientation and mobility skills for students who are deafblind.* Monmouth, OR: DB-Link—The National Information Clearinghouse on Children Who Are Deaf-Blind.

Giangreco, M., Cloninger, C. J., & Iverson, V. S. (1998). *COACH: Choosing outcomes and accommodations for children* (2nd ed.). Baltimore, MD: Paul H. Brookes.

Gill-Weiss, M. F., & Harris, S. L. (2001). *Reaching out, joining in: Teaching social skills to young children with autism.* Bethesda, MD: Woodbine House.

Gray, C. (1993). *Taming the recess jungle: Socially simplifying recess for students with autism and related disorders.* Jenison, MI: Jenison Public Schools.

Greenspan, S., & Wieder, S. (1998). *The child with special needs: Encouraging intellectual and emotional growth.* Cambridge, MA: Perseus Publishing.

Handleman, J. L., & Harris, S. L. (2001). *Preschool education programs for children with autism* (2nd ed.). Austin, TX: PRO-ED, Inc.

Hill, E. W., Guth, D. A., & Hill, M. M. (1985). Spatial concept instruction for children with low vision. *Education for the Visually Handicapped, 16* (4), 152–161.

Huebner, K. M., Prickett, J. G., Welch, T. R., & Joffee, E. (Eds). (1995). *Hand in hand: Essentials of communication and orientation and mobility for your students who are deaf-bind.* New York: AFB Press.

Huebner, R. A. (Ed.). (2001). *Autism: A sensorimotor approach to management.* Gaithersburg, MD: Aspen Publishers.

Hug, D., Chernus-Mansfield, N., & Hayashi, D. (nd). *Move with me: A parent's guide to movement development for visually impaired babies.* CA: Blind Children's Center.

Kalmeyer, D. (1998). *An introduction to applied behavior analysis.* Connecticut Families For Effective Autism Treatment. Available: www.ctfeat.org/ABA.html.

Kephart, J. G., Kephart, C. P., & Schwartz, G. C. (1974). A journey into the world of the blind child. *Exceptional Children, 40*(6), 421–427.

Kleiman, L. (1994). *Functional communication profile.* East Moline, IL: Lingui-Systems.

Koegel, L. K., Koegel, R. L., & Dunlap, G. (1996). *Positive behavioral support: Including people with difficult behavior in the community.* Baltimore, MD: Paul H. Brookes.

Kranowitz, C. S. (1998). *The out-of-sync child: Recognizing and coping with sensory integration dysfunction.* New York: CSK Publications, Perigee Books.

LaPrelle, L. L. (1996). *Standing on my own two feet.* Los Angeles, CA: Blind Children's Center.

Lieberman, L. J., & Cowart, J. F. (1996). *Games for people with sensory impairments: strategies for including individuals of all ages.* Champaign, IL: Human Kinetics.

Loumiet, R., & Levack, N. (1993). *Independent living: A curriculum with adaptations for students with visual impairments.* Austin: Texas School for the Blind and Visually Impaired.

Maurice, C. (1994). *Let me hear your voice: A family's triumph over autism.* New York, NY.

McAfee, J. (2002). *Navigating the social world: A curriculum for individuals with Asperger's syndrome, high functioning autism and related disorders.* Arlington, TX: Future Horizons, Inc.

McClannahan, L., & Krantz, P. (1999). *Activity schedules for children with autism: Teaching independent behavior.* Bethesda, MD: Woodbine House.

McMorrow, M., & Foxx, R. (1986). Some direct and generalized effects of replacing an autistic man's echolalia with correct responses to questions. *Journal of Applied Behavior Analysis, 19,* 289–297.

McVay, P., & Wilson, H. *Ideas, samples, & designs.* Portland, OR: Multnomah Education Service District.

Moore, S. (2002). *Asperger syndrome and the elementary school experience; practical solutions for academic and social difficulties.* Shawnee Mission, KS: Autism Asperger Syndrome Publishing Company.

Moyes, R. A., & Moreno, S. J. (1997). *Incorporating social goals in the classroom: A guide for teachers and parents of children with high-functioning autism and Asperger syndrome.* Austin, TX: PRO ED.

Myles, B., Tapscott Cook, K., Miller, N., Rinner, L., & Robbins, L. (2000). *Asperger syndrome and sensory issues.* Shawnee Mission, KS: Autism Asperger Syndrome Publishing Company.

Myles, B. S., & Simpson, R. L. (1998). *Asperger syndrome: A guide for educators and parents.* Austin, TX: PRO ED.

O.A.S.I.S. (Online Asperger Syndrome Information and Supports). (n.d.). *Behaviors that may be personal challenges for a student with autism spectrum disorder* [Online]. Available: www.udel.edu/bkirby/asperger/iep_Behav_Forms.html.

O'Neill, R. E., Horner, R. H., Albin, R. W., Sprague, J. R., & Storey, K. (1997). *Functional assessment and program development for problem behavior: A practical handbook* (2nd ed.). Pacific Grove, CA: Brooks/Cole Publishing Company.

Partington, J. W., & Sundberg, M. L. (1998). *The assessment of basic language and learning skills (The ABLLS).* Pleasant Hill, CA: Behavior Analysts, Inc.

Pefresson, R., & Dinner, P. (1989). *Semantic organizers.* Rockville, MD: Aspen Publishers.

Pogrund, R., & Fazzi, D. (Eds.). (2002). *Early focus: Working with young blind and visually impaired children and their families* (2nd ed.). New York: AFB Press.

Pugh, G. S., & Erin, J. (Eds.). (1999). *Blind and visually impaired students: Educational service guidelines.* Watertown, MA: Perkins School for the Blind.

Rowland, C. (1996). *Communication matrix. A communication skill assessment for individuals at the earliest stages of communication development.* Portland, OR: Oregon Health Sciences University, Center on Self-Determination.

Savner, J. L., & Myles, B. S. (2000). *Making visual supports work in the home and community: Individuals with autism and Asperger syndrome.* Shawnee Mission, KS: Autism Asperger Publishing Co.

Sewel, D. (1997). *Assessment kit: Kit of informal tools for academic students with visual impairment. Part 1; assessment tools for teacher use.* Austin: Texas School for the Blind and Visually Impaired.

Siegel, B. (1996). *The world of the autistic child: Understanding and treating autistic spectrum disorders.* New York: Oxford University Press.

Steinberg, A., Park, J., & Finkel, S. (2000). The diagnosis of autism spectrum disorders in children who are blind. *Journal of Developmental and Learning Disorders, 4,* 133–152.

Simpson, R., & Smith Myles, B. (1997). *Asperger syndrome: A guide for educators and parents.* Austin, TX: PRO-Ed.

Steinberg, A., & Marano, H. (2000). Autistic spectrum disorder and its identifcation in children who are blind: A clinical perspective from the field. *Journal of Developmental and Learning Disorders,* 153–183.

Stewart, R. (2002). *Motivating students who have autism spectrum disorder.* Retrieved 1/15/2002 from Indiana Resource Center for Autism Web site: www.isdd.indiana.edu/~irca/education/motivate.html.

Stokes, S. (2002). *Developing an intervention program for the verbal children with autism.* Retrieved 12/15/02 from: www.cesa7.k12.wi.us/sped/autism/verbal/verbal13.html.

Twachtman-Cullen, D. (2000). *How to be a para pro: A comprehensive training manual for paraprofessionals.* Higganum, CT: Starfish Specialty Press.

University of Michigan Health Services. *Developmental milestones.* Retrieved 12/30/03 from: www.med.umich.edu/1libr/yourchild/devmile.htm.

Wetherby, A. (Ed.). (1998). Preschoolers with autism: Communication and language interventions [Topical issue]. *Seminars in Speech and Language, 19* (4).

Wheeler, M. (1998). *Toilet training for individuals with autism and related disorders.* Arlington, TX: Future Horizons, Inc.

Willey, L. H. (1999). *Pretending to be normal: Living with Asperger's syndrome.* London, UK: Jessica Kingsley Publishers.

Williams, D. (1994). *Nobody nowhere: The extraordinary autobiography of an autistic.* New York: Avon Books.

Wing, L. (1991). *The relationship between Asperger's syndrome and Kanner's autism.* In U. Frith (Ed.), *Autism and Asperger Syndrome* (pp. 93–121). Cambridge, UK: Cambridge University Press.

Wolffe, K. (1998). Transition planning and employment outcomes for students who have visual impairments with other disabilities. In S. Sacks &

R. Silberman (Eds.), *Educating students with visual impairments and other disabilities* (pp. 339–365). Baltimore, MD: Paul H. Brookes.

Wolffe, K. (2000). Career education. In A. Koening & M. C. Holbrook (Eds.), *Foundations of Education, Vol. 2. Instructional strategies for teaching children and youths with visual impairments* (2nd ed., pp. 679–719). New York: AFB Press.

RESOURCES AND ADDITIONAL READINGS

This appendix provides sources for more detailed information about the topics covered in each chapter, including sources of any products and assessment tools or other instruments that might be mentioned. Most of the organizations listed have extensive web sites with information on a variety of aspects of autism and working with children who have autism spectrum disorders.

General Resources
The following organizations are good places to start when looking for additional information and resources on working with children with autism spectrum disorders, blindness and visual impairment, and children with multiple disabilities.

American Foundation for the Blind
11 Penn Plaza, Suite 300
New York, NY 10001
(212) 502-7600; (800) 232-5463; (212) 502-7662 (TDD/TTY)
Fax: (212) 502-7777
E-mail: afbinfo@afb.net
www.afb.org

A national organization serving as an information clearinghouse for people who are blind or visually impaired and their families, professionals, organizations, schools, and corporations. In addition to mounting program initiatives to improve services to visually impaired persons in such areas as aging, education, employment, literacy, and technology, conducting research, and advocating for services and legislation, AFB maintains the M. C. Migel Library and Information Center and the Helen Keller Archives; provides information and referral services; produces videos and publishes books, pamphlets, and videos on topics relating to blindness and visual impairment; the AFB Directory of Services for Blind and Visually Impaired Persons in the United States and Canada; Journal of

Visual Impairment & Blindness; *and* AccessWorld: Technology and People with Visual Impairments. *Maintains four National Centers in cities across the United States, and a Governmental Relations office in Washington, DC.*

Association for Education and Rehabilitation of the Blind and Visually Impaired (AER)

4600 Duke Street, Suite 430
Alexandria, VA 22304
(703) 823-9690
Fax: (703) 823-9695
www.aerbvi.org

A professional membership organization that promotes all phases of education and work for persons of all ages who are blind and visually impaired. It has a division that addresses the educational needs of infants and preschoolers, another that focuses on the needs of students with multiple disabilities, and an orientation and mobility division. AER organizes conferences and workshops, maintains job-exchange services and a speakers bureau, holds continuing-education seminars, and is involved in legislative and advocacy projects. Publishes RE:view, a quarterly journal, and AER Reports, a newsletter. There are state or regional chapters in the U.S. and Canada.

Autism Society of America

7910 Woodmont Avenue, Suite 300
Bethesda, MD 20814-3067
(301) 657-0881; (800) 3AUTISM (800-328-8476)
www.autism-society.org

A membership organization that promotes lifelong access and opportunity for all individuals within the autism spectrum, and their families, to be fully participating, included members of their community through education, advocacy at state and federal levels, active public awareness, and the promotion of research.

Centers for Disease Control and Prevention

Autism: Topic Home
U.S. Department of Health and Human Services
600 Clifton Road
Atlanta, GA 30333
(404) 639-3311; (404) 639-3534; (800) 311-3435
E-mail: ddbinfo@cdc.gov
www.cdc.gov/ncbddd/autism

Information about autism spectrum disorders with links to government research and other sources of information and resources for families and researchers.

Council for Exceptional Children
1110 North Glebe Road, Suite 300
Arlington, VA 22201-5704
(703) 620-3660; (888) 221-6830; (703) 264-9446 (TDD/TTY)
Fax: (703) 264-9494
E-mail: service@cec.sped.org
www.cec.sped.org

A professional organization for teachers, school administrators, and others who are concerned with children who require special services. Publishes position papers as well as periodicals, books, and other materials on teaching exceptional children. The Division on Visual Impairments focuses on educational issues and policies for infants, children, and youth who are blind or visually impaired.

National Dissemination Center for Children with Disabilities (NICHCY)
P.O. Box 1492
Washington, DC 20013
(800) 695-0285 (voice/TTY)
Fax: (202) 884-8441
E-mail: nichcy@aed.org
www.nichcy.org

A federally funded center providing information on disabilities in infants, toddlers, children, and youth, as well as programs and services; federal IDEA and No Child Left Behind legislation; and research-based information on effective educational practices. Publications and Web site include resources and information about autism and related disorders.

Texas School for the Blind and Visually Impaired
1100 West 45th Street
Austin, TX 78756-3494
(512) 454-8631
Fax: (512) 206-9452
www.tsbvi.edu

A source of extensive information about working with children who are blind and visually impaired, including professional publications, assessments, curricula, much of it available on the Web site.

Prologue: Learning, Teaching, Learning

INFORMATION ABOUT IDEA

Council for Exceptional Children
See listing under General Resources.

Families and Advocates Partnership for Education
PACER Center
8161 Normandale Boulevard
Minneapolis, MN 55437-1044
(952) 838-9000; (888) 248-0822; (952) 838-0190 (TTY)
Fax: (952) 838-0199
E-mail: fape@fape.org
www.fape.org

A partnership that aims to improve the educational outcomes for children with disabilities, linking families, advocates, and self-advocates to information about IDEA.

Federal Resource Center for Special Education
Academy for Educational Development
1825 Connecticut Avenue NW
Washington, DC 20009
(202) 884-8215; (202) 884-8200 (TTY)
Fax: (202) 884-8443
E-mail: jpatterson@aed.org
www.federalresourcecenter.org/frc

IDEA Partnership
National Association of State Directors of Special Education
1800 Diagonal Road Suite 320
Alexandria, VA 22314
(877) IDEA INF(o); 703-519-3800
E-mail: partnership@nasdse.org
www.ideapartnership.org

The IDEA Partnership housed at NASDSE unites 55 partner organizations in collaboration with states, districts, schools, and higher education in the implementation of IDEA.

National Dissemination Center for Children with Disabilities
See listing under General Resources.

National Early Childhood Technical Assistance Center
Campus Box 8040, UNC-CH
Chapel Hill, NC 27599-8040
(919) 962-2001; (919) 843-3269 (TDD)
Fax: (919) 966-7463
E-mail: nectac@unc.edu
www.nectac.org

An agency that supports the implementation of the early childhood provisions of IDEA.

Office of Special Education Programs
Office of Special Education and Rehabilitative Services
U.S. Department of Education
400 Maryland Ave., S.W.
Washington, DC 20202-7100
www.ed.gov/about/offices/list/osers/osep/index.html

The agency within the U.S. Department of Education that oversees education for infants, toddlers, children, and youth with disabilities ages birth through 2. IDEA resources are at www.ed.gov/policy/speced/guid/idea/idea2004.html.

Chapter 1: Autism Spectrum Disorders: An Introduction

PREVALENCE AND CHARACTERISTICS

Organizations

Autism Information Center
National Center on Birth Defects and Developmental Disabilities
Centers for Disease Control and Prevention
1600 Clifton Road
Atlanta, GA 30333
(404) 639-3534; (800) 311-3435
E-mail: ddbinfo@cdc.gov
www.cdc.gov/ncbddd/dd/ddautism.htm

A consumer Web site on Autism from the federal Centers for Disease Control and Prevention.

Autism Society of America
See listing under General Resources.

National Autistic Society
393 City Road
London EC1V 1NG
United Kingdom
+44(0)20 7833 2299
Fax: +44 (0)20 7833 9666
E-mail: nas@nas.org.uk
www.nas.org.uk

A membership organization that champions the rights and interests of all people with autism to ensure that they and their families receive quality services appropriate to their needs. The Web site includes information about autism and Asperger syndrome and about support and services available in the UK.

Articles

Common Characteristics of the Person with Autism. Available: http://autism .about.com/cs/whatisautism/l/blcharac.htm.

Prevalence of Autism in Brick Township, New Jersey; 1998: Community Report. Atlanta: Centers for Disease Control and Prevention, April 2000. Available: www.cdc.gov/ncbddd/pub/BrickReport.pdf or www.cdc.gov/ncbddd/ dd/rpttoc.htm.

Report to the Legislature on the Principal Findings of the Epidemiology of Autism in California: A Comprehensive Pilot Study. Davis: University of California, M.I.N.D. Institute, October 17, 2002. Available: www.dds.ca.gov/autism/ pdf/study_final.pdf.

GENERAL INFORMATION ON AUTISM SPECTRUM DISORDERS

Organizations

Center for the Study of Autism
P.O. Box 4538
Salem, OR 97302
www.autism.org

Provides information about autism to parents and professionals, and conducts research, in collaboration with the Autism Research Institute in San Diego, California, on the efficacy of various therapeutic interventions.

Articles and Books

Autism Primer: Putting a Face on Autism and Other Developmental Disabilities. (n.d.). Lombard: Autism Society of Illinois. Available: www.autismillinois.org/ autprimer.htm.

Frequently Asked Questions about Autism, by Temple Grandin, 1998. Available: www.autism.org/temple/faq.html.

An Inside View of Autism, by Temple Grandin, 1993. Available: www.autism.org/temple/inside.html.

Chapter 2: Identifying Autism Spectrum Disorders in Students with Visual Impairments

AUTISM AND BLINDNESS

Articles

Autism in the Visually Impaired Child. Paper presented by T. Pawletko & L. Rocissano at the Association for Education and Rehabilitation of the Blind, Denver, July 18, 2000. Available: www.tsbvi.edu/Education/vmi/autism-vi.htm.

Educational Implications of Autism and Visual Impairment. Paper presented by R. Jordan at the Scottish Sensory Centre Autism and Visual Impairment Conference, Edinburgh, Scotland, March 27, 1996. Available: www.ssc .mhie.ac.uk/archive/proceedings/jordan.html.

Visual Impairment and Autism—What We Know About Causation and Early Identification. Paper presented by H. Cass at the Scottish Sensory Centre Autism and Visual Impairment Conference, Edinburgh, Scotland, March 27, 1996. Available: www.ssc.mhie.ac.uk/archive/proceedings/hcass.html.

Chapter 3: Program Planning and Core Instructional Principles

PROGRAM DEVELOPMENT AND CURRICULUM

Articles and Books

Basic Skills for Community Living: A Curriculum for Students with Visual Impairments and Multiple Disabilities, edited by Nancy Levack, Susan Hauser, Lauren Newton, & Pat Stephenson. Austin: Texas School for the Blind and Visually Impaired, 1997.

Clinical Practice Guideline, Report of Recommendations. Autism/Pervasive Developmental Disorders. Assessment and Intervention for Young Children (0–3 Years). Albany: New York State Department of Health, Early Intervention Program, 1999. Available: www.health.state.ny.us/nysdoh/eip/autism/index.htm.

Educating Children with Autism, edited by C. Lord & J. McGee. Washington, DC: National Academy Press, 2001.

Educating Students Who Have Visual Impairments with Other Disabilities, edited by Sharon Z. Sacks & Rosanne K. Silberman. Baltimore, MD: Paul H. Brookes, 1998.

Essential Elements in Early Intervention: Visual Impairment and Multiple Disabilities, edited by Deborah Chen. New York: AFB Press, 1999.

LINKing Assessment and Early Intervention: An Authentic Curriculum-Based Approach, edited by Stephen J. Bagnato, John T. Neisworth, & Susan M. Munson. Baltimore, MD: Paul H. Brookes, 1997.

The STAR Program: Strategies for Teaching Based on Autism Research, by Joel R. Arick, Lauren Loos, Ruth Falco, & Dave A. Krug. Austin, TX: Pro-Ed.

Teaching Students Who Are Low Functioning: Who Are They and What Should We Teach? by Cathy Pratt & Rozella Stewart. Bloomington: Indiana Resource Center for Autism. Available: www.iidc.indiana.edu/ irca/education/teach.html.

Chapter 4: Assessment

BEHAVIOR OBSERVATION METHODS AND TOOLS

Assessment of Children: Behavioral and Clinical Applications, by Jerome M. Sattler. Circle Pines, MN: AGS, 2004.

Functional Assessment & Program Development for Problem Behavior: A Practical Handbook, by R. O'Neill, R. Albin, K. Storey, R. Horner, & J. Sprague. Independence, KY: Wadsworth Publishing, 1996.

BEHAVIOR RATING TOOLS

Asperger Syndrome Diagnostic Scale (ASDS), by B. S. Myles, S. J. Bock, & R. L. Simpson. Austin, TX: Pro-Ed, 2001.

"Autism Behavior Checklist" (ABC), in *Autism Screening Instrument for Educational Planning* (2nd ed.), by David Krug, Joel Arick, & Patricia Almond. Austin, TX: Pro-Ed (1993).

Autism Diagnostic Observation Schedule—Generic (ADOS-G), by C. Lord, M. Rutter, P. C. DiLavore, & S. Risio. Los Angeles: Western Psychological Services, 2000.

Childhood Autism Rating Scale (CARS), by Eric Schopler, Robert J. Reichler, & Barbara Rochen Renner. Circle Pines, MN: AGS Publishing, 1986.

Gilliam Asperger Disorder Scale (GADS), by James E. Gilliam. Austin, TX: Pro-Ed, 2000.

Gilliam Asperger Rating Scale (GARS), by James E. Gilliam. Austin, TX: Pro-Ed, 1995.

SENSORY ASSESSMENT

Adolescent/Adult Sensory Profile, by Winnie Dunn & Catana E. Brown. San Antonio, TX: Psychological Corporation, 2002.

Asperger syndrome and sensory issues: Practical solutions for making sense of the world, by B. S. Myles, K. T. Cook, N. E. Miller, L. Rinner, & L. A. Robbins. Shawnee Mission, KS: Autism Asperger Publishing Company, 2000.

Building Bridges Through Sensory Integration: Occupational Therapy for Children with Autism and Other Pervasive Developmental Disorders (2nd ed), by Ellen Yack, Shirley Sutton, & Paula Aquilla. Las Vegas, NV: Sensory Resources, 2003.

Infant/Toddler Sensory Profile, by Winnie Dunn. San Antonio, TX: Harcourt Assessment, Inc., 2002.

The Out-Of-Sync Child: Recognizing and Coping with Sensory Integration Dysfunction, by Carol S. Kranowitz. CSK Publications, 1998.

Sensory Integration Inventory—Revised For Individuals With Developmental Disabilities, by Judith E. Reisman & Bonnie Hanschu. Stillwater, MN: PDP Press, 1992.

Sensory Profile, by Winnie Dunn. San Antonio, TX: Harcourt Assessment, Inc., 1999.

OTHER ASSESSMENTS

Assessment Compendium Instruments for Assessing the Skills and Interests of Individuals with Visual Impairments, by Keith Benoff, Mary Ann Lang, & Michelle Beck-Viisola. New York: Lighthouse International, 2001. Available: www.lighthouse.org/assessment/index.htm.

Battelle Developmental Inventory. Itasca, IL: Riverside Publishing Co., 1984.

Bayley Scales for Infant Development, 2nd ed., by Nancy Bayley. San Antonio, TX: Psychological Corporation, 1993.

Brigance Diagnostic Comprehensive Inventory of Basic Skills—Revised Student Braille Edition, by A.H. Brigance. Louisville, KY: The American Printing House for the Blind, 1999.

Carolina Curriculum For Infants And Toddlers With Special Needs (3rd ed.), by Nancy M. Johnson-Martin, Susan M. Attermeier, & Bonnie Hacker. Baltimore, MD: Paul H. Brookes, 2004.

Functional Skills Screening Inventory: An Instrument to Assess Critical Living and Working Skills, by Heather Becker, Sally Schur, Michelle Paoletti-Schelp, & Ed Hammer. Amarillo, TX: Functional Resources, Inc., 1985.

Hawaii Early Learning Profile, by S. Parks, 1997. Palo Alto, CA: VORT Corporation.

Oregon Project for Vision Impaired and Blind Preschool Children (5th ed.), Medford, OR: Southern Oregon Education School District, 1991.

Vineland Adaptive Behavior Scale (2nd ed.), by S. S. Sparrow, D. A. Balla, & D. V. Cicchetti. Circle Pines, MN: AGS Publishing, 2005.

ASSESSMENTS OF FUNCTIONAL COMMUNICATION LEVEL

Several useful tools can assist the communication specialist, and other members of the team, in determining the functional communication level of the learner and also provide information for program planning. The following list will help the team select appropriate tools to assist in the assessment.

Autism Screening Instrument for Educational Planning (ASIEP) (2nd ed.), by David Krug, Joel R. Arick, & Patricia Almond. Austin, TX: Pro-Ed, 1993.
Addresses sample of vocal behavior.

Communication Matrix, by C. Rowland & P. Schweigert. Portland, OR: Design to Learn, Oregon Health Sciences University, 2004.
Addresses any form of communication, including presymbolic or alternative forms.

Communication and Symbolic Behavior Scales (CSBS), by Amy M. Wetherby, & Barry M. Prizant. Baltimore, MD: Paul H. Brookes, 1993.
Addresses communicative functions, gestural communicative means, reciprocity, social effective signaling, and symbolic behavior.

"Functional Communication Assessment: Informal Interview", in: *Understanding the Nature of Autism,* by Jan Janzen. San Antonio, TX: Psychological Corporation, 1996.
Addresses communication effort, functional communication use.

Functional Communication Profile, by Larry I. Kleiman. East Moline, IL: LinguiSystems, 1994.
Targets practical skills individuals with developmental delay encounter in their daily living.

Tangible Symbol Systems (2nd ed.). Portland, OR: Design to Learn, Oregon Health Sciences University, 2000.
Includes a process for determining level of representational communication (presymbolic, concrete symbols, abstract).

Test of Language Development–Primary (TOLD-P:3); *Test of Language Development*—Intermediate (TOLD-I:3) (3rd ed.). Austin, TX: Pro-Ed, 1997.
Measures components of spoken language.

TOPS-R Elementary: Test of Problem Solving—Revised by Linda Bowers, Rosemary Huisingh, Mark Barrett, Jane Orman, and Carolyn LoGiudice. East Moline, IL: LinguiSystems, 2005.
Addresses problem solving abilities; critical thinking skills.

OTHER COMMUNICATION ASSESSMENTS

"Assessment of Social Communication for Children with Autism". In: *DO-WATCH-LISTEN-SAY: Social and Communication Intervention for Children with Autism,* by Kathleen Ann Quill. Baltimore, MD: Paul H. Brookes, 2000.

Communication and Symbolic Behavior Scales (CSBS), by Ann M. Wetherby, & Barry M. Prizant. Baltimore, MD: Paul H. Brookes, 1993.

Chapter 5: Communication

GENERAL RESOURCES

Organizations

Closing the Gap
526 Main Street
P.O. Box 68
Henderson, MN 56044
(507) 248-3294
Fax: (507) 248-3810
E-mail: info@closingthegap.com
www.closingthegap.com

An organization focusing on computer technology to enhance the lives of people with special needs through its extensive web site, bimonthly newspaper, and annual international conference. Many resources related to augmentative communication are available.

Books

Assessment of Basic Language and Learning Skills (ABLLS) by J. W. Partington & M. L. Sundberg. Pleasant Hill, CA: Behavior Analysts, Inc., 1998.

Calendars for Students with Multiple Impairments, Including Deafblindness, by Robbie Blaha. Austin: Texas School for the Blind, 2001.

Do-Watch-Listen-Say: Social and Communication Intervention for Children with Autism, by Kathleen Ann Quill. Baltimore, MD: Paul H. Brookes, 2000.

A Picture's Worth: PECS and Other Visual Communication Strategies in Autism, by Andy Bondy & Lori Frost. Bethesda, MD: Woodbine House, 2002.

Tangible Symbol Systems (2nd ed.), Portland, OR: Design to Learn, Oregon Health Sciences University, 2000.

Teach Me Language: A Language Manual for Children with Autism, Asperger's Syndrome, and Related Developmental Disorders, by Sabrina Freeman & Lorelai Dake. Langley, Canada: SKF Books, 1996.

Teaching Language To Children With Autism or Other Developmental Disabilities, by M. L. Sundberg & J. W. Partington. Danville, CA: Behavior Analysts, Inc., 1998.

INSTRUCTIONAL STRATEGIES

Organizations

Judevine Center for Autism
1101 Olivette Executive Pkwy
St. Louis, MO 63132
(314) 432-6200
Fax: (314) 849-2721
E-mail: judevine@judevine.org
www.judevine.org

A center offering a full range of services and supports for children and adults individuals with autism spectrum disorders and their families based on the principles of applied behavior analysis, within a social exchange context.

Articles, Books, and Web Sites

Communication: A Guide for Teaching Students with Visual and Multiple Impairments, by Linda Hagood. Austin: Texas School for the Blind and Visually Impaired, 1997.

Creating a Need to Communicate; Fact Sheet 19. San Francisco: California Deaf-Blind Services, November 7, 1996. Available: www.sfsu.edu/~cadbs/Facts.html.

Developing an Intervention Plan for the Verbal Child with Autism. In: *Increasing Expressive Skills for Verbal Children with Autism,* by Susan Stokes. Green Bay, WI: Cooperative Educational Service Agency No. 7. Available: www.cesa7.k12.wi.us/sped/autism/verbal/verbal13.html.

Echolalia and Autism, by Gary J. Heffner, July 2000. Available: http://groups.msn.com/TheAutismHomePage/echolaliafacts.msnw.

Long and Short Term Strategies for Reducing Specific Repetitive Questions, by Beverly Vicker. Bloomington, IN: Indiana Resource Center for Autism. Available at: www.iidc.indiana.edu/irca/communication/longtermstr.html.

"Perspective Taking" in: *Inside Out: What Makes the Person with Social Cognitive Deficits Tick?* by Michelle Garcia Winner. Arlington, TX: Future Horizons, Inc., 2000.

A Standard Tactile Symbol System: Graphic Language for Individuals Who Are Blind and Unable to Learn Braille, by Linda Hagood. Austin: Texas School for the Blind, Life Skills Department. Available at: www.tsbvi.edu/Outreach/seehear/archive/tactile.html.

Tactile Symbols—Directory to Standard Tactile Symbol List. Austin: Texas School for the Blind and Visually Impaired Functional Academics and Basic Skills Department. Available at: www.tsbvi.edu/Education/vmi/tactile_symbols.htm.

SOURCES OF PRODUCTS AND MATERIALS

Different Roads to Learning
12 West 18th Street, Suite 3E
New York , NY 10011
(800) 853-1057; (212) 604-9637
Fax: (800) 317-9146; (212) 206-9329
E-mail: info@difflearn.com
www.difflearn.com

Products for children with autism spectrum disorders, including books, flashcards, puzzles and games, scheduling and PECS materials, videos, and software.

Enabling Devices
385 Warburton Avenue
Hastings-on-Hudson, NY 10706

(914) 478-0960; (800) 832-8697
Fax: (914) 479-1369
E-mail: info@enablingdevices.com
http://enablingdevices.com

Cheap Talk Communicators and other devices and toys for children and adults with special needs.

Inspiration Software
7412 SW Beaverton-Hillsdale Highway, Suite 102
Portland, OR 97225
(503) 297-3004; (800) 877-4292
Fax: (503) 297-4676
E-mail: webmaster@inspiration.com
www.inspiration.com

Inspiration and Kidspiration Software.

Mayer-Johnson
P.O. Box 1579
Solana Beach, CA 92075
(800) 588-4548; (858) 550-0084
Fax: (858) 550-0449
E-mail: mayerj@mayer-johnson.com
www.mayer-johnson.com/software/Boardmkr.html

Boardmaker a graphics database containing over 3,000 Picture Communication Symbols.

AUGMENTATIVE COMMUNICATION DEVICES

American Printing House for the Blind
1839 Frankfort Avenue
P.O. Box 6085
Louisville, KY 40206
(502) 895-2405; (800) 223-1839
www.aph.org

Motion PAD, motion activated memo pad, plays of 10-second voice message.

AbleNet
2808 Fairview Avenue
Roseville, MN 55113-1308
(651) 294-2200; (800) 322-0956
Fax: (651) 294-2259 (business)

E-mail: Customer Service@ablenetinc.com
www.ablenetinc.com

BIGmack: single switch device; Speak Easy: 12 Recorded Messages.

Attainment Company
P.O. Box 930160
Verona, WI 53593-0160
(608) 845-7880; (800) 327-4269
www.AttainmentCompany.com

Portable communication devices, including Personal Talker (single message device with one picture), and Go Talk and Pocket Go Talk (various numbers of messages).

Chapter 6: Social Interactions

ORGANIZATIONS

Gray Center for Social Learning and Understanding
4123 Embassy Drive, SE
Kentwood, MI 49546
616-954-9747
Fax: 616-954-9749
E-mail: info@thegraycenter.org
www.thegraycenter.org/Social_Stories.htm

An organization dedicated to individuals with autism spectrum disorders and those who work alongside them to improve mutual understanding. The web site contains information about guidelines for writing Social Stories and sample stories and additional resources for using them.

Indiana Resource Center for Autism
Indiana Institute on Disability and Community
Indiana University
2853 East 10th Street
Bloomington, IN 47408-2696
(812) 855-6508; (812) 855-9396 (TTY)
Fax: (812) 855-9630
E-mail: prattc@indiana.edu
www.iidc.indiana.edu/irca

A resource center that conducts outreach training and consultations, engages in research, and develops and disseminates information on behalf of individuals across the autism spectrum, including autism, Asperger's syndrome, and other pervasive developmental disorders to provide communities, organizations, agencies, and families with the knowledge and skills to support children and adults in typical early intervention, school, community, work, and home settings.

ARTICLES AND BOOKS

Comic Strip Conversations: Colorful, Illustrated Interactions With Students With Autism And Related Disorders. Kentwood, MI: Gray Center for Social Learning and Understanding, 1994.

Focused On: Social Skills [video and study guides], edited by Sharon Z. Sacks & Karen E. Wolffe. New York: AFB Press, 2000.

Inside Out: What Makes The Person With Social Cognitive Deficits Tick?, by Michelle Garcia Winner. Arlington, TX: Future Horizons, Inc., 2000.

The New Social Story Book, by C. Gray. Kentwood, MI: Gray Center for Social Learning and Understanding, 2000.

Reaching Out, Joining In: Teaching Social Skills to Young Children with Autism, by Mary Jane Weiss & Sandra L. Harris. Bethesda, MD: Woodbine House, 2001.

Taming The Recess Jungle: Socially Simplifying Recess for Students With Autism and Related Disorders, by C. Gray. Kentwood, MI: Gray Center for Social Learning and Understanding, 1993.

Teaching Children with Autism: Strategies to Enhance Communication and Socialization, by Kathleen Ann Quill. Clifton Park, NY: Thomson Delmar Learning, 1996.

Temple Grandin's "Hug Machine," by Stephen M. Edelson. Salem, OR: Center for the Study of Autism, 1996. Available: www.autism.org/hugbox.html.

SOURCES OF PRODUCTS

Therafin Corporation
19747 Wolf Road
Mokena, IL 60448
(708) 479-7300; (800) 843-7234
Fax: (708) 479-1515; (888) 479-1515
E-mail: info@therafin.com
www.therafin.com/squeezemachine.htm

Manufactures and delivers Temple Grandin's Squeeze Machine for deep touch stimulation, which produces a calming effect on some individuals with autism spectrum disorders.

Web Sites

www.barryprizant.com

www.tonyattwood.com.au
Web site guide for parents, professionals, people with Asperger's Syndrome, and their partners.

Chapter 7: Challenging Behaviors

FUNCTIONAL BEHAVIORAL ASSESSMENT

Organizations

Center for Effective Collaboration and Practice
American Institutes for Research
1000 Thomas Jefferson St., NW, Suite 400,
Washington, DC 20007
(888) 457-1551; (202) 944-5400
E-mail: center@air.org; cecp.air.org
http://cecp.air.org/fba/default.asp

An organization and Web site dedicated to the production, exchange, and use of knowledge about effective practices in fostering the development and adjustment of children with or at risk of developing serious emotional disturbance. The functional behavioral assessment section of the web site contains extensive information designed to provide resources needed to understand functional behavioral assessments as well as behavioral intervention plans.

Articles and Books

Asperger Syndrome and Difficult Moments: Practical Solutions for Tantrums, Rage, and Meltdowns, by Brenda Smith Myles & Jack Southwick. Shawnee Mission, KS: Autism Asperger Publishing Company.

"Assess and Plan Interventions for Severe Behavior Problems," In *Understanding the Nature of Autism: A Guide to the Autism Spectrum Disorders* (2nd ed.), by Janice E. Janzen. San Antonio, TX: Therapy Skill Builders, 2002.

Behaviors That May Be Personal Challenges for a Student with an Autism Spectrum Disorder. O.A.S.I.S. (Online Asperger Syndrome Information and Support). Available at: www.udel.edu/bkirby/asperger/IEP_Behav_Forms.html.

Solving Behavior Problems in Autism: Improving Communication With Visual Strategies, by Linda Hodgdon. Troy, MI: Quirk Roberts Publishing, 1999.

Chapter 8: Orientation and Mobility

O&M ASSESSMENT AND CURRICULUM

Finding Wheels: A Curriculum for Nondrivers with Visual Impairments for Gaining Control of Transportation Needs, by Anne L. Corn. Austin, TX: Pro-Ed, 2000.

Hand in Hand: Essentials of Communication and Orientation and Mobility for Your Students Who Are Deaf-Blind, edited by Kathleen M. Huebner, Jeanne G. Prickett, Therese R. Welch, & Elga Joffee. New York: AFB Press, 1995.

The Importance of Orientation and Mobility Skills for Students Who Are Deaf-Blind, by D. Jay Gense & Marilyn Gense. Monmouth, OR: DB-LINK, The National Information Clearinghouse on Children Who Are Deaf-Blind, October 2004. Available at: www.tr.wou.edu/dblink/lib/o&m2.htm.

Move, Touch, Do, by Wendy Drezek. Louisville, KY: American Printing House for the Blind, 1995.

Move with Me. Los Angeles: Blind Children's Center.

Oregon Project for Visually Impaired and Blind Preschoolers (5th ed.), by S. Anderson, S. Boigon, D. Brown, K. Davis, J. Methvin, & V. Simmons. Medford, OR: Southern Oregon Education Service District, 1991.

An Orientation and Mobility Primer for Families and Young Children, by Bonnie Dodson-Burk & Everett W. Hill. New York: American Foundation for the Blind, 1989.

Parents and Visually Impaired Infants (PAVII), edited by D. Chen, C. T. Friedman, & G. Cavello. Louisville, KY: American Printing House for the Blind, 1989.

Preschool Orientation and Mobility Screening, by Bonnie Dodson-Burke & Everette W. Hill. Alexandria, VA: Association for Education and Rehabilitation of the Blind and Visually Impaired, 1989.

Promoting Learning Through Active Interaction: A Guide to Early Communication with Young Children Who Have Multiple Disabilities, by M. Diane Klein, Deborah Chen, & C. Michelle Haney. Baltimore, MD: Paul H. Brookes, 2000.

Reaching, Crawling, Walking . . . Let's Get Moving. Los Angeles: Blind Children's Center.

Standing On My Own Two Feet. Los Angeles: Blind Children's Center.

Starting Points. Los Angeles: Blind Children's Center.

TAPS: Teaching Age-Appropriate Purposeful Skills: An Orientation & Mobility Curriculum for Students with Visual Impairments—Comprehensive Assessment and On-Going Evaluation, by R. Pogrund, G. Healy, K. Jones, N. Levack, S. Martin-Curry, C. Martinez, J. Marz, B. Roberson-Smith, & A. Vrba. Austin, TX: Texas School for the Blind and Visually Impaired, 1995.

MOBILITY DEVICES

Articles and Books

Mobility Devices for Young Children. New York: American Foundation for the Blind. Available: www.afb.org/Section.asp?DocumentID=804.

Standing on My Own Two Feet. Los Angeles: Blind Children's Center.

Sources of Products

AmbuTech
34 DeBaets Street
Winnipeg, Ontario R2J 3S9
Canada
(204) 663-3340; (800) 561-3340
Fax: (204) 668-9517; (800) 267-5059
www.ambutech.com

Mobility products, including canes and accessories.

MAPS

Sources of Products

American Printing House for the Blind
1839 Frankfort Avenue
P.O. Box 6085
Louisville, KY 40206
(502) 895-2405; (800) 223-1839
www.aph.org

Supplies for maps, including O&M Tactile Graphics, Quick Draw Paper, Picture Maker.

Chapter 9: Independent Living Skills

ORGANIZATIONS

Blindskills
P.O. Box 5181
Salem, OR 97304-0181
(503) 581-4224; (800) 860-4224
Fax: (503) 581-0178
E-mail: blindskl@teleport.com
www.blindskills.com

Publisher of Dialogue Magazine, *which includes information on adapting to life with low vision, techniques of daily living, career interviews, recreation and sports, technology tips and reviews, and descriptions of new products and services designed for visually impaired people.*

ARTICLES AND BOOKS

Applying Structured Teaching Principles to Toilet Training, by Susan Boswell & Debbie Gray. Chapel Hill: University of North Carolina's Project TEACCH (Treatment and Education of Autistic and Related Communication Handicapped Children). Available: www.teacch.com/toilet.htm.

Let's Eat: Feeding a Child with a Visual Impairment. Los Angeles: The Blind Children's Center.

Steps to Independence: Teaching Everyday Skills to Children with Special Needs (4th ed.), by Bruce L. Baker, et al. Baltimore, MD: Paul H. Brookes, 2004.

Toilet Training for Individuals with Autism and Related Disorders, by M. Wheeler. Arlington, TX: Future Horizons, 1998.

SOURCES OF PRODUCTS

Calm Comforts
1708 Cedar Glen Place
Cowichan Bay, BC V0R 1N1
Canada
(250) 746-1667
Fax: (250) 746-6337
E-mail: claire@calmcomforts.com
www.calmcomforts.com

Weighted vests, lap quilts, and blankets.

In Your Pocket
1508 Tackley Place
Midlothian, VA 23114
(804) 379-0944
Fax: (804) 379-9088
E-mail: weightedvest@comcast.net
www.weightedvest.com

Weighted vests and play clothes.

Quiet Quilts
1005 Goldeneye
Carlsbad, CA 92009
(760) 918-9555
www.quietquilt.com

Weighted quilts.

AUTISM AND DIET RESOURCE INFORMATION

Articles

Autism and the Gluten-Free/Casein-Free Diet. Glastonbury, CT: The Gluten-Free Pantry. Available: www.glutenfree.com/autism.htm.

Autistic Spectrum and Dietary Intervention. The Paleolithic Diet Page. Available: www.paleodiet.com/autism.

Web Sites

Autism Web. Special Diet for Autism and PDD. www.autismweb.com/diet.htm.

GFCF Diet. Gluten Free, Cassein Free: Dietary Intervention for Autistic Spectrum Disorders. www.gfcfdiet.com.

Chapter 10: Career Education

ARTICLES AND BOOKS

Parent Brief: Promoting Effective Parent Involvement in Secondary Education and Transition. Minneapolis: National Center on Secondary Education and Transition, Institute on Community Integration, University of Minnesota, February 2004. Available: www.ncset.org/publications/viewdesc.asp?id=1431.

Person Centered Planning: Building Partnerships and Supporting Choices. California Health and Human Services Agency, California Department of Developmental Services, 2001. Available: www.dds.ca.gov/publications/PDF/Person_Ctrd_Planning.pdf.

Person-Centered Planning: Maps and Paths to the Future, by Howard Garner & Lise Dietz. Norfolk, VA: Training and Technical Assistance Center, Old Dominion University. Available: www.ttac.odu.edu/Articles/person.html.

Resource List on Person Centered Planning. Napa, CA: Allen, Shea & Associates. Available: www.allenshea.com/resource.html.

ASSESSMENT TOOLS

Career Assessment Inventory—The Enhanced Version, by Charles B. Johansson. Minneapolis, MN: National Computer Systems, 1986.

Career Occupational Preference System (COPS). San Diego, CA: Edits Publishing.

McCarron-Dial Evaluation System. Dallas, TX: McCarron-Dial Systems.

SOURCES OF PRODUCTS AND MATERIALS

American Printing House for the Blind
1839 Frankfort Avenue
P.O. Box 6085
Louisville, KY 40206
(502) 895-2405; (800) 223-1839
www.aph.org

Prevocational Skills Developmental Materials kit and guidebook and Transition Tote System student kit and information supplement for teachers.

WEB SITES

Career Connect, American Foundation for the Blind, www.afb.org/careerconnect.

Division TEACCH Supported Employment Program, University of North Carolina at Chapel Hill. www.teacch.com/teacchsu.htm.

Chapter 11: Recreation and Leisure

ARTICLES AND BOOKS

Autism and Leisure Development: A Practical Approach for Home, School and Community, by P. Coyne, C. Nyberg, & M. L. Vandenburg. Arlington, TX: Future Horizons, 1999.

Introduction to Applied Behavior Analysis, by David Kalmeyer. West Hartford, CT: Families for Effective Autism Treatment. Available: www.ctfeat.org/Kalmeyer.htm.

Perkins Activity and Resource Guide: A Handbook for Teachers and Parents of Students with Visual and Multiple Disabilities (2nd ed.), by Charlotte Cushman, et al. Watertown, MA: Perkins School for the Blind.

Project Autism Guidelines Manual. Chapel Hill: University of North Carolina, Department of Recreation and Leisure Studies. Available: www.unc.edu/depts/recreate/crds/autism.

Suggestions for Recreation and Leisure Activities for Blind and Visually Impaired Children, by Debra Sewell. Austin: Texas School for the Blind and Visually Impaired, June 1994. Available: www.tsbvi.edu/Outreach/seehear/summer99/games.htm.

SOURCES OF PRODUCTS AND MATERIALS

American Printing House for the Blind
1839 Frankfort Avenue
P.O. Box 6085
Louisville, KY 40206
(502) 895-2405; (800) 223-1839
www.aph.org

On the Way Storybooks, a series of books featuring real objects and textures; adapted games.

LS&S
P.O. Box 673
Northbrook, IL 60065
(847) 498-9777; (800) 468-4789; (866) 317-8533 (TTY/TDD)
Fax : (847) 498-1482
E-mail: info@LSSproducts.com
www.lssgroup.com

Recreation and leisure games, equipment, and materials.

Media Access Group at WGBH
125 Western Avenue
Boston, MA 02134
(617) 300-3600 (voice/TTY)
Fax: (617) 300-1020
E-mail: access@wgbh.org
http://main.wgbh.org/wgbh/pages/mag/resources/dvs-home-video-catalogue.html

Described videos and accessible DVDs. To request a large-print catalog call (888) 818-1999. To request braille catalog call (888) 818-1181. To hear a listing of the latest DVS home video titles available or a listing of audio-described television programs broadcast, call (800) 333-1203.

Chapter 12: Classroom Supports

ARTICLES AND BOOKS

Calendars for Students with Multiple Impairments Including Deafblindness, by Robbie Blaha. Austin: Texas School for the Blind, 2001.

"Design Visual Adaptations & Routine Planning Chart," in: *Understanding the Nature of Autism, A Guide to the Autism Spectrum Disorders* (2nd ed.), by Jan Janzen. San Antonio, TX: Therapy Skill Builders, 2003.

Let's Play: A Guide to Toys for Children with Special Needs. (2005). New York: Toy Industry Foundation, Alliance for Technology Access, American Foundation for the Blind. Available: www.toy-tia.org/industry/publications/blindcurrent/cover.html or www.afb.org/Section.asp?DocumentID=2651.

Making Picture Recipes. Louisville, KY: American Printing House for the Blind.

Making Visual Supports Work in the Home and Community: Individuals with Autism and Asperger Syndrome, by J. L. Savner & B. S. Myles. Shawnee Mission, KS: Autism Asperger Publishing Co., 2000.

TEACCH Approach to Autism Spectrum Disorders, by G. B. Mesibov, V. Shea, E. Schopler. Chapel Hill: Division TEACCH, University of North Carolina, 2005.

Visual Supports: Helping Your Child Understand and Communicate. Gainesville, FL: Center for Autism and Related Disabilities (CARD). Available: http://card.ufl.edu/visual.html.

Words, Words, Words: Teaching Vocabulary in Grades 4–12, by Janet Allen. Portland, ME: Stenhouse Publishers, 1999.

SOURCES OF PRODUCTS

American Printing House for the Blind
1839 Frankfort Avenue
P.O. Box 6085
Louisville, KY 40206
(502) 895-2405; (800) 223-1839
www.aph.org

MasterPlan Calendar

Inspiration Software
7412 SW Beaverton-Hillsdale Highway, Suite 102
Portland, OR 97225
(503) 297-3004; 800-877-4292
Fax: 503-297-4676
E-mail: webmaster@inspiration.com
www.inspiration.com

Inspiration and Kidspiration software that use the principles of visual learning to help children develop early literacy skills, improve comprehension skills, develop ideas, and organize thinking.

Oriental Trading Company
P.O. Box 2308
Omaha, NE 68103-2308
(800) 875-8480
www.teachercentral.com

Catalog of inexpensive toys and games, craft supplies, costumes, novelties, etc.

INDEX

ABOUT THE AUTHORS

Marilyn H. Gense, M.A., is Special Education Coordinator with the Willamette Education Service District in Salem, Oregon, with responsibilities for coordinating services to children who are blind or visually impaired and children with autism spectrum disorders. She has been teaching in and coordinating programs for 28 years in residential programs, regional programs serving local districts, and statewide services as well as in university training programs. She is a past president of the Oregon chapter of the Association for Education and Rehabilitation of the Blind and Visually Impaired.

D. Jay Gense, Ed.S., is Director of Low Incidence Programs with the Oregon Department of Education in Salem, where he administers statewide services for students with visual impairments, hearing impairments, autism spectrum disorders, and deaf-blindness. He has been teaching in and administering educational programs for over 25 years in residential programs and itinerant-based regional services serving children and youths from birth to age 21 as well as teaching at the university level. He is a past president of both the Alaska and Oregon chapters of the Association for Education and Rehabilitation of the Blind and Visually Impaired.

Marilyn and Jay Gense have written numerous articles and presented widely at workshops and professional conferences on educational strategies for working with students who are blind or visually impaired and have autism spectrum disorders and on assessment and program development for students with low-incidence disabilities. They hope this publication helps disseminate more broadly information and resources about visual impairments and autism spectrum disorders.